A Guide To Reading The Entire Bible In One Year

a guide
to reading
the entire
Bible
in one year

68194

Webb Garrison

THE **BOBBS-MERRILL** COMPANY, INC.
A SUBSIDIARY OF HOWARD W. SAMS & CO., INC.
Publishers • INDIANAPOLIS • NEW YORK

Contents

Preface

This guide had a rather unusual beginning.

A small group of committed persons in Roberts Park Methodist Church, Indianapolis, set out to read the entire Bible. They quickly found that such a discipline requires planning and guidance. So, in response to this need, I agreed to prepare a reading guide.

Before the first monthly installment was finished, comparatively large numbers of persons in the congregation were showing interest. And brief mention of the reading program in the column that I write for the *Indianapolis News* brought queries from all over the state.

Within thirty days, therefore, it became evident that a purely local program for one congregation has more than local appeal. I soon found that the Biblical illiteracy of our times afflicts not only Methodists, but also Baptists, Disciples, Presbyterians, Lutherans, and others. And I was delighted to discover that surprisingly many persons of various denominational backgrounds are actually eager to know the Bible better.

As a result, this guide very quickly spread into other congregations and communities. And now, as I had hoped from the beginning, it is published as a hard-cover book.

—Webb Garrison

Introduction

Eager and excited, now that months of anticipation had given way to the reality of a trip, a group of New Jersey tourists pulled off the highway. It hardly seemed possible that, at last, they were in the Great Smoky Mountains National Park. As they had done four times in the last five miles, they jumped out of the car and started snapping their cameras at everything in sight.

Two mountaineers, rattling down the incline in their old car, looked at one another and laughed, seeming to say:

"Ha! Another first-time crowd! They're hardly out of sight of Gatlinburg, but they're using up their film mighty fast. It'll all be gone before they get halfway to the top, and you can't buy more in the park!"

On any journey through a land of wonders, it is a major problem to choose stopping places. Especially on his first half dozen trips through the Bible, a traveler may be so baffled by the wealth of vistas that he devotes too much time to the foothills and is weary before he reaches the first peak.

This guide is unlike any other in existence. It proposes to lead you at a pace that is appropriate to the stretch of highway being traveled. In some instances, you will be encouraged to skim through many pages in half an hour. At other times, you will be asked to read slowly and to meditate at length upon the message of a few paragraphs.

In order that individuals, classes, and congregations may

9

begin reading at any time during the year, the guide is divided into twelve months of thirty days each. In months that include thirty-one days, use the extra day to make a rapid review. In February, plan your reading to "catch up" with the outline during the last week of the month.

Whether covering little material or much in your daily reading, the goal is always your personal enlightenment.

This is not an academic or scholarly enterprise. Such questions as authorship and date of composition will not concern us. Throughout, we shall treat the Bible as a unique source of sacred light. Directed toward the path your feet are following, that light will transform your pilgrimage. Without exception, effects of such illumination are personal and practical.

As described in the Revelation (Chapters 6-8), a supernatural force breaks the seals on a book, and John's eyes are flooded with visions of things never before seen. The imagery is especially valid today. For of the many books whose contents are "sealed" to the majority of folk, the Bible now heads the list. We revere it; we study it, after a fashion, in Sunday school; we quote a few verses from it; we do everything but read the *whole* Bible with eager attention to highway information it offers throughout.

When seals are removed from Scripture, new understanding comes. Men become capable of seeing things they never before glimpsed. Some of these things are in the Book itself, some are in life. Always, there must be a two-way flow between life and the Book. Each can shed light upon the other, so that there is continuous increase in brilliance of the illumination.

Now, it would be utterly dishonest for me to pretend that you can claim the benefits of this light-bestowing process, without paying the price. In order to win the prize, you must run the race. Without expenditure of time and attention and interest, you cannot hope to claim the benefits of systematic Bible reading.

Just as is the case with food for the body, food for the soul must be eaten by the person who expects to gain the calories involved. That sounds simple—but the simplicity is deceptive. For the Gospel message that runs through the Bible from cover to cover is always proclaimed in the fashion of both/and. It is for everyone who will read it, yet it is also strictly personal. Its message is both universal and individual.

To make the Bible come alive, try to regard it as just off the press, with the ink still wet, having been prepared especially for your personal enlightenment. Do NOT read it for duty's sake. Do NOT read it as a discipline. Try to see it as inseparably linked with everyday events of your life. Try to regard it (though this is hard, hard, hard) as an on-the-spot news report of world-shaking events.

In the rare hours that you succeed in entering the mood and spirit of this Book, you will find it so full of action, so absorbing, so vitally informing, so urgent for YOUR LIFE TO-DAY that if you are called away from your reading to view a telecast of the launching of a satellite, you will tend to be nettled at intrusion of the trivial upon the cosmic.

Scripture's fundamental note is that of divine rescue. From the first page to the last, the Bible offers the incredible story of God's great acts designed to enable folk like us to burst the shackles of humanity. God opens for us a door that no person or event can close (Rev. 3:7-8); victory is the keynote of the whole incredible story. That basic Biblical note is sounded in as many fashions as air is expelled from the pipes of an organ—with its many different sizes and shapes of tubes. But there is unity in diversity. Each tube is like every other in emitting air in such a way that a musical note falls upon the human ear. Just so, every part of the Bible emits evidences pointing to rescue—suggested in a multiplicity of ways.

In your reading, be continually alert for signals that will deepen or clarify or re-direct your understanding of the

11

grand themes of life—such issues as the meaning of the human race, the "why" of our existence on a planet prepared especially for us, how to win in the ceaseless rat race of existence, and ways of running the race with joy and victory.

Read also with specific interest in the problems, triumphs, burdens, and joys of your everyday life. That is, do not read as an exercise in piety—but read as a bewildered (or elated or weary or lost or triumphant) traveler who must study his guidebook in order to get the most from today's journey.

If possible, secure a copy of the Bible (or individual books from it) that you will feel free to mark and underscore. Even slight notations, such as exclamation points and question marks in the margins, will help you to conserve your discoveries and turn to them again and again. The format of this guide was deliberately selected to provide plenty of space in which you may make notes as you use it.

Because the Bible comes out of life and is directed to life, it will speak most directly and clearly when USED DURING NORMAL ACTIVITIES OF YOUR DAILY LIFE. Do some of your reading at intervals between periods of work (regardless of whether you work at home, in a factory, shop, or office). Keep your Bible or Testament or individual Scripture portion conveniently at hand, so that you can turn to it as naturally as you would pick up the newspaper or pull your chair before the television set.

Probably you will find it fruitful to jot down some of your major insights. If so, follow whatever fashion is appropriate to your interest and experience. You may wish to keep a notebook, in which you will record the flood of new understanding that is certain to come during these months. Perhaps you will wish to write comments about questions that trouble you as well as discoveries that excite you.

If you become a part of a weekly or monthly discussion group, you will find that insights of others will both supplement your own and raise the level of your private reading. If you read alone, you will have the special joy of knowing that a substantial number of others are reading with you, day by day, and entering with you into a spiritual comradeship that overcomes all barriers.

During the exciting year that is ahead of us as we read and listen and rejoice together, I shall try to point out major landmarks. But the glory of the journey is such that you can see many a mountain peak from your own perspective, and, with these as points of reference, you will make every day—every hour—an exciting, joyful, victorious time of discovery.

A special reward grows out of the fact that hosts of other persons in many places are reading along with you. Every day, you can rejoice that you are not alone. You are part of a wide fellowship of kindred spirits—persons whom you will never know, but who are your companions along the daily journey.

At any earlier period, I would have used the beloved King James Version for my quotations. No other English translation is likely ever to challenge this classic one in terms of world influence or literary excellence. But the changing patterns of speech and of book-making have in the past five years brought me to increasing dependence upon the Revised Standard Version of the Holy Bible, copyrighted 1946 and 1952. It is therefore this version that is here employed. I am deeply grateful to the Division of Christian Education, National Council of Churches, for permission to follow this practice.

Genesis and Exodus

Genesis

Genesis is "the book of beginnings." Contrary to popular thought, though, it is not the beginning of the universe that is the most important part of its story. Rather, it is the beginning of God's dealings with mankind in general and with the Chosen People in particular, that makes this book so vital.

The story that unfolds is strictly and entirely the story of salvation—or the history of the manifold ways in which the Creator has offered rescue to men. From the beginning, the account is elaborate and tortuous. For the creature who is offered divine aid is the strangest mixture in creation. He is "made in the divine image." That is, he has inside him the potential to achieve God-likeness. But, because he is also of earth and from earth, he is confined and cribbed about by requirements of his body.

One half of this paradoxical creature, man, desperately wants to seize hold of divine gifts he can dimly see. But his other self—his earthly self—is lured by other goals. So he is in a state of ceaseless struggle. His responses to the overtures of God are never unmixed. He is sometimes eager, but he often balks and resists. Consequently, *salvation history* is a continuous series of ups and downs. At the very beginning, the climax—God's self-giving for the sake of man—is foreshadowed and hinted, though darkly, "like a lamp shining in a dark place" (II Pet. 1:19).

As you read the dramatic story of the beginning of God's striving to help us achieve our true goal, never forget that the world was created for this specific purpose. God's universe is a "university of life" designed to prod, to persuade, to awaken, and drive you and me to accept divine rescue. Therefore, the face of the whole world trembles in the balance as you prepare to accept or reject the good things offered you by God. What you do has a bearing upon the cosmic victory so vast that stars and planets and suns and moons are mere agents and instruments.

First Day	Read Genesis 1-2

Nothing that exists came into being by chance. God created the laboratory in which man is the inquiring experimenter. Because God's creative acts were deliberate and purposeful, it follows that the world and life are "good." Notice how many times this vital factor is clearly specified in the account of creation.

What does this have to say about your own burdens and opportunities today? What pressing problems that confront you will look entirely different if you can succeed in seeing them as co-operating in God's stupendous work of establishing a creative context for your life?

If you are confronted by difficult decisions, take heart! Notice that, from the first, the creature who names and controls all other creatures is incapable of living in a state of ease. For Adam and Eve are torn between desire to obey God and hunger for the forbidden fruit of "the knowledge of good and evil."

Do you think it is possible to escape tension and turmoil by any process short of erasing the divine image that is traced upon you?

Second Day   Read Genesis 3-5

Remember that we are dealing with *salvation history*. The Bible is not a text book of political history. Neither is it an encyclopedia of biology or astronomy or agriculture. From start to finish, the story told is that of the dealings of God with the sons of men. Always the emphasis is upon divine truths communicated through human words. Because the experiences and viewpoints and goals of the reader color every word he reads, the message of a given passage is not fixed and automatic. Instead, it varies from one person to another and from time to time in the life of one reader. You may take it as absolutely certain that during and after this year's reading you will frequently discover fresh meaning in passages long familiar to you.

In the story of Adam's fall, we find it to be a principle of life that no man can continue blameless in the sight of God. From generation to generation to generation, every son and daughter of every father and mother is *human*—that is, frail and limited and prone to stumble. That this always has and always will be the case is the burden of the story in which the serpent plays the role of the Evil One.

Third Day   Read Genesis 6-8

As with you and me, so with families and tribes and nations. How often God must have wearied of mankind!

But the darkness is never total. Always there is a Noah, standing for righteousness in the midst of a crooked and perverse generation. Always, the world's Noahs obey the voice of God, even when the message they hear seems to make no sense. Such obedience—in which you and I can participate in this our time of new deluges—is vital in *salvation history*. It is through an occasional truly obedient individual that God keeps the stream of grace flowing to quench the thirst of mankind.

17

Always, inevitably, without exception, the divine-human crisis ends in rescue and victory and joy. Anything resembling ultimate defeat simply is not conceivable. Though men in their freedom rebel and defy their Creator, he has so shaped his total creation that right and truth must triumph. Because that is the case, there is no hopeless situation under the sun. Whatever the nature of the flood waters that now roll over your soul, divine rescue and "a new beginning" await you if you will listen and obey.

Fourth Day · Read Genesis 9-11

Here we find the first clear witness to a central riddle of *salvation history*. For reasons never quite clear from our human perspective but entirely adequate for God's own purposes, the Creator has actually entered into a Covenant with mankind. Man did not earn or win or deserve the right to become a partner with God. This contract was entered into as a result of divine initiative and conferred upon man as a gift.

The entire Bible offers a running account of *salvation history*, so may be described as "the story of the Covenant." Not even the shameless conduct of a just-rescued Noah can cancel out the divine promise. Even the rebellious banding together of men, pooling human resources in an effort to build a tower to heaven and become more-than-human, does not void the contract.

The coming of Jesus Christ, at the time appointed by the Father, is the fulfilment of the Covenant from the divine side. At Calvary, the Creator makes good his word. Precisely because that is the case, no view of the Cross is adequate that does not see it as the culmination of age-long processes initiated by God "in the beginning" so that saved men may accept a glory no mere mortal can achieve.

18

Fifth Day   Read Genesis 12-14

In his acceptance of divine rescue and his entering into a
Covenant with God, Noah represents all mankind. But the
Creator's dealings with creatures made in his image are to
become more specific. Even God could not bring his Son
into the world in a vacuum, so to speak. For the Messiah to
enter history, it was necessary that a particular people be
set aside—chosen first by act of God and then by their response to the divine overture.

Without the slightest capacity to explain *why* they should
have been the Chosen People, we cannot escape recognizing
that the Hebrews actually *were* selected for a unique relationship with God. Their Covenant was entered through
Abraham, founder of the clan. God's special promises to
Abraham and his seed *forever* gain new and dynamic meaning in Christian thought, as we shall see before this year is
over. For the present, we can only confess with astonish-
ment that Covenant bonds are bound to produce a people
utterly unlike any other before or since.

Sixth Day   Read Genesis 15-18

From the beginning of the Covenant relationship, difficulties and delays and barriers are apparent. There is no quick,
smooth working out of the divine purpose even when it relates to the life of a single man. Over and over, there are
reasons to think God's promises are empty words. But the
very obstacles to fulfilment of these promises serve to dramatize divine power.

In several of his letters, Paul wrestles with the matter of
the Covenant between Jehovah and Abraham. The promise,
he concludes, was made to the spiritual rather than the
biological descendants of Abraham. Does this interpretation
add to your appreciation of the Old Testament?

Seventh Day **Read Genesis 19-22**

Scripture comes out of life, and is directed to life. These vivid chapters support the conclusion that the real issues of life change very little. Outward circumstances vary widely, but men of the atomic age face about the same temptations and testings and opportunities that confronted Abraham.

What ideas in today's reading are particularly pertinent to issues you face? Do you think Jewish interpreters of Scripture were right in regarding Abraham's sacrifice of Isaac as the spiritual mountain-top of the Old Testament? What parallels, if any, do you see with God's offering of his Son upon the mount of Calvary?

Eighth Day **Read Genesis 23-24**

While the Bible is immortal literature, it is much more than that. It is a faithful representation of man's dreams, frustrations, defeats, and victories. Instead of being a pretty-pretty story in which everyone is good, it depicts human nature exactly as it is. Some readers object to the frankness with which sexual lust and such matters are treated in Scripture. That is part of its glory: we are dealing with real persons, not characters out of fairy tales.

Notice that the haggling over purchase price of a burial ground is a delightful description of Near Eastern bargaining—helping to make Abraham a real person of flesh and blood rather than an idealized figure. Much the same thing can be said about Isaac's courtship, if it may be called that!

Ninth Day **Read Genesis 25-26**

By the standards of common sense, the birth of twins should pose insoluble problems about which boy would inherit the benefits and obligations of the Covenant. Faith of Israel leaped blithely over such difficulties and asserted that God's word is always gloriously victorious; nothing can thwart the working out of the compact. That is, in the triumph of the younger brother over the older, we see a demonstration of the way in which the promise made to the Chosen People overcomes even the obstacles of biology.

Over and over, the divine promises are repeated. Not only does every generation require a fresh assurance; at every crucial period in the life of a man who transmits the blood and the promise, he is fortified by hearing Jehovah repeat and underscore the fact that the Covenant still holds.

Tenth Day   Read Genesis 27-29

Part of the inner meaning of the strange story of Jacob and Esau rests upon reverence for the spoken word. It was through words, not through tangible agents or even angels, that God created the world and man. God spoke to Noah and Abraham, and his word triumphed over every obstacle. Psalm 29 gives a poetic description of the way Providence operates through God's voice. In John 1, as well as other less familiar New Testament passages, the Son of God is described in terms of his creative and revealing work as the Word of God. Even words spoken by humans are potent and enduring; once the decree of King Ahasuerus had been published, it could not be recalled (Esther 8:8). Having uttered a vow, Jephthah could not take it back even to save his daughter (Judg. 11:29-40). The word is the midwife who presides at the new birth (I Pet. 1:23-25). Coming from the mouth of the Saviour, it is a sword that makes holy war (Rev. 2:16).

Viewed from one perspective, it literally is true that no

word ever uttered can be taken back. So regarded, words actually are among the most dynamic factors in human life, and, tiny though it be, the tongue really is the organ that most clearly separates men from beasts.

Even though Jacob engaged in trickery, the promise of God, transmitted through the spoken blessing of Abraham's descendant, held good. Nothing, absolutely nothing, is powerful enough to cancel out the promises of the Covenant. Neither human frailty, nor family feuds, nor torturous marriage customs of a primitive clan can prevail against the divine word.

Eleventh Day   Read Genesis 30-31

The patriarchs took marriage and the family very seriously. Their views about sex do not coincide with those of the typical American. But, as a minimum, we cannot escape seeing that they regarded sex as participating in the mystery and grandeur of religious faith.

Nor can we fail to see that they were keenly sensitive to religious faith as a factor in every situation. They were not above engaging in what we consider shady tactics—but they were perpetually erecting altars, making sacrifices, and renewing their vows of fidelity to Jehovah. Do you consider them to have been hypocritical, or sincere? Why? What do you think of attempts to prepare an "edited version of the Bible," leaving out passages that shock the modern reader or "aren't fit for children to read"?

Twelfth Day   Read Genesis 32-33

All through the story of man's response to God's invitation, there is a back-and-forth movement. This is geographical as well as spiritual and intellectual. Especially in the time of the patriarchs, the called one is forever having to leave the comfort and security of home in order to go into some far country.

But there is equal stress upon the importance of returning home. Over and over, individuals and groups "go back." Jacob's exciting and dangerous return is repeated generations later by the return of exiles from Babylonian Captivity.

Some readers of the Bible are sure that this pattern of going out and returning home is a way of communicating a universal truth: in the providence of God, somehow and some day, all men will "return home" to enter into a saving relationship with the Father. So viewed, the going out and coming in of Old Testament individuals and groups serve to prefigure the message of salvation that is communicated through the Parable of the Prodigal Son. Maybe you will wish to debate this conclusion. Whatever you may think about it, do you consider the Biblical message to be essentially pessimistic, or overwhelmingly optimistic? What are the implications for your life this week?

Thirteenth Day	Read Genesis 34-36

Formally and informally, sometimes in solitude and sometimes through a public ceremony, the changing of one's name was a frequent Biblical event. Abram became Abraham, Jacob became Israel, and Saul became Paul. There are hosts of other examples.

Whatever else it indicates, the taking of a new name by an adult is a way of declaring to everyone in the family and circle of acquaintances that *a new person has come into existence*. That is, long before the Saviour spoke to all mankind through Nicodemus, the principle "You must be born again" was firmly established.

Jacob's change of name made public the inner transfor-

23

mation, long in process and often interrupted, by which a clever young rogue matured as one worthy to be in the ancestral list of the Christ. Mark well, however, that Jacob did not lift himself by his own bootstraps. His transformation was not merely one of "growth." Rather, he experienced a divine rescue whose effects were to make of him a person he could not become by any amount of striving.

Here is the eternal secret of the Gospel—proclaimed over and over in every section of Scripture, but perpetually hidden from those who have no eyes to see: GOD HAS CHOSEN TO DO THE IMPOSSIBLE FOR THOSE WHO ENTER THE COVENANT. HE WILL LITERALLY AND ACTUALLY RE-MAKE EVERY PERSON WHO WILL LET HIM. THIS COSMIC ACT OF "SALVATION" PRODUCES A TRANSFORMED INDIVIDUAL, SO DIFFERENT FROM THE OLD PERSON THAT IT IS AWKWARD OR IMPOSSIBLE FOR HIM TO ANSWER TO HIS OLD NAME. (*Compare* Rev. 2:17.)

Fourteenth Day   Read Genesis 37-40

Are you tempted to heave a sigh of relief?

"At last! We're on fairly safe, comfortable ground. Here is a story we can tell our children without blushing, and without their demanding too many explanations! The story of Joseph is vivid, dramatic, and not too hard to understand . . ."

Not so fast. Remember that the one true function of Scripture is to communicate truths of God to children of men. If some of the crude and bizarre stories we have read in recent days puzzle or disturb us, so that we have to search very hard to find any spiritual truths in them, we face an opposite danger here. We can regard the story of Joseph as being merely a historical record of colorful men and events. To treat it in that fashion is to destroy it as a pointer toward truths that transcend history.

24

What warnings or promises do you think God is making to all mankind, through the vehicle of an account of Joseph's adventures? How do events in the life of this ancient man yield clues for your own journey today? To what degree is some type of "going down into Egypt" a *necessary* prelude to acceptance of divine rescue and participation in an exodus from one's personal "land of corn and plenty . . . and fleshpots"?

Fifteenth Day   Read Genesis 41-43

Throughout Scripture, Egypt is a symbol of captivity to material things—"worldliness" in its most absolute form. It was the domination of "the world and the flesh," not simply the tyranny of Pharaoh, from which the Chosen People were rescued by mighty acts of God. Notice, too, that Joseph's success in the realm of politics and economics was the essential prelude to the captivity of Abraham's descendants. Grain and oil served as bait with which to lure Jehovah's Chosen into a trap from which they could not escape by their own power.

Sixteenth Day   Read Genesis 44-46

In recognizing the fearful threats posed by all the world's Egypts, never fall into the error of concluding that even a Pharaoh can reign apart from the Creator who sustains all that is. The Egyptian captivity of Israel's clan was to the development of the Chosen People what tragedy can be in the enlargement of an individual seeker for God.

Short of entering into a state of utter hopelessness, neither a clan nor an individual is likely to cease trusting in human resources. It takes desolation and helplessness to force that symphony of combined surrender and rescue, by which the offer of divine help is heard as attractive and acceptable. In this sense, it can be affirmed with absolute joy that God himself led his own people into the land of Goshen—because even God cannot rescue men until they enter a captivity so absolute that they recognize themselves as captives.

Seventeenth Day   Read Genesis 47-50

Enslavement in Egypt was gradual. At first, settlers in the land where men worshiped their ruler as divine considered themselves lucky. They did not lose their liberty all at once, but a bit at a time over a period of generations.

Here is a figure of the way men given freedom by their Creator, drift into slavery to false gods and dictatorship by habits and lusts. Yield a trifle here, retreat a bit there—nothing vital, mind you, just a reasonable concession to appetite or social pressure—and one day you will suddenly become aware of shackles that bind you hand and foot, fastened upon you so gradually that you hardly noticed them.

At this stage, the Chosen People have not yet learned to wear the chains of Egyptian bondage comfortably; though Joseph dandles his part-Egyptian grandchildren upon his knee, he never abandons the dream of being buried beside his father in distant Canaan.

Exodus

The Book of Exodus is an account of historic events that transformed an enslaved tribe into a free nation. But because tribesmen were people of the promise, the story is much more than mere "history." It represents a specific instance—*the* instance in Hebrew history—through which a fundamental truth is expressed: God the Creator perpetually rescues his own from captivity to material forces, and establishes them in a new land of promise so they may be free to keep their part of the divine-human Covenant.

Because Exodus uses events in the sphere of history as channels through which to pour deep truths of the faith, the book conveys its radiant message only when read with believing eyes. Among the rescued clansmen whose sandals were hardly dry from crossing wet sands of the Red Sea, only Moses listened intently enough to hear God reveal himself more fully than to Abraham. Among the individuals and groups reading Exodus during the next two weeks, only those who plod their way through the wilderness with eager certainty that God is leading them, will fall on their faces before the glory of the Creator revealed at some personal Sinai.

Eighteenth Day	Read Exodus 1-3

Marvels and wonders are essential ingredients in such a story. For it is an account of the Creator's dealings with creatures made in his image, and where there is no mystery or awe or transcendent glory there is no sense of the divine presence. So long as one regards the events of everyday life as wholly explainable—that is, not too large or complex for men to know them in their entirety—there is no sensitivity to the more-than-human.

Of all the incredible events in the career of Moses, perhaps the least emphasized is the paradox by which God used a prince from the household of Pharaoh as his agent. By all logical standards, we would be tempted to think such a man would be the least likely of instruments for the work of Providence. From the beginning of a career he did not choose but to which he was called, Moses was con-

27

scious that his highest task was obedience. It was divine power, not human, that was to set Abraham's descendants on the route back to the land of promise.

Nineteenth Day   **Read Exodus 4-6**

Whether it be social or individual, divine rescue is expensive. It costs a great deal in terms of suffering and struggle —both divine and human. Instead of coming easily and quickly, at the first response of an awakened one to the promise of liberation, rescue may be deferred through a series of interminable delays.

Indeed, the lot of the one seeking rescue may become successively worse as he makes his initial responses to God's overtures. No Egypt is left without struggle. No Pharaoh gives up his hold upon his slaves at the first sign of restlessness. One reason so many persons elect to remain in their personal Egypts, rather than be led out by God, is that freedom comes high, and it is not won without a long struggle, the plagues of which may be more agonizing even than endurable slavery.

Twentieth Day   **Read Exodus 7-9**

Reading about stupendous acts of God, worked in a strange and ancient land, the modern reader is likely to be baffled. Why on earth did Pharaoh prove so obstinate? How could he have been so blind? Is it possible that a man, with intelligence to rule a great civilization, refused to recognize God's sovereignty except in cataclysmic, death-dealing disaster?

Remember, that we are reading not merely the history of the Hebrews, but also *salvation history*. It is one of the

qualities of divine truth that it remains hidden from eyes
of unbelievers. Two men look at the same scene; one takes
off his shoes before the presence of his Creator, and the
other calculates the cost of laying out a subdivision. Perhaps the most insistent message of these chapters is in the
form of a warning: Are you playing the role of Pharaoh,
obstinately refusing to seek the work of the one true God
in events of your daily life? Will you stubbornly close your
eyes until tragedy strikes inside the walls of your own
house?

Twenty-first Day   Read Exodus 10-12

Have you been struck by the insistence that God repeatedly hardened the heart of Pharaoh? The story seems to
imply that divine forces were at work to prevent the
Egyptian from seeing God's hand in national troubles.
According to this line of thought, Pharaoh did not reject
his opportunities by free choice, but was forced by Providence to act as he did.

Such an interpretation by-passes the heart of the message. Faith asserts that NOTHING is outside the realm of the
Creator, and NOTHING is strong enough to defeat his purposes expressed in the Covenant. (Paul gives a detailed
interpretation of this matter in Romans 9.)

No matter how powerful or clever or stubborn he may
be, no human rebel against the government of God can
succeed in overthrowing the divine rule. Regardless of how
cruel or evil or warped a man may be, whatever he does
is done within the context of Providence and not outside
it. Because God's purposes cannot be thwarted, God succeeds in using any and all events for his glory and for the
fulfillment of his Covenant.

References to God's hardening of the heart do not relieve
any pharaoh from responsibility for free choice. Rather,

29

these are yet more triumphant assertions of faith, shouting that GOD IS NOT ALOOF EVEN FROM SUFFERING, TRAGEDY, AND DEFEAT. Regardless of what may take place within the stream of history, eyes of faith sparkle with joyous certainty that, somehow, this too is operating to effect rescue, exodus into a land of milk and honey, and ultimate glad victory.

Twenty-second Day   **Read Exodus 13-15**

Throughout the history of Israel, up to and including the twentieth century A.D., many ceremonies and symbols have been linked with the Exodus. The Passover feast is a solemn ritual that re-enacts God's "passing over" of the Hebrew houses on the night Egypt's first-born were slain by the angel of death. So, the seven days in which unleavened bread is eaten are days in which celebrants are reminded over and over that Jehovah is a God of rescue.

Any attempt to penetrate to the depth of New Testament thought without some understanding of Covenant events described in the Old Testament is utterly futile. At no point are bonds clearer than those between Calvary and the Exodus. Notice the clear foreshadowing of the Gospel's central promise in the triumph song of Moses and his followers, clearly emphasizing that the rescue from Egypt rested upon divine *purchase* (redemption) of the liberated ones (15:13, 16).

Holy Communion is an adapted and modified form of the Passover feast, pointing to and actually offering divine rescue through spiritual participation in the death and resurrection of God's supreme agent—his Son. The communion bread (or wafer) points back to the unleavened bread of the Jews and through it to manna eaten in the wilderness, as well as to Jesus Christ's broken body. The blood-red communion cup offers not only the rescue made available through the Saviour's shed blood, but also the leading out from Egypt of the Chosen People whose doorposts were smeared with blood. (In the same fashion, to eyes of faith, the waters through which Noah passed point to the saving water of baptism; *see* I Peter 3:21.)

Twenty-third Day   Read Exodus 16-18

Once the problems of captivity were solved by divine intervention, Abraham's descendants found themselves facing a host of new ones. Though liberated—made into a new people—by acts of God, they were not thereby freed of the limitations of humanity. Instead, they quickly discovered that, if they actually were to enter the land of promise, it would have to be as an aftermath of a long period of struggle.

Once more, group rescue has many qualities linked with individual salvation. Struggling with enslavement to forces in whatever Egypt happens to hold him captive, one pants for liberty. But when it comes, he who has become a new person in Christ Jesus quickly finds himself confronted by a host of new problems. Individually and collectively, therefore, to cross the Jordan and enter Canaan requires not simply a single parting of the Red Sea by the hand of God, but also a faithful forty-year struggle to walk in the pathway designated by God.

Twenty-fourth Day   Read Exodus 19-20

Probably you will wish to read these chapters more than once. For each time the account of the revelation to Moses is pondered, new truths emerge. A lifetime devoted to considering the Ten Commandments would not be sufficient to uncover all the spiritual treasure offered here.

31

Twenty-fifth Day **Read Exodus 21-23**

To a modern city dweller, these regulations seem more confusing than helpful. They simply do not apply to conditions of today's life. This is one of the insoluble problems linked with codes of law: we must have laws, in order to function as an organized society—but social changes quickly make laws obsolete. Here is eloquent testimony about man's incapacity to save himself! He cannot govern himself by abstract principles alone; regardless of how exalted these principles may be, specific laws based upon them must apply to specific conditions. Once those conditions change, the laws become empty.

It was the fatal mistake of institutional Judaism to become immersed in a sea of legalism. But it is far easier to recognize this error than to escape from factors that tend to force such conditions upon religious groups, cultures, and nations.

As you consider this phase of the human dilemma today, think of some specific laws of Christian conduct that are accepted by other persons but that seem to you no longer applicable to actual conditions. If even a Moses, face to face with God, is limited in ability to shape laws to govern human conduct, what does this say about a city council or a state legislature? Can you propose any human way out of the difficulty? Any divine solution?

Twenty-sixth Day **Read Exodus 24-27**

It is both the glory and the mystery of the Covenant that, although man can accept God's gifts and know God through belief-powered experience, man cannot by any means at his command describe or depict or represent God so that he can be known by persons who have not met him in experience. This is the root of the prohibition of graven images. However deep his own religious experience, however great his skill with mallet and chisel, no sculptor can communicate truth about God without also suggesting falsehood.

Today we readily accept this principle as applied to visual representation, or idols. But we do not always recognize that precisely the same difficulties attach to use of words. It is because any description or name may become an "idol" that God gives so mysterious a reply to Moses' question at his first response to the divine call (Exod. 3:13-15). Likewise, the name of the king of kings is known only to himself (Rev. 19:12). To say that God is the beginning, or that he is the end, is a kind of distortion: for at one and the same time, he is both beginning and end. He is Alpha and Omega *simultaneously* (Rev. 1:8).

But in order to speak to one another at all about God, in order to engage in anything equivalent to what we now stress as "Christian education," we must have visual and verbal pointers toward truths they do not fully contain. This is the function of the religious symbol. It serves as a handle, by which a novice can begin to grasp low-level truths that come in their fullness only through personal encounter with God.

For the Hebrew people, the Ark of the Covenant was high on the list of potent symbols: the visible one was simply a representation of the ark laid up in heaven (Rev. 11:19). Purposely made in costly and elaborate form, awe-inspiring and mysterious in its physical make-up, it was intended to point beyond itself to the divine-human Covenant that is basic to the experience of the Chosen People.

Twenty-seventh Day   **Read Exodus 28-31**

Ceremonies and clothing and furniture and food associated with religion (no matter how "primitive" or how "advanced") ALWAYS carry with them suggestions of the mysterious. That is also the case—indeed, particularly the case —with the vocabulary of religion. In worship we habitually and necessarily use words and phrases to suggest meanings not associated with those words and phrases in everyday speech.

This matter once more points to both the glory and the limited-ness of man. Through the symbols and ceremonies and vocabulary of religion, we can cultivate our own spiritual sensitivity and initiate beginners into mysteries of the faith. That is glorious. But the greater the degree of success achieved, the wider the gap between "insiders" and "outsiders." A stranger not familiar with the language of faith is bewildered by words and ceremonies and symbols of worship. For him, these serve as roadblocks rather than as highways.

In memory, take a quick survey of the physical surroundings at your church and try to decide which things mean most to you and what effect they would have on a person without experience in Protestant worship. Should there be fewer candles and crosses and flags, or more? Do you think verbal symbols that distract the novice should be discarded? (For example, "washed in the blood.") Or should we hold fast to inherited symbols and try to help others discover their deepest meanings?

Twenty-eighth Day   **Read Exodus 32-34**

Aaron's sin was not only a violation of the law against making an image of deity; it was also a frank concession to popular desire for good things associated with Egypt. Never lose sight of the fact that *salvation history*, or the account of the divine-human Covenant, deals as fully with man as with God. Divine readiness to rescue is ALWAYS matched by human reluctance to make a full surrender.

Were you and I less stiff-necked than we actually are, were the gap between God and man not absolute, there would be no necessity for a plan of *salvation*. It is part of the fallacy (or rather, heresy) of much modern churchmanship to minimize the radical nature of salvation and to proclaim a religion of achievement. Guard with your life against falling into this perversion of the Gospel. Today, this very hour, try to see more clearly what variety of golden calf you are tempted to worship in order to gain the bounty of the particular Egypt that beckons you most invitingly.

Twenty-ninth Day   **Read Exodus 35-37**

Repetition of rather monotonous details must not serve to blind us to deep truths in today's reading. Limited and prone to fail and fall though we are, men can yet have a part in the glorifying of God. We can make our offerings to God with such free will and glad surrender that we add not only to the tangible apparatus of worship, but also to the glory of the Creator! Even though our feet are prone to become entangled in details of cutting acacia wood or meeting quotas assigned by the denomination, faithful self-giving through such media is part of the fulfillment of the Covenant. It was for this that the world was established.

Thirtieth Day   **Read Exodus 38-40**

Provided we will open our eyes to God's presence in all that he has made, almost any event or object can serve to heighten our sense of wonder and mystery and holiness. From anointing oil to bronze fire pans, from fine-twined linen to gem-studded breastplates, any natural or manufactured thing whatever can point to the all-powerful God through whom it exists and by whom it is sustained.

Capacity to see God not only in holy articles associated with worship and inherited from previous generations, but also in the most commonplace and ordinary things of daily experience, is among the most sublime of belief-powered gifts (Rev. 5:13). Thanks be to God, here is a gift that can be cultivated! If you do not suddenly "see" God in fresh fashion today in some strange or some very familiar item of experience, it is because you are not eagerly straining to find evidence of the Creator in every aspect of his creation.

SECOND MONTH:

Leviticus, Numbers, Deuteronomy, Joshua, Judges

Leviticus

For most practical purposes, this book might as well not be included in the Bible. It has few points of contact with modern Christian thought or life, and is seldom opened. In our pilgrimage through the entire Bible, Leviticus can claim only the briefest pause.

It is startling to recognize the organic bond between Levitical laws and everyday life of the Saviour's people, as evidenced by the relationship between Lev. 12 and Luke 2:22-24. Yet we cannot ponder the message of this book paragraph by paragraph or even chapter by chapter. Instead, we must skim swiftly through many chapters in half an hour, looking for major landmarks that project above the surface.

First Day	**Skim Leviticus 1-14**

Fleeting pauses for quick glances at ceremonies of Israel lead to overwhelming recognition of blood's role in worship of the Chosen People. How many scores of times the word "blood" appears in these chapters! How few solemn rites proceed without ceremonial use of blood!

Central in the entire Old Testament and not merely the legal codes preserved here, blood's symbolism rests upon its role as the vehicle of life. Mysterious and elusive, life partakes of the nature of the Maker of life. Hence the carrier of life, blood, is forbidden as an item of diet; it is taboo. Even otherwise clean animals, those that die a natural death or are killed by beasts, are unclean because the blood has not been drained from their bodies. There is no atonement for murder, and the very land on which the blood of a man has been shed is polluted (Num. 35:29-34).

But, precisely because blood is the carrier of life and hence is the most precious part of an organism, it constitutes the ultimate substance for offering God the best one can give. Abraham's testing consisted of challenging him to sacrifice the blood of his only son. So just here, in the strangest of places, we begin dimly to perceive why blood symbolism should be so deeply embedded in the unfolding of *salvation history*.

Our Father's self-giving for the sake of humanity took the form of pouring out for men the most priceless item in the divine treasure house: the blood of his Son. Jesus' blood, voluntarily shed for men as a sin-offering and hence operating to cleanse men of guilt, becomes, in effect, the *modus operandi* of rescue. Just as blood coursing through the veins of a man conveys life, so the shed blood of Jesus Christ transmits spiritual life. In effect, that blood *is* grace (I John 1:7; Rev. 1:5), for it constitutes the purchase price of salvation (Rev. 5:9-10).

Blood symbolism is rooted in ideas and ceremonies whose origins are lost in antiquity, and so it appears crude and primitive to many modern eyes. Yet it is absolutely basic to understanding of the New Testament as well as the Old. So, in this "desert of dry bones" that is Leviticus, we can rise on wings of faith-founded metaphor to seize totally new understanding of Calvary and the Lord's Supper. From this perspective we gain fresh meaning from

Christendom's colossal repertoire of blood-centered meditations, prayers, and hymns, typical of which is William Cowper's glory song that begins:

> There is a fountain filled with blood
> Drawn from Immanuel's veins;
> And sinners, plunged beneath that flood,
> Lose all their guilty stains.

Second Day   Skim Leviticus 15-27

These chapters reveal a people acutely conscious of being set apart from the rest of mankind, and obsessed with zeal for observance of religious law. Instead of setting aside special places and occasions for obedience, Israel uses the law as social cement, holding society together. There is no hint of the modern distinction between sacred and secular; the law addresses everyone and deals with all aspects of life. The Sabbath is the pulse beat of the culture, as organic as the rhythm of the human heart.

Obsessed with religion, these folk, in conscious Covenant with their Creator, must always give him their *best*. Only unblemished male animals (prized by stock breeders then as now) may be offered. It is not just any handful of cereal, but fine flour that is used at the altar. Because the Lord accepts only the choicest, he requires that *unblemished* human males be set aside for the holy priesthood (21:16-24).

In a land perennially unable to feed all its hungry, the fear of God is brought into the kitchen by laws prohibiting many sources of food. No family can ever sit down to a meal without consciousness of religious overtones. This factor goes far to create a state of intoxication with the Lord. At the same time, there is an incredible degree of social solidarity. The descendant of Abraham is so con-

scious that he differs from other men that assimilation of the
"outsider" is slow and difficult. That is, a culture so permeated with religious rites actually constitutes a people
set apart (18:1-5; 20:23). But more is involved than conscious separation; Israel is *set apart to God.* This is symbolized by the tithe—through which one-tenth of the national
production is set aside; it is not actually an offering, for it
never does belong to men and is not to be put to ordinary
use even in dire emergencies.

Incredibly difficult to comprehend from the modern
viewpoint, almost weirdly "out of this world" through absolute domination of religious law, the Israel so formed
constituted the people through whom God would pour
himself into history in the person of his Son.

Numbers

As in the case of Leviticus, we must skim this little-read
book very swiftly. Its English title comes from Moses'
census, or numbering of the tribes. Hebrew editions call it
"In the Wilderness," for the book deals with Israel's life
during her forty years of wandering. Word-for-word reading in meditative fashion would be worse than barren. But
a swift over-all look reveals powerful and fascinating
qualities in the life of the Covenant people, destined to be
the social womb through which the Son would be delivered
to effect salvation.

Third Day	**Skim Numbers 1-10**

Israel's whole life was permeated by God-consciousness.
Still, some areas of experience and conduct were especially
holy and hence potent. (*See,* for example, 3:38; 4:15, 19-20.)
Potency of the holy is the base on which the ceremony of
lie detection rests. (*See* Chapter 5.) Power so permeates

the holy that it is explosive. Dealing with it, a novice may bring disaster upon himself and all his people.

Partly for this reason, and partly because complex ceremonies required discipline and training for the leader, there developed special classes of men "set apart." Priests, considered to be descendants of Aaron, became specialists in worship. Other descendants of Levi were designated as their assistants. As guardian and manipulator of the holy, the priest could, to a degree, direct the flow of divine power. He was not a servant of the people, not a paid official of the tribe, but an earthly representative of the Most High.

Christendom has tried to preserve something of this quality through the practice of ordination. Far as he is from belonging to the house of Aaron, the modern ordained minister is also a priest. Within the life of the congregation, he alone administers the sacraments—of which Holy Communion and baptism are especially important among Protestant Christians. Do you think of your minister chiefly as a priest, or as a friend? Is he an employee of the congregation, or an appointee of God? What are the implications for the life of the Church? How important do you consider sacraments to be, in the process of salvation?

Fourth Day   **Skim Numbers 11-21**

Interspersed with sections of religious law and descriptions of ceremonies, there is a thrilling and frightening account of the rescued people as they react to their new freedom and responsibility. Not once, but over and over, the people who so recently thought they wanted liberty more than life, complain at their new lot. Not satisfied with grumbling, they repeatedly engage in active rebellion.

These incidents take place against the backdrop of Providence, as it were. For their miraculous feeding in the wilderness is calculated to make them sensitive to God's concern, and aware that they are totally dependent upon him.

No matter how earth-shaking a miracle may be, it is likely to be taken for granted when it becomes an item of daily experience. Abraham's descendants marveled the first few times they gathered manna, but soon wearied of it and cried for good red meat. Though this was only one of many sources of complaint and rebellion, it is symbolic of them all.

Over and over, God punished them: through sickness, natural disasters, and military defeat. But they never learned. Over and over, the cycle was repeated: divine bounty and forgiveness soon were taken for granted; men complained and rebelled; God punished them sorely and then forgave the repentant ones; for a while, they rejoiced and offered noble sacrifices—but soon slipped back into sin to launch another cycle.

Fifth Day	**Read Numbers 22-24**

In a way, it is a shame we ever began telling the story of Balaam and his ass to Sunday school tots. For many have come to think of it as nothing more than a glorified fairy tale. So regarded, it is interesting and amusing, but has little significance for the lives of educated adults in the age of science.

Actually, the story of the prophet and his beast is a vivid case history in divine revelation.

A fundamental note of Scripture sounds precisely here. For the entire Bible is founded on the conviction that God actually communicates with men. Moreover, asserts faith, the Creator is not limited to the vehicles of man-to-man communication. He of course uses inspired prophets and seers, whose words challenge and guide less sensitive men.

But in addition to these comparatively clear channels for divine-human dialogue, God actually uses everything in existence. EVERYTHING IN CREATION HAS CAPACITY TO WITNESS ABOUT THE CREATOR (Ps. 19:1-4).

There are hosts of Biblical instances in which a sensitive soul hears God "speak" to him without being exposed to sounds of human speech. To Noah, the rainbow "says" that God has entered into a compact with men. Attuned ears of Jeremiah, exposed only to the squeaking of a potter's wheel, "hear" divine warnings and promises. And that passionate listener, St. John, reports in the Revelation how in quick succession he heard God's voice poured out through a trumpet's blast, thunder, and the cry of an eagle.

Do you think Balaam's ass spoke an early Hebrew dialect—or did his actions simply so point the prophet to God that Balaam had to resort to human words to report the message he received? Have you ever been "spoken to" through an event or thing that did not employ language? Is God less eager and able to speak to us today than during the time of the patriarchs? How literally shall we take the idea of a sword's serving to convey a message? (Judg. 3:20).

Whatever you may conclude about the mystery of Balaam's beast, this I should like to declare as a personal conviction:

If you will deliberately tune your ears to God's wave length, there will be many days when you will hear life-changing messages from heaven, and rarely will your Creator fail to whisper in your ear during a day.

Sixth Day   **Read Numbers 25-36**

Internal solidarity, evidenced by adoption of yet more elaborate laws, continued to mature during the desert wanderings. It was this factor that transformed Israel from a

43

motley band of refugees into a stalwart group of tightly-knit clans.

But there was no advocate of world peace among the people of the Covenant! Fierceness of their warriors was matched only by cruelty with which conquered foes were treated. There was almost fiendish exclusiveness: come what may, the blood of the Chosen People must not be contaminated. There could be no compromise with worshipers of false gods; those who could not be assimilated—i.e., brought into the life-stream of Israel—must be exterminated.

The whole idea of a divine-human covenant with a Chosen People requires that they be set apart, fiercely exclusive, totally unwilling to enter into compromise with "the world." For, in order to give his Son to all mankind, God had to take for himself an earthly bride in the person of an Israel who would remain true to him, rejecting all the amorous advances of those who bowed at the altar of Baal and other pagan gods.

Deuteronomy

This set of codes whose Hebrew title describes it as "The Second Law" is the last of the five Books of Moses. In clear contrast with much earlier religious law directed to desert tribesmen, it deals largely with the life of an agricultural people settled in villages and towns. Influence upon New Testament writers has been immense, with St. Matthew and St. Paul especially vocal in their tribute to Deuteronomy's spiritual power and witness to the Saviour dimly glimpsed.

Seventh Day	Read Deuteronomy 1-4

Here reported as a formal address by Moses, these chapters give a capsule interpretation of divine law. It rests entirely upon God's promises, which he made voluntarily. But, in order to gain the rewards that are offered, the Covenant people must act boldly and faithfully.

God's word stands forever; the Covenant cannot be destroyed. Ultimate fulfillment is more certain than the coming of morning after the night with which the Hebrew day begins. But both individuals and the Chosen People (functioning in many respects as a sort of corporate individual or "social person") are prone to turn aside from God and bring down wrath. Such fire from heaven, poured out not once but over and over, serves to convict and convert erring ones. Here is the womb from which the transformed soul must be born: the Covenant state, with all its paradoxes and alternating currents, its inevitable human failures, mingles with assurance of absolute victory through divine rescue.

Eighth Day   Read Deuteronomy 5-7

Moses' second "public address," as transmitted by generations of the pious, is essentially a commentary upon the Ten Commandments. Notice particularly the winged words of 6:1-15, and repeated emphasis upon Israel's unique role as a Chosen People set apart.

Ninth Day   Read Deuteronomy 8-11

Promise and warning . . . warning and promise! How the two aspects of the Covenant relationship do continually alternate!

Viewed from a perspective other than that of a brief human life, promises and warnings actually coexist and thereby establish a field of tension whose intensity may vary, but whose fierce tuggings never cease. Establishment

45

of this environment for development of souls is basic to God's creative work. Only in such a context can the creature made in the divine image so respond to the Creator that he shakes off the limitations of the dust from which he came, and enters into endless glory in the company of the Father.

Tenth Day   Read Deuteronomy 12-15

Even in the time of joy and victory that is symbolized by entrance into Canaan, the rescued one is never wholly free of the tendency to bow down before false gods. The lure of Satan and the world is ceaseless. In this life, spiritual power never reaches such a point that the Covenanter, with Egypt still fresh in his memory and the glory of rescue still vivid, can bask at ease.

Relax for a new moon or two, cease to be on the aggressive against the forces of evil, drift into contentment . . . and defeat is near. That is why scrupulous attention to the law is vital when security threatens; awakening and convicting statutes cause fresh winds to blow over the soul.

Eleventh Day   Read Deuteronomy 16-19

Part of the eternal human dilemma lies in the relation between individual and group. True human individuals cannot develop in isolation: a social as well as a biological womb is necessary. But the impact of the group upon the individual is such that we are continually trying to "improve" society for the sake of the persons whom it includes and shapes.

To have a king, or not to have a king? In one form or another, that is a perennial riddle. (See especially 17:14-20.)

We cannot function as an organized society without a power structure—but poor leaders are worse than none. Once more, we recognize that we are incapable of saving ourselves; if we are to enter an ideal state, it must be by God's grace and not by our own cleverness.

Twelfth Day	Read Deuteronomy 20-23

No activity, no event, no circumstance is outside the area of the Covenant and its concerns. Conduct of battle, siege of a city, discipline of a son, finding of a stray farm animal, and robbing of a bird's nest are activities within the law and not apart from it.

Thirteenth Day	Read Deuteronomy 24-27

Never under any circumstances must Israel forget that she has been redeemed—not by her own power, but by the favor of the Lord. At every time of harvest, the rejoicing at earth's bounty can be a special occasion for remembering divine rescue (26:1-11). Every occasion of remembering can be the stimulus for erecting altars and memorial stones —which, in turn, serve to evoke new rememberings.

It is such remembering and dedicating, over and over, through all the activities of a God-intoxicated culture, that gives Israel her unique nature and constitutes her as the bride of Jehovah (26:16-19).

Fourteenth Day	Read Deuteronomy 28-29

Blessings or curses . . . bliss beyond imagination, or afflictions severe and lasting . . . in the Covenant relationship, there is no middle ground of neutrality.

Fifteenth Day   **Read Deuteronomy 30-31**

Man's freedom comes at the point of moral and spiritual choice. We are not free, in the sense that we can do anything we please. We are of earth, and chained to earth with bonds far stronger than those of iron. Even in the Space Age, we shall take our earthliness with us, if and when we transcend the physical limits of our planet.

It is our glory that we can shake off the shackles of earth in the realm of the spirit. Each of us has set before him "life and good, death and evil" (30:15). Each of us not only *may* make this cosmic choice; each of us *must* make it.

Sixteenth Day   **Read Deuteronomy 32-34**

Few passages in literature exceed the power and sweep of the songs of Moses. As you revel in their magnificent promises, remember that Christian thought makes each individual follower of the Son the recipient of all the bounty promised by the Father. Israel's whole history, God's entire Covenant of Grace, comes to focus in you. Hence you may read these glory songs with your own name inserted; it was in order that *you* might accept the Father's good gifts that the heavens and the earth were created!

Joshua

Historical books of the Old Testament present a strange combination. They depict the growth of a family (Abraham's descendants) into a group of tribes, and then into a nation. Throughout, there is enormous stress upon the importance of the group. It is the collective Israel, "bride of Jehovah," with whom the story is concerned.

Yet it is at the same time a story centering upon a few individuals. Joshua, successor of Moses, is one such stalwart leader. Just as we associate Moses with the divine deliverance that produced the Exodus from godless Egypt, so we associate Joshua with the fulfillment of God's promise to establish his Chosen People in a land of abundance. Not merely once or a few times, but over and over God raises up a Joshua to play a vital and dramatic part in leading masses of persons into some Canaan.

That is to say, God is never an absentee landlord. He not only creates and sustains the physical environment essential to human existence, he also has an organic role in human history. God's absolute entrance into that history is through the person of his Son who came in the fullness of time. But it did not take the first Christmas and the road to Calvary to initiate divine-human encounter. Always, God is in history as a power-conferring and shaping agent working through some Moses or Joshua.

Seventeenth Day   Read Joshua 1-4

It is a somewhat ironic commentary upon all that we call "progress" to reflect upon the role of national leaders, then and now. Joshua's rise to leadership is the fruit of his response to a divine call. His first duty is that of obedience to God. His most pressing daily task is that of meditating day and night upon the book of the law.

In our epoch of "enlightenment," where leaders derive their power from voters rather than from God, the first duty of the elected officer is that of pleasing the persons who can keep him in office. His most pressing daily task is that of inquiring what the majority of voters want, and trying to act accordingly.

In these thousands of years, how far have men come, really? Is there any reasonable hope for development of an ideal society—Utopia—on this planet? Do you accept or re-

49

ject the notion that social dilemmas, like individual ones, remind us of our limited-ness and can serve to persuade us to seek divine rescue rather than human achievement?

Eighteenth Day   **Read Joshua 5-7**

Every advance is achieved at a price. Even in the process of accepting and acting upon divine help, men remain men. But we are prone to forget our limitations when we are relatively comfortable. This is the perennial error that we make, individually and socially. Over and over, God leads his own out of their personal Egypts and, by the thunder of his trumpets, causes the walls of fortified cities to fall. Over and over, rescued ones cease to "hearken to the voice of the Lord," break faith, and, in their self-sufficiency, rebel against their deliverer. Over and over, proud ones are denied entrance into the Canaan for which they set out in their enthusiasm at being led over some Red Sea.

Hence it is that, perpetually and perennially, children and grandchildren can actually settle in lands of promise never entered by those who "grow up" and cease to think of themselves as little children in the sight of a Father who demands absolute obedience as the price of rescue.

Nineteenth Day   **Read Joshua 8-10**

We are inclined to remember Joshua largely for his role in that strange battle when the sun stood still. This memorable event, like the rain of stones from heaven, was a dramatic message conveyed through deeds rather than words. (*See* comment on Num. 22-24, 5th day.) Translated into language, these marvelous signs of God's special concern for Israel would simply "say" that the Lord is fighting on the side of the Chosen People.

Today's middle-class churchmen tend to use the marvelous events of Joshua's military campaigns simply as interesting and vivid stories—and frequently fail to show Sunday school pupils how they are outward fruits, as it were, of individual and national faithfulness to God. For the real message of Joshua's story centers in his ceaseless search for greater obedience (1:8). His building of an altar, offering of sacrifices, and reading of "all that is written in the book of the law" (8:30-35) are the central public events of his colorful career. Supernatural aid in battle was simply a visible and tangible effect of his far more important campaigns in the realm of the spirit.

Twentieth Day   Read Joshua 11-13

Bloody and cruel as the account is, the record of the wars of Joshua is not to be struck from the Book that deals with *salvation history.* In our present-day recoil from the horrors of war and our enthusiasm for world peace, we tend to adopt a point of view in which wars are fought in a vacuum, as it were. That is, we are prone to regard war as taking place outside the ongoing creative work of God.

Here is a wholesome corrective.

Let us never fall into the error of believing that anything whatever can exist "in its own strength." God is maker of all that has been; God sustains all that is. Even when men, in their freedom, fall upon one another and slaughter the innocent with the guilty, God has not turned his back upon his creation. Providence is ever-present and exalted, operating on so vast a scale that eyes of men perceive details only with difficulty.

But, were we sufficiently sensitive, we could see the Creator in every aspect of creation. That is essentially the witness of these chapters. Blithely indifferent to contrary arguments, rising on wings of belief above all the objections of logic and doctrine, they declare that God is *the* active agent in human history. God is working out his purpose even in our darkest hours. For those who accept his offer of redeeming grace, every circumstance whatever is an agent operating to strengthen the bonds of the Covenant.

Twenty-first Day   **Read Joshua 14-20**

Assignment of territory by lot is still another evidence of absolute dependence upon divine guidance. Such a notion sounds strange today. We are prone to rely upon the wisdom of a human expert, or to call upon some "impartial jury" of average men and women who will arrive at a verdict—i.e., "the truth."

Only in a God-centered culture is it possible to seek the will of the Creator through what we are likely to consider pure chance. Israel found it wholly logical to make important decisions upon the basis of the fall of Urim and Thummin—small stones that functioned somewhat like dice.

Casting of lots was a standard religious ceremony. (*See* Exod. 28:29; Lev. 8:8; Num. 27:21; Deut. 33:8.) It was actually employed by Jesus' Apostles to select a successor to Judas (Acts 1:26). Gideon's fleece was simply another device for "testing God," or seeking to know his will (Judg. 6:36-40). Some device for casting lots was probably used in such crises as that described in Judg. 20:23. The apron-like *ephod* of the priest (influential in freemasonry as well as ecclesiastical garments) was used to determine God's will in cases of doubt. See, for example, David's employment of it to decide whether or not to attack in battle (I Sam. 30:7-9). It was frightful to be unable to get any answer through the use of such devices; this "crisis of silence" sent Saul in disguise to consult the witch of Endor (I Sam. 28).

I think the point of view (*exceedingly* difficult for us to grasp) was roughly this: NOTHING WHATEVER TAKES PLACE APART FROM GOD. THEREFORE, GOD AFFECTS THE OUTCOME OF CASTING LOTS AND THROUGH THIS PRACTICE "SPEAKS" TO THOSE WHO HAVE ENOUGH FAITH AND SKILL TO UNDERSTAND WHAT HE SAYS.

However you may react to so primitive a view of Providence, it nevertheless remains provocative. For if you and I can become convinced that a given outcome represents the will of God, and if we order our conduct in the light of this conviction, then it follows that, for us, whatever comes is bound to bring us closer to God rather than cause us to turn aside from seeking him. Such a point of view is radically different from fatalism—passive acceptance of whatever comes, resignation that "what will be, will be."

Vital trust in providential ordering of life's events, even to the assignment of a place to live (about which we moderns fret so much), produces individual and cultural "peace of mind" of a variety far deeper than that of shallow contentment.

Twenty-second Day   Read Joshua 21-22

Even the assignment of territory is conditional; even the blessing of a Joshua rests upon acceptance of terms. Those terms, in the present case, are no less than scrupulous daily concern for God's will as expressed through religious law (22:5).

Twenty-third Day   Read Joshua 23-24

Once more, the people of the promise hear a warning that their special relationship with God is like a two-edged sword.

53

Obedience to God alone will bring blessings, but loyalty to any other god or goal will arouse God's anger and cause his wrath to be poured upon the heads of his people. There is no safe middle ground; it is either/or (24:15).

As a small boy learning the catechism, I was bothered by the idea that God is "jealous." But the sense of that adjective is positive rather than negative. God so yearns to give us all his good things that he frets and chafes every time we turn aside from him to seek a "foreign god." Let us not fall into that delusion of Satan according to which idols and false gods have vanished from this age of enlightenment; to put any other goal ahead of the desire to know and please God is to bow down at the shrine of some modern Baal and thereby to invite the wrath of Jehovah.

Judges

Having settled in the Promised Land, the people of the promise developed a town culture that contrasted sharply with that of wandering shepherds. Heads of clans could no longer govern the people satisfactorily—but it would be many generations before a true nation could take shape. In this interim period of several centuries, tribal chieftains and heroes, or "judges," were important and colorful leaders. Hence their title attaches to the book that preserves many records from the period.

Twenty-fourth Day   **Read Judges 1-3**

It was the role of the judge not only to lead in battle and govern in time of peace, but also to serve as "agent" or spokesman for God. (See 8:23.) That is, during the period of the judges, the distinction between "religious" and "political" leadership hardly existed. Part of the power of the judge, even when a man of violence like Ehud or Shamgar, derived from his conviction that he was first a messenger of God and second a leader and governor of his fellow men.

Twenty-fifth Day   Read Judges 4-5

Sisera, most powerful Canaanite chieftain of the period, had no stockpile of atomic bombs. He commanded nine hundred chariots of iron, however, and military force alone could never defeat him.

To bring the mighty warrior and his iron chariots low, God raised up—not a stronger fighting man, but a woman! Deborah might be described as an ancient forerunner of Joan of Arc; her weapons were words and moral certainty. To complete the irony of divine retribution, the great Sisera died at the hands of a woman! (*See* also Abimelech's end, Judg. 9:50-54.)

You recognize, of course, that such accounts represent history interpreted from the viewpoint of absorbing belief in all-inclusive Providence. This is only one of many ways in which history can be viewed and reported; it is quite alien to the method of most present historians. But the important thing for us to underscore here is the fact that all historical reports are shaped by beliefs of the historian. There is no such thing as "impartial and objective reporting of what happens."

We are dealing with *spiritual history*, in which events of every area of life are interpreted from one of many possible viewpoints—namely, absorbing certainty that God is the decisive agent in all that takes place. Precisely that certainty is the message of the Song of Deborah.

Twenty-sixth Day   **Read Judges 6-8**

Have you noticed how many paragraphs and chapters begin with the same note? Just as military victory is credited to the work of Providence, so defeat is regarded as a call to self-appraisal and repentance.

Whatever else you may think of Israel's philosophy of history, this much is beyond dispute: in a culture where disasters are regarded as divine punishments, complacency is impossible. Over and over, men and tribes are driven to their knees. From that perspective, they look up and out to be overwhelmed with consciousness of having wandered from the path that leads to life. Confessing guilt and begging forgiveness, they rise to serve God with fresh ardor.

This cyclical pattern, already noticed, is one of the chief characteristics of the record of deeds among the people of the Covenant.

Twenty-seventh Day   **Read Judges 9-11**

"God sent an evil spirit between Abimelech and the men of Shechem" (9:22); . . . "God requited the crime of Abimelech" (9:56); . . . when Israel served false gods, "he sold them into the hand of the Philistines" (10:7).

What do such statements mean, for understanding of Israel's inner life? What significance for our life today is there in the point of view here expressed?

Twenty-eighth Day   **Read Judges 12-15**

Divine intervention—or, better, participation—in human procreation is a recurrent motif in Scripture. You will instantly see major parallels between the birth stories of Samson, Isaac, and John the Baptist.

56

As is the case with the multitude of instances in which God is reported as acting in ways we today would prefer to think God does not act, we must try not to become so interested in details that we overlook the underlying point of view which guides reporting of details.

What really matters here is the basic conviction of the Covenant people that the birth of a son or daughter is neither accidental nor casual. Rather, God the Father is both interested and involved. No baby comes into the world apart from the work of Providence. Human mothers and fathers are merely agents—essential ones, to be sure, but only agents—for the working out of the divine will as it moves through the stream of human heredity.

Whether they be orthodox or heretical, no interpretations of the Virgin Birth of our Saviour are really coherent unless they take into account the basic Biblical attitude about God's role in human procreation.

Twenty-ninth Day   **Read Judges 16-18**

For the typical movie-going, Bible-neglecting church member, Hollywood has succeeded in greatly distorting the Old Testament. Samson's goings-on with Delilah, LIKE EVERYTHING ELSE IN THE OLD TESTAMENT, find a place in the sacred record only because the account has power to communicate truths about God in his relationship with mankind.

Do you find it difficult so to focus your reading that you rise above absorption with the sordid, in Samson's brief biography? If you succeed even briefly in using the story as a lens for high-level seeing, what vivid new truths emerge here?

Thirtieth Day   **Read Judges 19-21**

Flagrant sexual perversion . . . bloody civil war . . . near-extermination of blood descendants of Jacob's youngest son. . . .

All this within a score of generations after God reached down into Egypt to rescue Abraham's seed. All this from the people set apart—holy, dedicated to the Lord. All this within the framework of the continuing Covenant between God and the people whom he called to be his own.

Ending as it does on a note of near-despair, the record of the days of the judges offers hope in every time of national and international darkness. For this is not the end. More is yet to be. God has not turned his back upon the world. In the fullness of time, the Saviour will surely come. Victory, not defeat, is the ultimate assurance.

Ruth, I and II Samuel, I and II Kings, I and II Chronicles, Ezra, Nehemiah

Ruth

A hasty glance at this little book suggests that while it has a certain sentimental appeal as a very early romantic short story, there is little religious content.

But underneath, the currents run deep. For Ruth gives an account of events central to the family history of David, greatest of Hebrew kings and ancestor of the Saviour. Through the marriage of a foreign woman with a man who stands in the line of succession from Abraham, the Covenant is given new breadth. At least in potential, it now beckons all men, and not simply those who have inherited the bloodlines of Israel. That is to say, Ruth becomes "an inheritor of the promise" by her own act of choice; that she should thereby become an ancestress of the Saviour adds mightily to the power of the drama that involves heaven as well as earth, God as well as men.

First Day   **Read Ruth 1-4**

Because Israel is the bride of Jehovah, Ruth deals with the divine-human marriage as truly as with that between a Hebrew man and a Moabite woman. Ruth's entrance into

59

the Covenant relationship is a harbinger of the "New Israel" of which St. Paul makes so much in his Letter to the Romans. Inheritors of the divine promise are not simply those who have Abraham's blood in their veins. Rather, all who will may enter the Covenant state as freely as Ruth accepted God's lordship along with Hebrew law and culture.

I and II Samuel

When the sounds of Hebrew speech are transcribed into written words, only consonants are used. This primitive form of shorthand is a considerable space-saver; a document occupies almost twice as much space when written in Greek as when written in Hebrew. A group of scholars centering in Alexandria prepared a famous Greek version of the Old Testament, the Septuagint, during the third century B.C. Because the Hebrew book of Samuel doubled in size during translation, it was for convenience divided into our present two volumes.

In some respects it is strange that the prophet Samuel, and not the great king David, should be named in the title of this history of the early kings of Judah and Israel. Seen through eyes of faith, however, history is as truly a record of the mighty acts of God as of the doings of kings and warriors. Hence, unless a political leader is also a religious prophet (often the case with great names of Israel), prophet takes precedence over king. It was David, and not Samuel, who was destined to advance the bloodline leading to the Saviour; but it was Samuel, and not David, who came to symbolize religious fervor not adulterated by secular ambition.

Second Day   **Skim I Samuel 1-9**

Instead of concentrating upon the familiar and often sentimentally interpreted story of Samuel's birth and boyhood, notice why he *had* to be raised up to judge the land. It is the old, old story—the doctrine of absolute human depravity, here revealed through the vehicle of the religious institution. Given power, the religious leader always tends to fall away from God. Self-interest of the official (2:12-29) takes many forms, but is never permanently curable. Corruption in the religious institution leads to a break in the dialogue of God with men (3:1, 21); social rottenness develops and then spreads through the whole culture like a cancer.

But this is not the only convicting and humbling note sounded here. Let men beware of thinking that they or their institutions can manipulate divine power. Whether symbolized by the Ark of the Covenant or by some other "dwelling place of God," the ongoing work of the Creator is bigger than men. It is lethal, and to men seems erratic; even priests must not think they can control and direct God's power, but must themselves bow down before it and confess their limitations.

Third Day   **Skim I Samuel 10-15**

Man's rebellion against God, even within the Covenant relationship, is as inevitable and continuous as the divine movement of rescue. In these vivid chapters the little kingdom just established on the strength of divine blessings totters under the effects of disobedience to God. No one remains guiltless. By acting as a priest to make offerings (13:8-14), Saul foolishly claims powers that do not belong to him; later, he permits his men to keep booty he was told to destroy (15:3, 10-31) and victorious Israelite warriors commit the great sin of eating blood (14:32).

Over and over, repentant ones offer sacrifices and set up stone memorials. But no degree of contrition can wipe out the offense. Obedience, not sacrifice, is demanded by God— and men cannot give it. So it is mercy that they must ask of God, and not justice.

Fourth Day   **Skim I Samuel 16-22**

As with many Biblical stories such as those of Joseph, Samson, and Ruth, there are subtle dangers here. Color, vividness, and power of description give these chapters some qualities of good fiction. Precisely because it is easy to become absorbed with David's adventures and interpret them upon the human level, there is danger that we overlook spiritual overtones.

Notice that the most powerful motivating factor here is the divine will. God is at work in the unfolding of Israel, and it is he who elevates and deposes kings; battles, friendships, and intrigues are simply instruments that serve to implement the purposes of the Creator.

Again, let us not become so absorbed with delight in David's exploits that we fail to see their symbolism. In offering himself as champion of his people, to give his life for them if need be, David is a forerunner of the Saviour. That is, he serves as a *military substitute*. In stepping forward against Goliath he takes upon himself as an individual the risks that belong to the nation, collectively. So he points, though dimly, to Calvary—where One serves as a spiritual substitute. In and through the Cross, our divine-human Champion steps forward to do battle with Satan, taking upon himself the sins of the whole world.

Fifth Day   **Skim I Samuel 23-31**

While human heroes and villains are the most conspicuous characters walking the stage of history, their freedom to "make history" is limited. God acts in every situation and through every event. It is he, for example, who sends Abigail to feed and placate David (25:32). Though the pride and stupidity of Saul are agents working to put him at the mercy of David, it is the Lord who actually gives him into the young rebel's hand (26:23).

God being *the* decisive agent in the outcome of any event, cosmic or trivial, it follows that those who fear him will try to discover the divine will in every situation. David's perpetual inquiring of God (23:2-3; 30:7-8; II Sam. 2:1; 5:19; 5:23; for example) seems to us to have been on a crude level; we would not today cast lots or consult oracles. In your opinion, is the difference between such inquiring and the use of prayer a difference of degree or of kind? Why?

Whatever you may think about methods of asking for divine guidance, notice that the outcome is very different when one fails to seek it and lets himself be guided purely by his own wants and wishes. Literature includes no more suggestive contrast than that between David's taking as wives the two women, Abigail and Bathsheba. Notice that both were earlier wives of other men. But in the case of Abigail, there is encounter between man and woman based upon mutual surrender to God. (*See* especially 25:23-35.) In the case of Bathsheba, the encounter is the fruit of concession to lust. That Bathsheba rather than Abigail should enter the bloodline of the Saviour does not excuse the sin of David. Rather, it witnesses with dramatic eloquence to the fact that God's power to rescue men, and his willingness to use their failures as well as successes, is without limit.

Sixth Day   **Skim II Samuel 1-6**

Earlier, we have noticed the vital power of words—through which humans gain powers not granted any other creatures. We have seen the significance of those special words we call names, and have noted ways in which metaphors can point to truths they are too small to contain.

These chapters are rich with the power of symbolism. For it is David, the shepherd king, who prefigures and points to the coming of the Shepherd of Men and the King of Kings. It is the Canaanite stronghold of Zion, or Jerusalem, that

David captures and makes his capital. Ever afterward, the City of David, however designated, will be a central symbol of the Hebrew-Christian faith. To those who have ears attuned for messages from God, "the sound of marching in the tops of the balsam trees" speaks more forcefully than any words (5:24); to those who use their literal meanings as bases from which to leap forward in faith, radiant truths are seized through such symbols as: the Good Shepherd, the New Zion, and the City of David.

When religious symbolism is concentrated, as it were, in persons or things rather than in words, we have visible and tangible "vessels that contain the holy." A king who has been anointed by God's priest is such a vessel. Therefore to slay him—even in righteous wrath—is to rebel against God, to take the work of Providence into one's own hand (1: 13-16; 4:10). As the supreme tangible example of the holy, the Ark of the Covenant is actually dangerous. Regardless of how good his intentions are, Uzzah's stumbling against it constitutes an act of suicide (6:6-7).

Do such notions appear utterly strange to you? Or has our journey through this portion of the Old Testament increased your capacity to wonder at the work of God? Is human knowledge almost at the point of absolute mastery of the world and life—or in this Space Age are we still babes lost in the woods of life and requiring rescue to reach a goal we can never attain in our own strength?

Seventh Day   **Skim II Samuel 7-13**

Success is the road to failure.

But conscious failure and repentance offer a new start; no failure is final unless we choose to make it so. Having gone down into the Egyptian captivity of adultery, and having had the angel of death enter the royal household, David accepts the forgiveness that even he cannot win with his sword.

It is then, and only then, that the new man, who can pour out his penitence in Ps. 51 and who is to be used by God to bring Solomon into the world, enters into the new Covenant. Instead of speaking directly to David, as was the case with Abraham, God this time utilizes an agent: Nathan the prophet. Modified and expanded, the new promise to the new human partner—the nation of Israel rather than the family of Abraham—preserves the original qualities of boundlessness and limitedness, coupled with assurance of absolute victory (*See* Chapter 7.)

Lust, greed, vanity, perversion, and hate pervade these chapters. God is not working through plaster saints, but through flesh-and-blood humans whose wars are as savage and whose murders are as brutal as any history records. Yet the promise cannot be defeated. The Covenant is so strongly maintained from the side of God that nothing man can do is sufficient to shatter it. Israel, the Bride of Jehovah, will in due time bring forth the divine-human Son, whose role will be that of overcoming Satan and canceling the effects of sin so that men, made in the image of God, may accept the prize they can never win.

Eighth Day   **Skim II Samuel 14-19**

These chapters, too, depict colorful men in a brawny era. In the fast-moving story of intrigue that sets father against son, there are few references, direct or indirect, that we can consider "religious." God is in all that occurs, to be sure (17:14), but the chief emphasis here is upon the character of David—destined to become idealized as "the perfect ruler."

No matter how hard it may be to see his movements, God is
the source of all that is. Nothing exists apart from the ongoing work of creation, and the sustaining hand of the
Creator. Every victory and each deliverance is actually the
work of God, not man who enjoys his moment of triumph.
Hence an occasion of "success" is a time that demands one's
gladdest and most fervent praise—even if few can match the
winged words of David as reported in his song of praise.
(*See* Chapter 22.)

By the same token, God is always deeply involved in
tragedy and trouble (21:1; 24:10-15). Days of tribulation
are heavenly traffic lights, as it were, calling on men and
nations to stop their mad rush for gain. A time of distress
can function to drive even a king to his knees and send him
out to erect an altar and make a special offering to God
(24:18-25). For the faith of Israel, this is the meaning of
tragedy: sons of the Covenant suffer in return for sin, and
their suffering is redemptive because it can turn them back
to God, humble enough to accept his rescue.

I and II Kings

These two books made up a single volume in the Hebrew
original, and the actual division was not made until the
sixteenth century. Most Greek Bibles prefer the title "Kingdoms," which in them is applied to these books and to the
books of Samuel.

Like the books of Samuel, these are filled with details—
sometimes vivid but often all but meaningless to us today.
Here are accounts of the most glorious decades of Israel as
a political community. And here is the so-human story of
civil war, military defeat, and foreign captivity.

While these books have even less "surface" evidence of
conveying deep spiritual truth than do the books of Samuel,
they are nevertheless vital to the unfolding story of the

Covenant. For they tell us (often in what seems to us tiresome detail) how Israel's material success led to her spiritual decay. In order to be reawakened, the Chosen People had to be led into a new Egypt, as it were, that, from bondage in Babylon, a new rescue could revitalize their sense of destiny.

Tenth Day   Skim I Kings 1-7

These chapters symbolize both the individual and the national paradox: eagerness to serve God and him alone, combined with a tug from sin that is too strong to resist.

Solomon receives from his dying father a challenge so powerful that it reads almost as though from a Shakespearean play (2:1-4). He accepts as the chief principle of his kingdom the fact that God "has established me, and placed me on the throne of David my father" (2:24). Yet, in the next breath, after making a solemn vow of loyalty to God, he sends his agents to slay his ambitious brother and hurries to contract an alliance with Egypt (2:25; 3:1).

It is to the eternal glory of Solomon that he, not David, becomes the builder of the temple. But that same great king, made wise because of his earnest prayer for wisdom and not long life or riches (3:11), is careful to make sacrifices and burn incense at the "high Places" whose shrines long competed with the Temple for allegiance of the people. In old age, he will degenerate into open idolatry (11:1-8).

Eleventh Day   Skim I Kings 8-14

Solomon's great public work, the Temple, is built to house the Ark. But this holiest of Israel's inheritances (deadly when touched carelessly) is merely a receptacle for the

67

stones on which the Ten Commandments are written. These stones, in turn, are merely pointers to the God of whom they speak, but who is too glorious to be contained in anything visible (8:27).

It is the Covenant, no word of which has failed (8:56), to which all these tangibles witness. By the glory of the Temple and all its contents, men are impelled to bow down at the greatness of Jehovah—and to wonder why he should have chosen Israel for his bride. Always, there is clear recognition that the principle of the Covenant makes it a conditional instrument (8:25). (*See also* 2:4; 6:12; 9:4-9.)

But in practice, the best men in the nation, deliberately set apart to follow God, repeatedly fall and fail. Both in Judah, loyal to David's seed, and in rebellious Israel following after Rehoboam, the Covenant is repeatedly broken from the human side. Though the Hebrew calendar begins with the year of the Exodus from Egypt (6:1) somewhat as the Christian calendar begins with the birth of our Saviour, Jeroboam erects golden calves and calls upon all Israel to worship them (12:25-33). It is the repeated and flagrant breaking of the Covenant that will send the Chosen People into new captivity where, battered to their knees, they will once more long for divine rescue rather than boast about their human achievements.

Twelfth Day   **Skim I Kings 15-22**

How very brief is any human hour of glory! Kings were a dime a dozen in these years; Zimri conspired, murdered, and made war—in order to reign for seven days (16:15). As with individuals, so with nations. David's kingdom began to break up even before his death, and the once-powerful nation degenerated into mutually hostile states.

God's power no longer being especially evident in political leaders, prophets such as the "troubler of Israel" (18:17) had to speak against the idolatry of the times. Even smashing victory over the prophets of Baal, with fire called down from heaven by an Elijah, could not bring lasting reform; "the people still sacrificed and burned incense on the high places" (22:43).

What parallels do you see between this Hebrew period and United States life since 1914? What major differences do you see? If history teaches any absolute lessons, how greatly dare we trust in the White House, the Pentagon, or the United Nations?

Thirteenth Day   Skim II Kings 1-7

Miracles of the New Testament have attracted great interest, and have been the subject of bitter debate. Probably because the accounts are seldom read, mighty works of Old Testament prophets are not widely discussed. Notice, however, that under Elijah and his successor, Elisha, all the great categories of the miraculous are reported: healing of illness, marvels in the natural world (iron floating, water mastered), and the dead raised to life. Prophetic calling down of heavenly fire to strike opponents dead has no counterpart in the New Testament. To center upon minute details of such accounts is fatal to discovery of their inner meaning. One and all, these startling events play the role of witness. To the ear of belief, they shout about the majesty and wonder and infinite power of God. As you ponder these strange stories, are you bewildered and repelled by them—or do you, at least faintly, hear in a new way the central motif of the Biblical symphony?

Fourteenth Day   Skim II Kings 8-12

Having sunk into the pit of infamy, the descendants of Abraham wallow in their own filth. If history should be interpreted in terms of individuals, we should have to confess that there are many periods of utter hopelessness.

But viewed from the perspective of God's total dealings with mankind, darkness is never absolute. God is active, even in defeat and tragedy (10:32). God will continue to raise up reformers who will abolish whatever pagan altars dominate their cultures. Such reform, however, is itself always limited and never absolute.

These bloody pages therefore speak a queerly paradoxical verdict: man can never sink so low that he slips through the fingers of Providence, nor can he ever climb high enough to achieve a God-centered culture from which all the pagan shrines have been banished.

Fifteenth Day   **Skim II Kings 13-18**

To read *spiritual history,* as revealed through the pages that record the deeds of Hebrew kings, is to become wholly pessimistic about human nature, and at the same time utterly optimistic about divine love. For the long, sorry story tells us (over, and over, and over, and over, as though repetition is necessary to drive home the truth) that men always fall and fail. No reform is absolute or enduring, no progress is unqualified. In our own strength we cannot—we simply *cannot*—achieve anything approaching an ideal, Godly society.

Yet God does not cancel his promises. He reaffirms the Covenant, punishes in wrath only to forgive again in redemptive love, and refuses—absolutely *refuses*—to write off the human race as an experiment that has failed. Over, and over, and over, and over, as though no number of repetitions can cause him to waver, he holds out forgiveness and offers rescue that can lead to absolute spiritual victory.

Sixteenth Day   **Skim II Kings 19-25**

These tumultuous generations were marked by two sets of events that were to affect the whole course of Covenant history.

First, the book of the law was discovered in the Temple. Lost or hidden during long periods when kings sank so low that they even practiced human sacrifice, the written code was the basis of Josiah's sweeping reforms. Note, however, that the sun of fidelity to God peeped out from clouds of idolatry only briefly; the nation returned to its pagan practices upon the death of Josiah.

The second crucial set of events centered in the realm of international affairs. After being threatened by Assyria and becoming tributary to Egypt, the people of God were overwhelmed by soldiers of Babylon. Their Temple sacked, their cities burned, Abraham's descendants were carried away bodily into a second great foreign captivity.

Note, however, that every page of the record affirms the clear conviction that God is the decisive agent in all that takes place. When national victory comes, it is because he has given it. But disaster is equally his work! FOR EYES OF FAITH, WHATEVER COMES WILL SERVE TO CONVEY A GOD-CENTERED MESSAGE. EVERY EVENT, WHETHER IT LEADS TO REJOICING OR MOURNING, SERVES AS AN AGENT OF REVELATION AND "SPEAKS" ABOUT GOD TO THOSE WHO LISTEN WITH EARS ATTUNED TO THE STILL, SMALL VOICE.

I and II Chronicles

These volumes constitute a rough parallel with much that is included in the books of Samuel and Kings. Like all historians, the chronicler selects his evidence to defend a particular point of view. He presents an overwhelming case for the conclusion that kings (and their people) incurred divine wrath by failure to worship God without compromise.

Such visible and tangible sins as the making of alliances with foreigners were simply results of the inner decay: breach of the Covenant by which the children of the promise owed ABSOLUTE trust and loyalty to God.

Seventeenth Day   **Skim I Chronicles 1-10**

To us, these chapters constitute a valley of very dry bones. But to the devout Hebrew, and to Christians of early decades, the genealogies here included were of absorbing interest. For it was considered vital to trace the transmission of the Covenant and its promises through unbroken lines of descent. The normal pattern was that of the bloodline: from father to eldest son. But there were numerous exceptions. Reuben's adultery (Gen. 35:22) cost him his place in the line of succession and the birthright went to his youngest brother, Joseph (I Chron. 5:1). Though the story of David's many marriages is hopelessly scrambled, it is clear that he had a number of sons before Solomon (I Chron. 3:1-9); to seek a wholly logical explanation for Solomon's place in the *salvation history*, to which genealogies merely point, is to become entangled in fruitless speculation. Divine choice, not man's doings, is at work here (I Chron. 28:5-7).

However devious the pattern of descent, faith has an explanation that covers every situation in principle. Sin on the part of the human recipient of divine grace—breach of the Covenant by the partner of God—deflects *salvation history* from its normal course.

In many instances, such as that of Reuben, the sin is specified; in others it is only implied. Saul's disobedience and his dabbling in the occult cost him the throne and his life (I Chron. 10:13-14). David's scorn for God's unqualified demands cost him the life of his first son by Bathsheba (II Sam. 12:13-20). Solomon, without parallel among kings, succumbs to the lure of foreign women (Neh. 13:26). Judah's faithlessness sends the whole nation into Babylonian captivity (I Chron. 9:1).

Unlike any other collection of sacred literature, the Bible underscores the limited-ness of its heroes, prophets, and holy men. Instead of elevating its chief figures into divinities, the Bible perpetually reminds us that there is no one faithful—no, not one (II Chron. 6:36). It is this perpetual and inevitable human factor that accounts for the erratic and sometimes inscrutable path of the *salvation history* that is its absorbing theme.

Eighteenth Day   **Skim I Chronicles 11-19**

Woven into this account of David's personal and national triumphs, there is a strand that runs through the entire Biblical record. Precisely because of the Covenant relationship, and not in spite of it, the Chosen People (individually and collectively) live in a state of paradox and of tension. They must be in perpetual fear of God; if they happen to become callous they are warned by some mighty event to return to a saving state of dread (I Chron. 13:12). Yet at the same time, they must continually be in a state of ecstatic joy, powerful enough to evoke such praise as David's song of thanksgiving (I Chron. 16). (*See also* Ps. 100.)

This double orientation of life carries over into the realm of signs, portents, revelations, and words. We have already noticed Old Testament emphasis upon the power and mystery of these devices for communication between God and man as well as between man and man. In our reading of the Psalms and especially in our New Testament reading later this year, we shall be reminded over and over that words are frequently employed to convey meanings at two or more levels. It is not strange, therefore, but natural and

73

logical that Nathan's vision of glorious kingship on the part of David's offspring (I Chron. 17:11-14) should (to faith-directed eyes) be a harbinger of the coming Saviour who will occupy the throne of David and establish the new Zion.

Nineteenth Day   **Skim I Chronicles 20-29**

No man, asserts the Scriptural record, ever gets all he wants. Our capacity to yearn always exceeds our ability to perform. Even David cannot build the temple of which he has dreamed; he must go to his grave denied this central satisfaction of his life.

How do you account for the emphasis upon his sin in making a census? Did Satan tempt him to rebellious pride, so that he numbered his subjects in order to magnify his own importance and thereby to reduce his fear of God? What is the divine message here, for the statistic-minded modern Church?

Twentieth Day   **Skim II Chronicles 1-9**

Solomon's encounter with the Queen of Sheba is colorful and easy to read. Details of his economic and military exploits, and especially the long lists of materials and furnishings for the Temple, are all but meaningless to us today. We tend, therefore, to skip over the account of years in which the house of the Lord was translated from a dream into reality.

Woven into that tedious story, however, there are warnings that temple-builders and God-seekers need perpetually repeated. Glorious as the Covenant is, wonderful as its promises are, the divine-human contract is conditional. Punishments for faithlessness are on the same grand scale as rewards for fidelity (II Chron. 7:11-22).

Even a Solomon cannot win or achieve the right to build a house for the Creator of all houses (II Chron. 2:6-16). Sublime and mysterious divine *glory* (II Chron. 5:14; 7:2), conferred by the presence of God himself, is what sets his house apart from all others; the visible Temple, no matter how costly and beautiful and magnificent, means nothing unless God is in it. And no matter how close the bonds between God and priests of his Chosen People, God is always withdrawn, hidden "in thick darkness" (6:1), forever beyond such intimacy that men can successfully manipulate him. Let Solomon's people, therefore, guard with their very lives against the danger of thinking that, because they have erected the Temple, they control its Lord and may relax in their passionate striving to know and serve him better.

Twenty-first Day　　　　　　　　　**Skim II Chronicles 10-19**

Clearly, there is nothing "new" in these chapters; they simply repeat almost to the point of boredom the basic notes sounded in many chapters of the books of Samuel and of the Kings.

Why do you suppose there is so much Biblic repetition? Would it not be equally convincing, and more readable, to present just two or three vivid case histories that communicate a given message? Is it really necessary to overwhelm the reader with literally dozens of instances that tell the story of divine constancy . . . of human failure . . . of mutual pledges between Creator and creatures . . . of faithlessness that leads to religious reform (always incomplete) and re-affirmation of loyalty? Even with all these repetitions of a few fundamental notes, do you think they are heard and heeded by most church folk today? If there is a cure for the basic human dilemma, what is it?

Twenty-second Day   **Skim II Chronicles 20-28**

Whatever else it communicates, this record of the rise and fall of kings and the coming and going of national attitudes shouts very loudly about the limited-ness of man's influence. Nothing human is permanent. Whether a change be in the direction of evil or of good, it is fluid and transient.

Yesterday's spiritual victories do not carry over into to-day's life. Baal must be overthrown again in every generation (II Chron. 23:17). Social salvation is a myth; mankind can never hope to arrive at an ideal society by means of human progress and reform. Man cannot save himself. Society, like the individuals who constitute it, is limited and fallible. Divine rescue is a social as well as a personal necessity; no reform is absolute or eternal, no progress is great enough or enduring enough to eliminate the need for divine intervention in the affairs of men and nations.

Twenty-third Day   **Skim II Chronicles 29-36**

Repeating, for the most part, details already reported in portions of II Kings, these chapters simply document the verdict which we arrived at yesterday. Hezekiah's clean-up is followed by Manasseh's orgy of idolatry; we are impelled to join our own voices to the plaintive cry that "men never learn; . . . men never, never learn."

Queerly, however, this is the one source of valid hope. Because we cannot put any trust in ourselves, we are forced to trust in God. When we have failed on a sufficiently conspicuous scale to recognize our own failure—and only then—we are ready to join Manasseh in the humble entreaty for divine rescue that leads to overpowering recognition that the Lord really is the one true God (II Chron. 33:10-13).

Ezra

Ezra, the valiant priest, probably author of the Chronicles as well as the little book that bears his name, here records a new exodus on the part of a new Chosen People. Instead of Egypt, the captor has been Babylon. Instead of a great horde of liberated ones, there are just 1496 men and their families. Instead of a whole people (all the seed of Abraham), the rescued ones are merely the righteous remnant of a once-great nation.

Besides these factors, there is the important difference that "going back" cannot be identical without going out to a new land. This time, the people led by God are returning to their old home in hopes of restoring some of their past glory. So their whole orientation is different from that of Moses' people, eager to claim a God-promised land and in it to grow from a group of families into a nation.

Twenty-fourth Day   **Read Ezra 1-4**

Here we find tears mingled with shouts of joy (3:12-13), for the new Temple is hardly under construction before human adversaries, moved by jealousy (4:1-5), succeed in stopping the work. But the combination of weeping with rejoicing, symbolic of man's incapacity to achieve a tension-free state, cannot silence the praise of these people. Their glad song (3:10-11) comes from the lips of men just back from exile. Even overwhelming national disaster cannot shake their faith in divine love, or their confidence in divine favor.

Part of their delight stems from the fact that a new note has been sounded in the old symphony of the Covenant. Cyrus of Persia—a man outside the ranks of God's people—plays a major role in the building of the new Temple. Even though Abraham's descendants are employed as his agents

77

to perform the work, we here begin to get a hint that the whole concept of the Chosen People is in process of radical revision.

Twenty-fifth Day   **Read Ezra 5-7**

First-person comments are rare in the Old Testament, so the almost casual personal remarks of Ezra (7:27-28) are a bit startling. Devout and courageous as this priest certainly was, we cannot avoid recognizing that at its highest and noblest, *rebuilding* is not identical with building.

So the whole movement of Ezra and his people witnesses to preoccupation with the past (return of part of the gold and silver vessels that long adorned the Temple, for example). Such looking backward always involves some degree of hardening, intellectually and spiritually. It involves some degree of inhibition of the novel—even when originating from God.

In the end, this "looking back" is to prove the undoing of the Covenant people. They will become so zealous to interpret the inherited law that they refuse to participate in the new revelation offered through incarnation of the Creator in the person of Jesus of Nazareth.

Twenty-sixth Day   **Read Ezra 8-10**

Here we are confronted by the concept of social guilt. According to it, all in Hebrew society (even Ezra himself) are stained by the sins of their fellows (9:1-7). The great sin involved is that of contamination—failure to remain deliberately set apart from all other peoples.

As a result of recognized guilt on the part of the whole Chosen People, there arises a new understanding of the divine-human contract. Since God has chosen to destroy the nation that developed in the land of promise, human understanding of the Covenant must have been in error. It is not the entire Hebrew people who will inherit the promise— but only a righteous minority, a *remnant.*

Subsequent generations will see the visible remnant dwindle in number until at last it includes, strictly speaking, only one member: Jesus of Nazareth. But his victory over Satan and death leads to a new revision of the Covenant idea, so that after Calvary the Chosen People (made up of all who accept the salvation offered by the risen Lord) will rapidly expand in number and will include men of all races and nations—the new "family of God" raised up to take the place of the Israel who played her essential role by giving birth to the long-promised Son of God.

Nehemiah

This earliest of Hebrew autobiographies, coming from the pen of a layman rather than a priest or Levite, is essentially a story of action on behalf of God as contrasted with meditation about the nature of God.

Twenty-seventh Day   **Read Nehemiah 1-4**

The vivid and often emotion-colored words of Nehemiah witness that action can never be divorced from principles that motivate it. To build for God is to evoke jealousy, ridicule, and opposition. Such building is therefore costly and dangerous.

This case-history therefore poses some basic problems. Is persecution by foes of God an inevitable mark of genuine devotion to God alone? Are there any situations in which public opinion is so overwhelmingly on God's side that one can build a genuine temple without opposition?

Twenty-eighth Day   **Read Nehemiah 5-7**

Few portions of Scripture even approach these chapters in preserving spontaneous conversation with God, woven into reports of daily events (5:19; 6:9, 14; *see also* 13:22, 29, 31). Nehemiah speaks to the Lord as naturally as to any human companion. So his account is an ancient forerunner of "he walks with me, and he talks with me; he tells me I am his own."

To a unique degree, the Hebrew-Christian stream has produced witness of men and women having so entered into personal relationship with God that the gulf between the divine and the human has been bridged.

Twenty-ninth Day   **Read Nehemiah 8-10**

Periodic rediscovery of the written law is basic to Israel's cycles of regeneration. That is, from floundering without any sure guide, the society a few generations away from fervent dedication to God "finds" a source of certainty in the law. Such discoverings and enterings into new covenants always involve both promise and warning—"an oath and a curse" (10:29).

Precisely here, we find light shed upon a dilemma of Protestant Christianity in our time. There are but three great streams from which spiritual vitality may flow: holy ceremonies and the institution that transmits them, a body of holy writings, and religious experience. Large segments of Protestantism have practically abandoned the authority of the Church and her holy ceremonies. Religious experience still suffers from the excesses of a kind of evangelism that elevated emotional factors at the expense of intellectual ones. And insistence upon verbal literalism, followed by a wave of purely literary and historical study, has cut the foundation from the Scriptures in many communions.

For new hope in the Church, we today need precisely what the returning exiles found: a holy Book to which we can turn with the delight of new discovery, from which we can draw authority and through which we can come into personal encounter with the God to whom it points. That is the real purpose of this discipline in which we are now engaged—an all-too-hasty survey of the Bible in one year.

Thirtieth Day   Read Nehemiah 11-13

Discovery of a long-lost holy code is not, in itself, any guarantee of lasting gains. It is vital that those who ponder the sacred writings shall find in them new meanings that apply to the current situation (13:1-3), and as a result of those insights order their lives differently.

When "study of the law" degenerates into making commentaries upon what men of earlier generations found, the spirit is dead and the letter reigns. Our year's reading has reached a significant milepost: one-fourth of our time is gone, and we have surveyed considerably more than one-third of our total material.

Yet it is that which is ahead, not that which is behind, that calls! We dare not play the part of returning exiles who seek to recapture a recent past, romantically interpreted. We must be divinely-led immigrants, consciously called to enter a new Canaan whose wonders we shall never exhaust. That land of promise lies ahead of us, across the intellectual-spiritual Jordan that separates the New Testament from the Old. Though we are led by a more-than-earthly light, we have yet some time of preparation and of hardening before we shall be ready to cross that river.

FOURTH MONTH:

Esther, Job, Psalms 1-89

Esther

This little book is among the most colorful in the Bible. It reads almost like good fiction, with a fast-moving plot. But, though there are many impressive lessons in the realm of ethics and morals, the spiritual content is far below that of most Scripture. For religious purposes, its chief role was that of giving support to the observance of the feast of Purim. It is neither quoted nor mentioned anywhere in the New Testament.

First Day   Read Esther 1-5

Persecution of the Jews began early, frequently became intense, and has continued across more centuries than the mind can readily bridge. Whatever else may be said for them, the Jews are absolutely without counterpart. Not a true racial group, but a community held together by religious ties, their very survival is one of the marvels of human history.

So this exciting account of ancient plots and counterplots is a sort of capsule summary (better, a symbol) of Jewish survival during most centuries that these people have existed. Haman's role is also symbolic, for economic and political factors have often motivated the Jew-baiter.

The writer of the Book of Esther is absolutely sure that
the Lord of hosts, Creator of the heavens and the earth, has
a keen personal interest in these Chosen People. What do
you think of that idea?

Second Day   **Read Esther 6-10**

In every culture, social change gives a degree of instability
to the meaning of all words, names, symbols, ceremonies,
and customs. This is true "across the board": change operates in such realms as economics, politics, science, literature,
and music as well as in religion. Hence it is not unusual but
actually commonplace for folk suddenly to wake up to the
fact that they are using words or practicing ceremonies
without fully understanding why.

Such a situation creates an intellectual vacuum, as it were.
We are so made that we are dissatisfied without explanations. Consequently, "history is written backward" through
development of stories to account for the origins of customs,
ceremonies, names, and words that have been transmitted
from the past.

Celebrated by Jews on the fourteenth and fifteenth days
of the twelfth month, Adar, Purim's origin is lost in antiquity. This important but otherwise unintelligible name is
in Esther explained by its connection with the Persian word
Pur, used to name the device for casting lots (Esther 9:26).
It was Pur, the divining tool, that in Haman's hands deter-
mined the date set for slaughter of the Jews, and hence for
the two days of celebration when the king changed his
mind.

Biblical interpretation is greatly complicated by this process. Many names, words, and ceremonies of Scripture are
accompanied by accounts that grew up generations or centuries after the items which they seek to explain. Known as

83

"folk etymology," such evidence is often a red herring on trails of history; but, as in the case of the present account of the origin of the feast of Purim, it may be of tremendous interest and value.

Job

If this ancient drama had to be summarized in one sentence, perhaps the most nearly suitable one would be the question of 4:17. (*Compare* 15:14; 25:4.) For the entire action, like the argument of St. Paul's Letter to the Romans, revolves around the question of how a creature can enter into the righteousness demanded by his Creator.

There are but two basic answers to that question. Many religious systems teach that righteousness is a goal to be won by dint of great striving. Dozens of brief passages in the Old Testament, considered without regard for the larger context, support just such a view. Many critics of Jewish thought assert that Judaism is essentially a legal system that interprets a religion of achievement.

At opposite poles to any view by which a creature can by striving succeed in escaping the limits of creaturehood is that by which righteousness is an unearned gift of God. It is a fruit of mercy, or grace, and operates through the process of salvation, or rescue. So regarded, religion is a goad that continually pricks man and urges him to accept from God the "acquittal by mercy" that he can never win through justice.

Because the entire Bible deals with this fundamental issue, and because the Book of Job presents most of the basic arguments, all neat summaries of its message are suspect. Here, questions are more basic than answers. This is a book to make one examine his surest convictions; instead of becoming simpler, it becomes more profound each time it is read.

Third Day   **Read Job 1-5**

Suddenly plunged from peace into tragedy, the upright Job reacts by entering black despair. Though he speaks more fluently than we tongue-tied ones, I wonder if his vivid imagery (Chapter 3) leaves any mature person untouched? Have we not all felt utter defeat that makes us wish we had never been born?

Out of his despair, Job raises the fundamental questions of human existence: Why am I here? Is there any purpose to my life?

His "comforter," Eliphaz, presents one of the stock arguments central to many religious systems and prominent in much Old Testament thought. Trouble and suffering, he says, are direct results of sin—which may be deliberate, or unconscious. That chastened one, who uses tragedy as a lens with which to magnify his view of Providence, gains marvelous new power by which he wins prosperity and peace.

Fourth Day   **Read Job 6-10**

Eliphaz' promise of prosperity in return for righteousness is empty, Job asserts. Man's meaning is centered in a life span whose end is bound to be (cannot escape being, simply because it is a terminus) futility. To die is to go to "the land of gloom and deep darkness" (10:21-22). To die is to cancel out having lived. Therefore, all striving is useless.

Furthermore, Job says, if a man does his absolute best so that he is spotless by comparison with other men, he is no less guilty in God's sight than is the most wanton sinner. That being the case, what is the use of trying? (9:29)

As though this ancient prototype of "Sixteen Tons" were not a sufficiently troubling line of thought, Job adds to it his realization that God actually does concern himself with

85

man. This futile one, soon to be put back in the ground from which he came, is the object of divine visitation so ceaseless that a man is never alone long enough to swallow his saliva. Why this absorption of the Creator with so futile a creature? Why? Why? Why?

Blithely leaping over Job's main argument, Bildad reiterates Eliphaz' assurance of future material blessings *in this life* as a reward for righteousness. Job retorts with a fresh statement of a major motif of the whole drama: "How can a creature attain acquittal, when the Creator is judge?"

Fifth Day   **Read Job 11-15**

Zophar shakes his head to silence Job and repeats the assurance that if he will just cease sinning, God will bless and prosper him.

"Your answer is too simple," Job retorts. "With one eye shut, I can see flagrant sinners (robbers and idolaters) who are enjoying peace and prosperity. God, the omnipotent and ever-present, obviously has a hand in such victories by evil men."

Despairing of help from human wisdom, Job yearns to take his case before God. If permitted to do so, he will argue that man's days are numbered (14:1-2, 10-12). Man is actually impotent, a helpless bit of flotsam moved hither and thither by tides that the Creator directs. Therefore, it is an absurdity—a travesty upon the idea of justice—that God should require righteousness of man.

Sixth Day   **Read Job 16-20**

Job's reasoning continues along these lines:

God has attacked me; there is no doubt of it. My superhuman adversary (no saviour, he) has overwhelmed me.

There is no use for me to yearn for death, since I cannot take hope into the grave with me. If God is going to give me justice, it will have to be soon—for life ebbs away daily, hourly. To tell me that I am suffering for my sins is a waste of words and simply puts my friends on the side of the persecuting God. How I do wish my claims could be written to last forever! I know that, someday, God will assess the evidence and declare me guiltless.

Zophar by-passes the main issue and suggests that apparent prosperity of the wicked should not trouble a good man, for it is sure to pass and be followed by woes sent from God.

Seventh Day   **Read Job 21-25**

Still angry at divine injustice, by which all the enterprises of the wicked seem to thrive, Job protests once more that it is useless to struggle for righteousness. Death treats all men alike and wipes out all differences between the good and the bad.

Eliphaz repeats the basic argument of all the "comforters." It is sin, he insists, that causes Job's woes. If he is not guilty of deliberate acts of rebellion, he is certainly guilty of sins of omission. In order to gain peace and prosperity, he must make peace with God.

Job cries that the accusation is false. He is innocent, and would give his life to confront God to his face in order to defend himself. But the hope is futile; with half an eye, one can look at the way evil flourishes and wicked men prosper, and know that God is an absentee landlord who cannot be found in order to be called to account.

Bildad's answer, in Chapter 25, once more repeats the fundamental question of the drama—whether or not righteousness is possible to man. (See 4:17; 15:14.)

Eighth Day   **Read Job 26-28**

Windy words of Bildad and his comrades, according to Job's reply, have added nothing to the God whom they would defend. God is Lord of all, and needs no human champion.

Job insists that this great God is his persecutor, who has attacked an innocent and righteous man.

Returning to the persistent question of life's meaning in the face of inescapable death, Job concedes that death actually does make null and void all present triumphs of the wicked. But this fact simply underscores the deeper riddle. Man, the magnificent master of all things, has seized every treasure but one—understanding of himself and his meaning. Hidden from the eyes of every creature, "the place of understanding" is known only to God. The closest man can come to wisdom is to fear the God who alone possesses it.

Ninth Day   **Read Job 29-31**

In these closing chapters of Job's great argument in his own defense we find some of the most stirring lines of the entire drama. For here (as, indeed, in all his protests) Job speaks for all mankind and not simply for himself. Looking back upon his life, necessarily viewed through his own eyes, he repeats his plea of innocence and his demand for a meeting with his divine adversary. Summarized, his plea runs:

Though I was a knight in shining armor of righteousness, revered among the leaders of men, I have become a joke to rabble—and this by the hand of God. It is his purpose to bring me (along with all living) into the house of death. Yet I cannot keep silence. I must cry out, though I know I will not be heard. I cannot refrain from protesting my innocence and challenging God to meet me so that I may answer all his charges and be pronounced guiltless.

Tenth Day   Read Job 32-35

So far, the great themes of the drama have simply been repeated over and over. Though expressed quite differently each time, the arguments of Job and of his "comforters" have not changed substantially since first advanced. With the entrance of Elihu, the son of Barachel, the tempo changes and new motifs begin to appear. Brushing the older men aside, Elihu addresses Job in a symphony of words whose burden runs:

The fault lies with you, Job, rather than with God. You say God does not answer you. That is absurd. The silence stems from your dull ear. God speaks in more ways than one —through terrifying dreams, for example, and especially through suffering that leads to despair. Not once, but over and over, God speaks through acts of rescue.

You, Job, have concluded that there is no justice under the sun. In doing so, you dull-eared one, you have simply added rebellion to your other sins. Take a look at the glories of creation, and recognize your folly. For neither your sin nor your righteousness can touch the Creator of all. You say God does not hear you? It is because you do not call in the right way. In rebellious pride you dare to challenge your God—and then to wonder that he does not bend his will to yours!

Eleventh Day   Read Job 36-38

Continuing his powerful argument in three chapters that form one of the most moving of all tributes to life-shaping belief in providence, Elihu asserts:

Instead of being withdrawn, as charged by Job, God is actually central to every event whatever. Providence permeates all situations, without exception. God conceived and sustains all natural processes that give and take life, that bless and curse. He is so wholly unsearchable that it is impious folly to challenge him; "he does great things which we cannot comprehend" (37:5). "God is clothed with terrible majesty" (37:22); he is to be worshiped ("feared"), not challenged by proud and rebellious men whose sole claim to wisdom is conceit.

Twelfth Day   **Read Job 39-42**

Human argument having ended, the Lord himself at last confronts Job. But instead of commending him for his righteousness or chiding him for his guilt, God underscores the gulf between creature and Creator. Chapters 38-39, showing Job how very little he knows about the world's origin and operation, are among the most sublime of all tributes to the God who shaped and sustains all that we call "the natural world."

Momentarily stunned, Job is further challenged in Chapters 40-41 to demonstrate power like that of God, if he is to dare challenge or question God.

Prostrate, literally overwhelmed by face-to-face encounter with God, Job blurts out a moving confession of his own impotence and repents of having played the rebel by questioning the will of his Maker (42:5-6). Here the drama proper comes to a stunning and climactic end.

There are two schools of thought concerning the epilogue (42:7-17). Some interpreters take it literally, holding that the man Job was showered with material blessings as a reward for his faithfulness. Others hold that the passage is symbolic, promising God's richest rewards (not necessarily material ones, conferred in this life) to those who learn life's most paradoxical lesson: the one road to righteousness is that of contrition for inability to achieve righteousness.

Psalms

More than any other book of the Bible, that of Psalms has its modern counterparts. For in the case of religious bodies with a history of several centuries, the hymnal relates to public worship much as the Psalms related to Temple rites in Israel. To recognize the Psalms as religious poetry adapted for public worship and set to music is to see that this book is radically different from, say, II Chronicles. So the reader who seeks the deepest meanings from individual Psalms must bring his own dedicated and inspired imagination to the reading of them.

It is a delightful paradox (true of all Scripture, but especially vivid here) that, to a startling degree, one gets from his reading what he seeks. "Truth" and "meaning" do not reside in words in the way eggs nestle in a cardboard carton. Rather, meaning is a product of the meeting between message and seeking mind. This has the startling effect of making the meaning a variable, so that two readers (or one reader at two periods of his life) will get quite different sets of meaning from a single Psalm or other Scripture passage. Recognized everywhere in the Bible and stressed throughout the New Testament, this fundamental aspect of communication was expressed for all time by Elihu when he told Job that "the ear tastes words, as the palate tastes food" (Job 34:3).

If you have not already recognized this factor, which at one blow demolishes all views according to which the literal meaning of the words of Scripture is fixed and final for all persons and all time, this fresh reading of Psalms may help you seize upon "dynamics of meaning and interpretation" as forces offering you breathtaking new truths from old and familiar groups of words.

Thirteenth Day   **Read Psalms 1-7**

All through your reading of Psalms, try to be alert for vivid examples of poetic imagery. Through metaphor and other poetic devices, it is possible to express profound truths that cannot otherwise be conveyed by words. Yet, taken literally, the statements are not "true." Deliberate stretching of words is one of the several factors that make the Psalms so breathtaking. Try, for example, to communicate the meaning of Ps. 7:14 in literal, non-poetic fashion, and then compare your effort with the lines of this verse as it stands.

Notice how many of these seven Psalms are evoked by trouble, tension, and danger. Notice also how frequently the words of a Psalm "speak for you and me" by expressing our private thoughts more vividly than we can.

Now turn back to Ps. 1 and put in writing your idea of the two distinct ways in which its promises and warnings may be understood. Do you think Israel's devout ever stopped with taking this Psalm literally at the level of material blessings? Can you think of a way to express hope for spiritual blessings, so phrased that no one could interpret the promise on lower levels?

Fourteenth Day   **Read Psalms 8-14**

How strife and wickedness do flourish! Is there any social order, any system of government, under which evildoers will be subdued while those who seek the Lord bask in peace?

Whatever answer one may give, the meaning of life and of civilization is at stake. This is precisely the focus of many Psalms. Such powerful ones as Ps. 8 deserve to be memorized. Committed to memory or read frequently over a period of years, a passage like this demonstrates the fluid nature of meaning—for its riches will never be exhausted. Just when you conclude that, finally, you fully understand what Ps. 8 says about God and man, you are likely to be flooded with fresh insights persuading you that as yet you have hardly made a beginning!

Fifteenth Day   Read Psalms 15-19

Many devout persons have been troubled by emphasis upon blood and battle in the Psalms. According to this point of view, many passages portray God as cruel and vindictive—ready to hear prayers for rescue and vengeance that are essentially pagan in tone.

To what degree do you think these matters reflect the limitedness of men who wrote and sang the psalms? Do failures and imperfections on the part of even zealous worshipers reflect upon the character of God? Mentally stepping outside our own culture and viewing it from a distance, what do you see about our public worship that you would like to change? Can you discover any prejudices and blind spots that affect your own prayers?

Ponder the verdict of Ps. 18:25-26. What bearing do you think it has upon the deep questions suggested here?

Sixteenth Day   Read Psalms 20-23

Today's reading provides an especially vivid example of a feature that marks the entire Psalter. Throughout, there is the dramatic alternation between exultation and despair that puts Ps. 21 in sharp contrast with Ps. 22. Both triumph and tragedy are prominent in these ancient songs—for both moods have a place in every normal life. It is part of the timeless message of Psalms that tragedy and triumph alike may be creatively related to God.

No situation, no event, no circumstance can cut off dialogue with God, so long as man fervently wants it! We can

take both our woes and our ecstasies to God, and in both
moods can hear the still, small voice. Sharp contrast between Pss. 21 and 22, forming a prelude to Ps. 23, can
hardly be accidental. Rather, this arrangement is an example of the very highest literary artistry—demonstrating
the fact that only one who has cried to God from both the
pit of despair and the pinnacle of success, and been answered in both situations, could possibly witness through
such a set of lines as those that form the Shepherd Psalm
(Ps. 23).

Seventeenth Day   Read Psalms 24-29

There are times when the devout find praise to be their
chief employment; instead of asking God for things, the
loosened tongue can only pay tribute to divine glory as in
Pss. 24 and 29.

At other times and in other moods, however, prayer becomes a process of telling God about the affairs of everyday
life. Such conversation with God is dominant in Pss. 25, 26,
27, and 28. Notice how these inspired verses show us the
way of prayer. Nothing is too big or too little to find a place
in one's prayers; we can talk with God about anything and
everything: our longings, our youthful sins, guilt, loneliness,
plots of our enemies, our dark hours, and our radiantly
joyful days. Prayer, as demonstrated in the Psalms, is as
broad as the human spirit and as deep as life itself.

Eighteenth Day   Read Psalms 30-34

Notice today how the language of devotion reflects the
circumstances under which prayers and praises are framed.
From these Psalms alone, we can get a coherent idea of
the land and culture from which the Psalmists speak. Some

of the pertinent allusions in today's reading are: strong mountain, sackcloth, rock of refuge, pit, fortress, a broad place, a broken vessel, a besieged city, the heat of summer, the rush of great waters, lyre, harp of ten strings, war horse, famine, young lions. Such a list could be compiled from any half-dozen Psalms, and from many passages in the historical and prophetic books of the Old Testament.

Once more, we are made vividly aware that God speaks to particular men in particular places. He never broadcasts a verbal message to all men everywhere—but relies upon sensitive individuals to hear his non-verbal messages and translate them into the words and images and thought-forms that prevail in the time and place. This aspect of divine revelation presents both major difficulties and monumental opportunities in Bible study. Always, it is the reader's task to find in his own vocabulary some equivalents for words and concepts that flourished in the climate of thought from which written Scripture sprang.

Nineteenth Day   Read Psalms 35-37

Evil, wrongdoers, and enemies *always* beset those who try to follow the path of righteousness—whether in a shepherd culture or in an industrial age.

Is it chance, or deliberate arrangement by ancient singers, that accounts for the fact that these three Psalms are grouped together?

In Ps. 35, the singer (whose pleas readily become my own) begs God to join the battle of life—on his side. Reflection tells me, in Ps. 36, that God actually does rule the world and me, no matter what circumstances may prevail for the moment. In Ps. 37, I conclude that I must be more patient. I must cease my groaning and let God act in his own good time. Measured against the time scale of the Creator, everything human is like a puff of smoke or like flowering weeds that adorn the pastures for a few hours in the spring. Let my own effort, therefore, be directed toward holding fast in my place of refuge; God will take care of the wicked without my help.

Twentieth Day   Read Psalms 38-41

All four of these Psalms are in the first person. All four are both individual and universal, for through each of them there runs a note of victory in dire distress.

Let me never forget that it is not success, but stress, that turns me to God confessing my failures and weaknesses as a prelude to pleading for divine forgiveness and rescue. In this sense, trouble (as a basic ingredient in human life) is one of God's richest gifts.

In your own next period of overpowering distress, even despair, you will find it helpful to remember this quartet of songs. Read them with your own name substituted for the "I" of the ancient singer; make David's lamentations, pleas, cries of victory your own.

Twenty-first Day   Read Psalms 42-48

Every seeker for God goes through periods of darkness and doubt. It is normal to experience some protracted "dark night of the soul" in which all spiritual striving seems useless. Pss. 42, 43, and 44 come from a mood of near-despair. But the rest of the Psalms in today's reading reflect a different mood.

God is an active agent in whatever happens, these Psalms declare. Whether one experiences victory or defeat, he is not outside the realm of providential purpose and care. So the real secret of happy and victorious living is not to get what one wants—but to use every situation as a lens through which to see God. Calamity, earthquake, and defeat can be used as avenues through which to approach God more closely. Treat every situation from joy to anguish as an opportunity to know God better, and you will find joyful victory no matter what life may bring.

Twenty-second Day   Read Psalms 49-53

Throughout the Book of Psalms, there is recognition of the grand issues and dark riddles of human existence. Today's reading centers here. Since all men (good and bad alike) must die, the inspired singer ponders life's meaning and finds that it resides in God above.

Before an all-powerful God, good men and evil men are alike. God in his heaven looks down and laughs at man's struttings, pretensions, and mighty strivings directed toward ephemeral goals. Enduringness attaches to God, not man. Hence it follows that the only human effort of more than fleeting significance is that aimed at permitting the Creator to impart his own qualities to his creatures in greater measure.

Twenty-third Day   Read Psalms 54-59

As with the case of two or three earlier readings, today's group of Psalms reflect the constant turmoil that marks human life. Though the nature of one's enemies may vary widely, conflict is as basic to existence as air and water. So these Psalms are universal—above and beyond time and circumstance. They speak for all troubled men everywhere.

How could a man so plagued and tormented as the writer of these Psalms have produced these and even greater hymns of praise and confession? In a sense, the answer to that question is the central "hidden secret" of the Psalter. For, though reason and logic can never quite build up a convincing case, faith asserts that the only person who will accept God's best gifts is the person who is desperate because all his own resources have failed. Consequently, only a context of tension, trouble, and disappointment can serve as soil to yield a crop of timeless songs, prayers, and praise.

Twenty-fourth Day   **Read Psalms 60-66**

To be human is to be involved in stresses and tensions. But these need not be endured as purposeless, nor suffered in solitude. God is in every situation of tragedy, exile, and turmoil. He tries his own as the silversmith tries his precious metal; he takes us through fire and water because he loves us.

There is no state or condition which does not permit prayer. To enter into dialogue with the Creator—symbol of permanence in contrast with impermanence of all human and created things—is to "feast on marrow and fat" even though fainting in a waterless desert. So all the earth can join in joyful praise to our great God—praise that echoes through terrible affliction, and provides automatic reward, because this crying-out-in-trouble strengthens bonds of fellowship with God.

Twenty-fifth Day   **Read Psalms 67-69**

Is God the ruler of nations as well as individual men? Does he literally affect the course of world history—wars, conquests, treaties and alliances—or has he delegated control in these areas to man?

The whole history of Israel, and the whole Bible as a record of the covenant between God and a particular people, are at stake here. Whatever else these Psalms may do, they insist (sometimes to the perplexity of peace-minded moderns) that God is not far off in some abstract heaven. Rather, God is involved in the "blood, sweat, and tears" of both individuals and nations. That nation, or that person, who has a life-directing relationship with God gains some human friends and makes some mortal enemies thereby. All life is affected here and now, not simply in some non-physical hereafter.

If this outlook is accepted, it seems natural that the God-fearing one should pray heaven's vengeance upon his enemies, as a prelude to rescue. Do you consider such bloody petitions as included in these Psalms to be pagan, or Christian? Why?

Twenty-sixth Day   **Read Psalms 70-72**

It is something of a Biblical landmark to come to the end of the prayers of David, the son of Jesse and symbol of royalty who gave Jesus Christ one of his chief titles. Whether or not David himself wrote all the Psalms to which his name has become attached is beside the point. What matters for us is the vivid fashion in which they portray the problems and challenges of life.

On the surface, it seems that for a mighty ruler, who has been "a portent to many" (71:7), David is strangely obsessed with his need for divine aid. This powerful warrior before whom strong men quail is perpetually calling for help!

Not simply in today's readings, but in many of David's prayers—as well as in Solomon's Psalm 72—there are suggestive undercurrents. Perhaps these inspired men glimpsed

99

more clearly than ordinary folk the paradox by which human need for divine protection increases rather than decreases as a man gains prestige, power, and wealth. Of all men, the king is actually most needy! Material success, whatever its form, constitutes a source of danger that has no equal. Measured by whatever human standard, achievement is "a rise to a height" at which a man easily becomes dizzy and may fall to his injury or death. Instead of relaxing in your quest for divine guidance and protection during periods of success, if you follow David's rule of thumb you will search and ask and pray with new fervor every time you score a triumph.

Twenty-seventh Day   **Read Psalms 73-77**

Why are godly men so restless and troubled, and godless ones so often complacent if not actually triumphant?

All religious systems must face that question, and none offers a universally acceptable answer. Perhaps there is a clue for us in the very frequency and fervor with which it is raised throughout the Hebrew-Christian Scriptures, and especially in Psalms such as these. Can it be that discontent with things as they are is a mark of the God-seeker? Is it possible that a sensitive soul, attuned to the voice of God, simply *cannot* be completely at ease in the world of flesh and of things?

Whatever your conclusion, notice that the very process of wondering why God does not act to bring about justice and right has ways of yielding answers. Over and over here, the Psalmists, who cry out in their impatience over injustice and wrong, answer themselves by taking a look at history. It is the verdict of the ages, they conclude, that God actually is in control. Through faith, we must hang on to that belief, even when events of the present moment (viewed from our limited human perspective) seem to challenge the notion that God, truth, and right really do rule.

Twenty-eighth Day   Read Psalms 78-80

Delete from these Psalms a few references to long-vanished ways, and they become contemporary. So far as their basic theme is concerned, these lines might have come from twentieth-century U.S. life as appropriately as from that of ancient Israel.

For a basic characteristic of the divine-human Covenant is especially prominent here. We have noticed earlier that in the relationship of individuals and peoples with their Creator, the characteristic mood is change rather than constancy. *Salvation history* is marked by ebb and flow, by advances and retreats, by new surrender to God and fresh rebellion against him.

So vivid is this quality that today's reading hints that the Covenant is almost an organic state, whose pulse-beat is essential to its existence. The periodic cry, "Restore us, O God of hosts," is as fundamental to seeking and serving God as the heart's pounding is to the human body. That person or group who succeeds in maintaining a placid and undisturbed state is likely to be spiritually dead; no matter how vigorous the outside appearance, his blood is no longer circulating.

Twenty-ninth Day   Read Psalms 81-86

Not simply in today's reading, but throughout the Book of Psalms, there is much testimony to the reality of divine-human dialogue. Many of these passages point to heights and depths that we dull and timid ones today hardly dare

101

seek in our prayers. Burning, life-directing hunger for an answer from the lips of God (85:8; 86:1) creates conditions in which prayer ceases to be monologue and becomes dialogue.

Oh, the grandeur and sublimity of direct quotations from the lips of God! Passages such as Ps. 81:6-16 gain in power each time they are read. It is a major role of the Psalter to persuade you and me that in rare and exalted moments we can hear God speak directly to us, too.

Thirtieth Day   **Read Psalms 87-89**

Speaking in the mood of this closing section of the third "book" of Israel's songs of praise, a modern poet has suggested that God is closer than a man's breath, nearer to him than his own hands and feet. That is a way of acknowledging that Providence is so fundamental to existence that every situation and circumstance is pervaded by divine purpose and care. You cannot get away from God, no matter how hard you try. He is involved in all.

God gives singers and dancers their bounce (87:7). God is in the personal "dark night of the soul," using a man's despair as a context in which to create hunger for light. God is in the tragic eras of his own Chosen People; in periods that seem to challenge the very notion of a divine-human Covenant, the Creator is at work stirring men to enter the mood in which faith defies logic in order to cry triumphantly: "Blessed be the Lord for ever! Amen and Amen." (89:52)

FIFTH MONTH:

Psalms 90-150, Proverbs, Ecclesiastes, The Song of Solomon

Even in the Book whose function is to stir the mind and heart, these Psalms represent a mountain top. All of them, but especially Pss. 90, 91, and 95, include so many sublime ideas so magnificently expressed that every doubting and troubled soul can find new life here. If you have not already done so, you will surely want to memorize one or more of these Psalms.

You have noticed, have you not, how they permit you to breathe the crisp, clear air of the mountains? When you are so troubled that life seems useless, these Psalms will help you find strength to keep inching upward until you actually enter the place of refuge and find yourself made invulnerable by shelter behind the rock of salvation.

Men and their doings pass away. Friends and foes alike have a life span like that of autumn weeds. All human institutions, including powerful nations that strike terror into the hearts of the whole world, will vanish like puffs of smoke. God alone is enduring. God alone is powerful.

God give me vision to see that my only refuge is in him, and God give me courage to accept that refuge. In the place that is at one and the same time hidden from sight and visible to all who will consent to see it, I can sing glad praises.

103

Here, nothing can touch me. Weak and puny creature that I am, during every hour that I linger here, qualities of the Creator himself attach to me.

Second Day   Read Psalms 95-100

There are many other joyful passages in Scripture, some in verse and some in prose. Nowhere, though, does any group of half a dozen chapters rise higher than these triumphant ones. Maybe you will want to make a note inside the cover of your Bible, reminding yourself to turn to them when you have had a special blessing and cannot find words to express your joy and gratitude.

Joy so great that it can be poured out only through song is the dominant note from the first line of Ps. 95 to the last line of Ps. 100. That the Lord reigns, absolutely, is *the* fundamental fact of existence. During the rare hours that I really know this, I cannot keep from singing! Life's circumstances, no matter what they may be, simply serve to magnify the utterly unbelievable wonder that I, a creature, may know the Creator! Glory be to him; in knowing my God I bring to life those divine qualities that lie dormant inside me!

Third Day   Read Psalms 101-104

Notice how intensely personal these (and many other) Psalms are. In today's reading, no poem of praise omits the wee words that point to one of the axles on which my world turns—words like "I," "me," and "my." Though the ancient seekers, sometimes puzzled and sometimes overjoyed, are speaking for themselves, they are also speaking for *me*. To the degree that I succeed in making their lines not words in

104

a Book but outpourings of my own heart, I shall enter into their experiences and victories.

Throughout these Psalms, humanity and divinity are contrasted. A particularly vivid description of man's utter futility occurs in Ps. 102:3-11, and a spine-tingling tribute to the unspeakable glory of God is found in Ps. 104:1-30; briefer and less exalted passages of both sorts abound here.

Instead of leading to despair, as would be the case with an agnostic, recognition of the gulf between God and man is for the believer a source of triumph. Mentioned briefly several times in these Psalms, faith's note of victory is trumpeted full blast in Ps. 103. The net result of belief-powered scrutiny of the incalculable gap between the divine and the human is overpowering. It makes me recognize that, by crossing that gap, a man really can gain significance in the midst of our chaotic world. Glory! A human being—I myself —can become at least a tiny bit like the God whom I both revere from a distance and meet face to face!

Fourth Day   Read Psalms 105-106

We have here, in a sense, a poetic summary of *salvation history*. In relation to secular history, the time span is limited from the days of Abraham to establishment of the Chosen People in the Land of Promise. But, as an expression of the Covenant relationship between God and man, this summary is timeless.

God initiated the Covenant, not man (105:8-11). God is faithful in every situation; Providence is involved in all possible circumstances, from famine (105:16) to plague (106: 29). Whether through negligence or outright rebelliousness, man can neither escape nor flee from the hand of God.

But, though he is the beneficiary of this Covenant relationship, man is by nature incapable of keeping his part of the bargain. Man cannot help being a rebel. Overpowered for a time by consciousness of deliverance, man soon forgets. He tests and tries the God who has saved him, fashions idols and pollutes the very land with monstrous deeds performed in the name of piety.

Is there, then, any solution? Yes! The heart of the Covenant relationship, the secret shouted so loudly that few men succeed in really hearing it, is the fact that God does for his own what they cannot do for themselves. God is perennially busy in the cosmic process of rescue. Here is reason enough to praise him and rejoice "from everlasting to everlasting!" (106:48).

Fifth Day   **Read Psalms 107-109**

Turn where you will in Scripture, if you stay with a passage long enough and really open your mind and heart, you will find a personal message that applies directly to your life.

At first look, the diversity of these Psalms is discouraging. They are alike in only one respect: each voices a note of praise to God. You and I cannot avoid noticing that the praise of Ps. 107 with its theme of divine deliverance in response to human pleas (verses 6, 13, 19, 28), and the praise of Ps. 108, sound from a higher plane than that of Ps. 109. Almost, it seems that the violent language of Ps. 109, with its fervent pleas of vengeance upon the heads of enemies, is out of place in Scripture.

But maybe its very inclusion has a purpose. Maybe the sharp contrast between these Psalms is a way of calling upon you and me to examine our own ways of praising God. How ready we are to feel that *our* praise is pure, while that of someone else is tainted! How easy it is to see the fly in the ointment—provided it is someone else's ointment!

Just how pure is your everyday run-of-the-mill praise of God? Compared with the lowest and most selfish notes sounded in Ps. 109, are your prayers lofty and selfless? How do they sound by comparison with the praises voiced in Ps. 108:1-4?

Sixth Day   Read Psalms 110-115

Winds of eternity blow through these Psalms. Different as they are in other respects, each of the six suggests or refers directly to contrast between God's enduringness and the instability of men and nations.

Vividly to recognize that God's great Covenant with mankind is established *forever* is to discover an escape hatch in the roof of the dungeon of life. Or to change the figure of speech to a more contemporary one, personally to set out upon the adventure of praising God's name "from this time forth and for evermore" is to enter a bomb shelter that no number of megatons can threaten.

Given such a source of security, you do not need to fret over whether to trade your concrete tank for a newer model, or whether to investigate buying a fallout shelter that can be stocked with supplies for a whole month instead of a mere two weeks. Really to know the everlasting God and fully to praise him is so absorbing a task that anyone joyfully engaged in it has no time or energy left to worry about Russian bombs.

Seventh Day   Read Psalms 116-118

One of the rewards of patient, systematic reading of the entire Bible is the frequent discovery of familiar lines in strange settings. Today, perhaps the most vivid example of such discovery is Ps. 118:24. These words, publicly recited at frequent intervals in many congregations, take on new power when recognized as linked with divine rescue in time of distress.

Even in today's brief reading, there are other much-quoted verses such as Ps. 116:15 and Ps. 118:22. The latter is a famous figure of speech applied by early interpreters to the Saviour. Here, in a setting that seems very far removed from proclamation of the Good News of Christianity, we find that the central idea of divine rescue is already well developed. *Salvation history* is the story of the development of that idea into a rounded system of thought that comes to focus in the person of a divine-human Saviour.

Any point of view, according to which the Old Testament and the New Testament are poles apart with no common core, must be rejected in favor of recognizing the subsurface unity of the entire Bible. "From cover to cover" it proclaims that God does for man what man can never do for himself.

Eighth Day   **Read Psalm 119**

This Psalm, famous as the longest chapter of the Bible, is also some of the most highly stylized poetry in Holy Writ. There are twenty-two stanzas—one for each letter of the Hebrew alphabet—and each stanza has eight lines, all of which begin with the appropriate Hebrew letter.

These impressive features of the Psalm disappear with translation into English. So we are once more confronted with the riddle of language. This theme runs all through Ps. 119, preoccupied as it is with God's testimonies, statutes, and *words*. God has so made men that ideas may be expressed through patterns of conventional sounds (spoken words) and shapes (written words). Within a given language group, meanings can be expressed fairly accurately. But translation from one language to another always involves losses as well as gains. Those well-meaning but misguided persons who are ready to fight to defend one of several meanings of a word or verse in the English Bible have failed to reckon with the intricacies of translation. It is beyond the limits of human skill to produce a modern-language version of Holy Writ that is identical with ancient Hebrew versions.

Yet the riddle and marvel of translation has its positive as well as its negative side. Through our God-given capacity to work with words, we can transmit sublime truths and poetic images "sweeter than honey" (Ps. 119:103), not simply from one generation to another, but from century to century. Civilizations, different in almost every other respect, can unite in seeking and in praising God with words that do not look or sound alike, but which somehow succeed in expressing the same longings of the creature made in God's image.

Ninth Day   **Read Psalms 120-129**

All these Psalms, as well as the next five, bear a special title. Regardless of how that title may be rendered in translation, it seems to have applied to special pilgrim songs of the Hebrews. Travelers who climbed Temple Hill, about 2,500 feet above sea level, "ascended by degrees" as they approached the central shrine of Israel.

That pilgrim who ceases to climb upward is not actually headed toward the holy place of the Lord God of Hosts, no matter what he may think of himself, and regardless of how other men judge him. Climbing is integral to the religious quest. No matter what level one may reach, to cease ascending, however gradually, is to die inside.

But this aspect of the human response to the divine overture is no cause for melancholy and weeping. Rather, it is a basis for great joy! Though born of struggle, these songs of the upward-climbing pilgrim are triumphant. They suggest that simply to join a band of like-minded seekers and with them strive to ascend the holy hill is to enter a state of victory. It is not arrival at a given goal that constitutes religious success—but the ardent, joyful process of struggling to get a little higher every day.

Tenth Day   Read Psalms 130-135

A quick look at these Psalms, mostly very brief ones, gives a first impression of diversity almost to the point of confusion. Just about anything, it seems, can form a subject for a holy hymn of praise!

Here we have agonized personal longing (Ps. 130), followed by a wee stanza of humble praise (Ps. 131). National destiny of the Chosen People (Ps. 132) seems so grand a theme that praise of community harmony follows a bit lamely (Ps. 133). And, almost it appears that a brief exhortation to take part in public worship (Ps. 134) has nothing in common with poetic praise of God the Creator contrasted with impotent pagan idols (Ps. 135).

A second reading reveals that there is unity even in diversity. For the constant factors here are God and man. However much they differ in length, style, and subject-matter, these Psalms are alike in treating the divine-human relationship as the most important aspect of existence. Regardless of how stirring or sublime it may be, no piece of literature or work of art or system of thought can deserve the label "Biblical" unless it is true to this standard: dealing not with God in the abstract or with man in the concrete, but with God-and-man in a state of conscious relationship.

Eleventh Day   Read Psalms 136-139

It is impossible for man, formed by God to become like God, to enter any situation from which the steadfast love of

110

the Creator is absent. Divine love permeates the total environment, affects both societies and individuals every moment of existence. In this respect, the history of civilization, with all its varieties of Babylonian Captivity, is cut from the same cloth as that woven by the workings of one individual.

From the cradle to the grave, mankind and individual men are swathed in protective layers of providential care. From the dim, lost beginnings of civilization to those far-off days when earthmen may form colonies on other worlds, the Covenant relationship shapes my destiny and your destiny and the corporate destiny of all the upright creatures made in the image of their Creator.

Twelfth Day   Read Psalms 140-144

No matter how hard we try, you and I cannot fully enter the situations from which our Psalms came. Distance gives the Old Testament world a halo all its own; we are inclined to think it natural that immortal songs of praise should have taken form in those glorious days when it was easy to obey God. For simple men of simple times, we say, it was as though heaven and earth were closer together than they are now.

Let us be done with such empty musings!

Samuel and David had to wrestle with the world, the devil, and the flesh just as strongly as you and I! Regardless of the times or circumstances, every man who tries to know and serve God is sure to be dogged by evil men. Every drama has its villains who "spread a net" (140:5), offer banquets featuring forbidden "dainties" (141:4), set a hidden trap in the pathway (142:3), overwhelm the innocent and make them "sit in darkness like those long dead" (143:3), speak lies and offer a right hand that is actually "a right hand of falsehood" (144:8).

111

Away with explanations and excuses for failing in this our own day to rise to the level of God's heroes of other days! They had their trials and troubles, too. Certainly, the trail that leads to the city built without hands is rough and dangerous now—but it was no smoother, no straighter in the days of Abraham and Isaac and Jacob. If, as a highly-advanced Christian civilization, we must view the spiritual achievements of ancient Israel with wonder from afar, it is not because they had things easier then. In contemporary America as truly as in ancient Israel, God will raise up men—if, in surrender, men will accept from him the rescue they cannot win through striving.

Thirteenth Day   Read Psalms 145-150

I sometimes fear that too much of the time and energy of the typical modern Christian is devoted to trying to understand God, and not enough to voicing praise of the God who is beyond understanding. The Psalter begins with a promise of bliss to the person who learns to enjoy seeking the hidden things of God, and ends on a full-throated chorus of praise.

All that God has created reflects the greatness of the Creator. (*See* Ps. 19.) But among created things, man is unique in his capacity for formal praise of the Creator through words and melodies. Until one engages in such creative praise, he has not accepted the full legacy that is due him. A living creature with upright posture and bloodlines that label him *homo sapiens* does not automatically rise to the level of one "made in the divine image"; to make the latent image real he must exercise his capacity for praising his Maker.

So viewed, the Book of Psalms contains the key to life. Everyone who accepts and uses the God-given key enters into a life of creative delight that constitutes manhood at its best. Praise the Lord that this is so!

Proverbs

Every culture develops its own collection of capsule sayings, or proverbs, that offer folk wisdom in condensed form. A hasty look at the Proverbs of Israel might lead readers to conclude that they are very much like those of other peoples and other periods, and so hardly deserve to be given the rank of sacred Scripture.

While there is a degree of evidence for such a conclusion, it is challenged by slow and meditative reading of the Book of Proverbs. Most of the individual sayings can be interpreted on two or three levels. As is the case with folk wisdom in general, there is much word-play and employment of figures of speech. Such material is not intended to be gulped down in huge chunks, but to be sucked and chewed in tiny morsels. When treated in this fashion, the Proverbs yield a great deal of spiritual nourishment. It is true that few of them are on the exalted level of, say, the Sermon on the Mount. But it is equally true that such passages as the Sermon on the Mount must rest upon solid foundations long a-building. The Book of Proverbs is such a foundation for Christian thought and experience.

Fourteenth Day   **Read Proverbs 1-3**

As sought passionately by generations of the Chosen People, wisdom is *not* identical with knowledge or skill. It is possible for a man who is very ignorant, as the world measures learning, to be profoundly wise in the sense of the Biblical quest.

God is intensely masculine, but Wisdom is personified as

feminine. She is a co-worker with the Creator, and plays a vital part in the work of bringing the world into existence (3:19). That work, you will recall, is accomplished by the power of words; as creation is described in Genesis 1, God *speaks* the world into being.

Wisdom is an agent of God—an intermediary who communicates the things of God to the sons of men. In this respect, she is a sort of dim prototype of the Holy Spirit.

Because Wisdom has fabulous gifts to confer, she must be eagerly sought over long periods. Any man who devotes his life to courting Wisdom can become so infatuated with her that he is not tempted by the shiny baubles that constitute bait in the traps set by the adversary (personified as an adventuress in Prov. 2:16-19). To achieve a state of yearning for Wisdom is to enter the bliss of Ps. 1. It is, by a great paradox, at one fell swoop to achieve the impossible: by virtue of yearning for the divine gift of Wisdom, to rise above the limitations of creaturehood.

Fifteenth Day   **Read Proverbs 4-7**

At the level on which literal meanings of words govern interpretation, these chapters are a damning indictment of lust and immorality. On the higher level of theological interpretation, they offer a profound analysis of the cosmic drama in which the forces of good and evil fight for the prize of the human soul.

Wisdom is on the side of God and of right, and does everything in her power to hold any man who is attracted to her. But she is opposed by the evil woman, "the adventuress with her smooth words" (7:5), who represents the attractive tug of tangible goals. The struggle between these two women is somewhat like that between Christ and Satan, for, in both instances, the fate of a man made in the image of God is at stake. Far from being a helpless pawn, man actually decides the issue. He can succumb to the seductive speech of the woman of the world and follow her like an ox going to the slaughter (7:21-22). Or he can so seize hold of Wisdom, hanging on grimly and sleeplessly, that he actually saves himself "like a gazelle from the hunter" (6:5).

The fight is on, and it is a fight to the finish! Withdraw from it, no man can. Win it by the grace of God and the power of his agents, any man may!

Sixteenth Day   **Read Proverbs 8-10**

God's first great act of creation was that of establishing Wisdom (8:22-31). As a go-between, offering the Creator's good things to creatures made in his image, Wisdom is perpetually beguiling. Wisdom does not wait for men to become enamored of her, but takes the initiative and stations herself where the pilgrim cannot fail to hear her pleading voice (8:2-3).

Wisdom never gets an uncontested hearing, though. Her opponent, the foolish and noisy "wanton" who personifies Worldliness, actually imitates her manners and repeats her invitation verbatim. (*Compare* 9:4, 9:16.)

Therefore, the pilgrim is never safe and secure; his journey toward the holy city is never finished. Life is a perpetual battle in which spiritual victory is beyond achievement. The most that a man can do is to busy himself in ceaseless seeking, occupying himself so fully with the courtship of Wisdom that he remains "on the path to life" (10:17).

Seventeenth Day   **Read Proverbs 11-13**

No compartment of life is sealed to the influence of a man's faith. What one deeply believes, and what one seeks as his

115

life's goal, will affect everything he does: the way he uses his money, his tongue, his time, and even the way he dresses and walks.

Consequently, a dividing line runs through society, separating men into two distinct categories: the righteous and the wicked. Life attaches to the former, and death to the latter. Challenge this as "too neat and too simple" if you like—but, by whatever standards you arrive at your own classifications, use your God-given freedom to make today a time when your personal scales are tipped toward righteousness and life.

Eighteenth Day	Read Proverbs 14-16

Much twentieth-century religious thought emphasizes difficulties and dangers in arriving at clear-cut definitions. According to this view, right and wrong are not absolute but relative. Gray, in a wide variety of shades, is far more common than either black or white.

No such doubts plagued the culture out of which the Book of Proverbs came. The characteristic structure of a wise saying is that of deliberate antithesis between two (and only two) alternatives: "A fool despises his father's instruction," "but he who heeds admonition is prudent" (15:5). Here there are no shades of gray, no in-between stages; it is either/or. However persuasive the arguments that challenge such an outlook upon life as being oversimplified and dogmatic, the fact remains that the viewpoint that produced the Proverbs of Israel is calculated to make men realize that life is a constant succession of choices, and that the decision to walk toward the light rather than toward darkness does affect the goal that a pilgrim reaches.

Nineteenth Day   Read Proverbs 17-20

This collection of brief sayings touches most areas of life. Yet it is not so formless and chaotic as it seems at first look. Through the whole there runs the unifying thread of emphasis upon man's capacity for speech. This great gift, rightly employed, can make life sublime; misdirected, it makes life futile.

He whose whole life is a courtship of Wisdom will find delight in brief maxims that represent the distilled thought of the past. Perhaps he will even succeed, himself, in producing a few well-phrased formulas. Poles apart from the outpourings of a fool's mouth, each such Proverb is a spiritual-intellectual mine, whose richest treasures come only after much digging. (*See,* for example, Prov. 17:3, 16; 18:18; 19:16; 20:24, 30.) Brief as they are, such sayings challenge one to examine his whole system of values and conduct.

Twentieth Day   Read Proverbs 21-23

To a degree that is both fascinating and astonishing, twentieth-century Americans accept the idea that change brings progress. As a culture, we are thoroughly committed to the notion that the forward movement of time brings improvement—"every day, in every way, we are getting better and better."

Israel's Proverbs challenge this whole outlook. For though they speak across 4,000 years, and from a wholly alien culture, the voice I hear is that of my own heart. Only externals change. Man himself is the same in all generations. The lure of alcohol, as a way of escape (23:29-35), is the same among desert nomads of Abraham's day and apartment dwellers of a modern city. Regardless of techniques that may be used, no modern philosophy of education rises one inch above that of Prov. 22:6. Though we now focus upon atomic

117

weapons instead of war horses, the verdict of Prov. 21:31 is for all ages and conditions—past, present, and future.

Twenty-first Day   **Read Proverbs 24-26**

To court Wisdom instead of living with that contentious woman, Worldliness, is to enter into dialogue. Wisdom is not limited to the words of human speech as a means of communication; she can whisper in her lover's ear through any event or experience whatever. Everything that God has made has capacity to convey divine messages to that seeker who looks and listens for late word from God in every situation.

Tasting honey, the awakened one makes a great leap of understanding and in a flash "sees" that Wisdom is like this sweet stuff (24:13-14). Observing a costly piece of jewelry, he cocks his ear and listens as Wisdom whispers that stinging reproof from a friend is like this thing of beauty (25:12). Aghast at hearing of a practical joker who throws firebrands at the innocent, Wisdom's courtier knows she is using this experience to warn him against tossing fiery words (26:18-19).

Twenty-second Day   **Read Proverbs 27-29**

We are not alone. We are social as well as solitary. It is a major paradox of that strange creature, made in the divine image but bound to earth by feet of clay, that full development requires a man to be at one and the same time an unduplicated individual and a unit of organized society.

Though specific patterns change, man's social structures pose about the same problems and opportunities in every age. How to get along with one's friends, relatives, neigh-

118

bors, king (or boss) is as basic a problem in the Atomic Age as in an age when iron was rare and wonderful (27:17). Then and now, a man's relationship with his God is the basic factor that governs the way he will get along with his fellow men.

Twenty-third Day   **Read Proverbs 30-31**

The beginning of Wisdom is to realize how little one knows. It takes only a casual glance, just an instant of direct attention, to be bowled over by mystery. The wind, the waters, a soaring eagle, a lizard taking a sun bath in the courtyard of a palace . . . any one of these is enough to convict the wisest man of gross ignorance. We know so little, and God knows so much.

To recognize our littleness, to bow down before the awe-full greatness of God who made and sustains the total universe and us within it, is to begin to escape from the clutches of that wanton woman, Contentment.

Ecclesiastes

Ecclesiastes, or "The Book of the Preacher," is as puzzling as it is intriguing. Highly-distilled theology and philosophy are presented here, now in verse and now in prose that has many qualities of poetry. Modern readers are tempted to by-pass this little collection of Wisdom's formulas because of its obscurities, or hastily to conclude that it is too cynical to be included in a Christian's spiritual diet. A careful and sympathetic reading, approaching the book as an instrument through which God will speak directly to you about the affairs of your life, is likely to yield such thrills that you will feel cold shivers run up and down your spine as you stand with bowed head in the presence of the Most High.

119

Twenty-fourth Day   **Read Ecclesiastes 1-2**

There are two ways to view life. One may examine it on the horizontal plane, where visible and tangible things reign supreme. Or life may be seen with a vertical as well as a horizontal dimension.

Anyone who really takes a good look, limiting it to those things that can be touched and tasted, seen and sold, is driven step by step to an inevitable conclusion. That conclusion is summarized in Eccles. 1:2, and repeated from the same outlook in Eccles. 2:24.

If truth and meaning and joy are inseparably linked with life in the physical body, then all striving really is busy-work (1:13). If the intangible and invisible do not have eternal significance, if human logic rules supreme and belief deals only with chimeras, then the epitome of success really is to eat, drink, and be merry.

Twenty-fifth Day   **Read Ecclesiastes 3-5**

God, who made man in such fashion that he can devote all his time and energy to busy-work, also "has put eternity into man's mind" (3:11). This is where the trouble arises. Man might be satisfied with enjoying his work—planting and plucking up, casting away stones and gathering them together—were it not that he has been given a glimpse of the eternity he cannot grasp with his hands. As it is, the man who wins only tangible successes (whether in terms of ancient vineyards or modern corporations) reaches the end of his days realizing that he really has "toiled for the wind" (5:16).

This utterly frustrating situation, says the Preacher, is the work of God. God has deliberately arranged things so that men will sooner or later come to see that their furious strivings are futile: "I said in my heart with regard to the sons of men that God is testing them to show them that they are but beasts." (3:18)

120

Twenty-sixth Day   **Read Ecclesiastes 6-8**

Emotionally and intellectually twisting and writhing, doubling and redoubling upon the trail of his own thought, the Preacher repeats his earlier arguments in different form. Neither material success nor length of days actually contributes one iota to life's meaning. Neat answers simply are not to be found; even the pursuit of wisdom is futile, for it perpetually eludes the seeker (7:23). Everything seems to be topsy-turvy; wicked men are rewarded, and righteous men are punished (8:14).

Troubled, perplexed, and burdened, this mixed-up seeker gets his answer in a flash of insight. The truth is, ultimate answers are hidden from men; the earth-bound creature who toils to discover how the Creator orders his universe is doomed to disappointment. "However much man may toil in seeking, he will not find it out; even though a wise man claims to know, he cannot find it out." (8:17)

Twenty-seventh Day   **Read Ecclesiastes 9-12**

Since the dozen chapters of this brief book are absolutely without form or order (so far as modern Western minds can determine), it is useless to seek for a clearly-visible positive conclusion in these final pages. But I believe the last two verses actually do answer the riddle. Coming after the Preacher's breathtaking vision of the end of things, they form a sort of denouement in which the central theme of the drama is condensed.

Convinced of the futility of every human activity, the overwhelmed one is in a mood to turn to God for divine gifts he must accept in lieu of personal achievements.

It is only out of the pit of despair that one is impelled to look up and out. Until a struggling seeker descends to rock-bottom defeat, where all human activity spells "vanity

121

of vanities," he simply will not cast himself utterly upon God. So long as man retains the least glimmer of hope in his own strength and efforts or the progress of society, he will not make divine rescue his one goal. No man in his senses will put the fate of his soul into the hands of a male-factor dying upon a cross; to do that, he must have de-spaired of every other source of help.

So viewed, this dark and difficult little book suddenly glows with more than earthly light. Though he never spells out his message in a few easy sentences, the Preacher in-sists throughout that a more-than-logical act of rescue by the Creator is the one thing that can give significance to the creature made in the divine image.

The Song of Solomon

Chances are, here is a little book that you have never studied in Sunday school! There are two widely divergent positions concerning it.

Many modern Christians (probably the majority of Prot-estants) take the "literary" view. According to it, this is a pagan love song—no more and no less—which won a place in the Bible only because Solomon's name is attached to it. So regarded, it is poetry of a fairly high grade whose sub-ject matter makes it quite unfit for any religious use.

But this point of view has been prominent for only two or three centuries. During more than fifteen hundred years the Song was generally regarded to be the love song between Jehovah and the Chosen People (or between Christ and the Church). So viewed, the lines are not sensuous, but exalted enough to occupy a central place in the devotional life of such a great leader of Christendom as Bernard of Clairvaux.

Twenty-eighth Day **Read Song of Solomon 1-3**

For my part, I shall take the position that those who long ago helped shape the contents of the Bible were not schoolboys, but great and godly men. Consequently, I shall insist upon reading the Song as the love plaint of Israel, daughter of Zion (Isa. 16:1) for her divine Lover. Here is the nuptial music of the Covenant!

So viewed, the placement just before the Book of Isaiah is deliberate and tremendously significant.

Israel and her divine Lover engage in the fervent and secret language of love. Their rapid exchanges defy logical outline. Each sometimes whispers sweet nothings, sometimes bursts into lyric praise. It is not possible in some instances even to say which of the two is speaking.

This much, however, can hardly be overlooked: the vocabulary of love-making actually *does* convey high-level ideas about the exotic, delightful, and creative state produced by union of God and man. In more direct language (and more exalted poetry), we have here an ancient forerunner of Christian love songs such as "In the Garden" and "The Lily of the Valley."

Twenty-ninth Day **Read Song of Solomon 4-5**

In every age and among all circumstances, sensitive men and women have had a sense of being *sought after* by God. This is the basic idea in all considerations of the "call" to religious service, for example. That is, God is seen as taking the initiative. He does not wait for men and women to seek him, but continually beguiles us to come to him.

Artists have expressed this compelling concept through such paintings as those which depict Christ knocking at the door of the heart. In his famous poem, "The Hound of Heaven," Francis Thompson suggests that God chases the wayward soul as a hound follows his quarry.

Today's reading employs softer and warmer imagery. The divine Lover described in the thrilling words of Song of Sol. 5:10-16 is not stern or fearful. Rather, he is engaged in eager courtship! Now pleading, now chiding, now tenderly pursuing, he devotes all his ardor to the task of *wooing* the soul of man!

Thirtieth Day   **Read Song of Solomon 6-8**

Fervent and ceaseless as it is, the wooing of the divine Lover will not lead to union until the soul responds in kind. For really fruitful and transforming encounter with God, one must literally pant for the instant of embrace. With every fiber of her being, the soul must focus upon the coming of the Lover in order to surrender to him. She must cry with all her heart:

> Make haste, my beloved,
>   and be like a gazelle
> or a young stag
>   upon the mountains of spices. (8:14)

When such a mood dominates the hungry soul, when yearning for God is so intense that it cannot be haltingly expressed except in the language of romantic love, then the soul is ready to enter into the transforming surrender that the Bible exalts as the apex of human achievement.

Isaiah and Jeremiah

Isaiah

In order to play the role of prophet, a person must have a sensitive ear and a nimble tongue. It is his function to hear and understand the divine messages that folk in general fail to notice, then put those messages into such form that they have public influence.

Because of the nature of prophecy, it is inevitable that dozens or scores of would-be "proclaimers of divine secrets" are forgotten, for every one that is remembered. Many a self-styled prophet is more keenly attuned to his own inner groanings than to the voice of God. Hosts of others, who really do succeed in hearing messages from on high, lack capacity to communicate those messages in such form that masses of listeners are impelled to take heed.

Messages that form the Book of Isaiah stand in the front rank of Jewish-Christian prophecy. It takes only a casual reading to discover that, though all the garments are cut from the same bolt of cloth, the hands of more than one tailor have been used by God. There are three natural divisions in the book: Chapters 1-39, 40-55, and 56-66. Respectively, they deal with: Judah in the eighth century B.C., the sixth-century Babylonian Exile, and the fifth-century "return to Jerusalem."

What matters, for our purposes, is the remarkable fashion in which a stream of prophecy that flowed across three pre-

Christian centuries served as a herald of the coming Good News. Jesus Christ, the supreme agent of communication between God and man, so embodies the divine that we revere him as "the Word of God." Everything that he does, as well as all that he says, *speaks* to us about the Father. No previous channel conveyed so full, so overwhelming, and so definitive a stream of revelation.

But the essential central truths, according to which men and God are in a Covenant relationship such that God rescues those men who will accept his unearned Grace, resound throughout Scripture. In this sense, the Old Testament is precisely like the New Testament. Indeed, without the centuries-long work of Providence by which a Chosen People were prepared to hear the definitive message from God, it would have been futile for that message to have been sounded.

The Book of Isaiah stands in the front rank of the agents of preparation. Isaiah foreshadows much that is clearly articulated in the Son of God. Isaiah is to the solemn movement of *salvation history* as John the Baptist is to Jesus Christ in person. Read as an unequaled "preparer of the way," this noble book will bathe your whole understanding of the Gospel with brilliant new light.

First Day   **Read Isaiah 1-4**

Whatever else he may be, Isaiah is a man with a message! Sometimes he spews out challenges that sting; sometimes he pours out promises that soothe. But in both instances he requires that we who read shall take a stand; neutrality is not an alternative.

God's own people have rebelled against him, the prophet charges; Zion's haughty daughters "walk with outstretched necks" (3:16) while they deliberately explore the depths of iniquity. So great is their sin that Jerusalem has become a new Sodom.

Though it is seldom expressed explicitly, Isaiah everywhere implies that his prophetic warnings are voiced in a time of prosperity. Having grown strong and comfortable, the people of the Covenant have ceased to rely upon divine help. They worship the fruits of their own labor. They do not need any gifts from God; they are getting along quite nicely on their own, thank you.

All this will change in "the day of the Lord," the prophet declares. Then things will be reversed, with the proud laid low and God alone exalted. Boys will play the role of princes (3:4) and the latest arrangements from the beauty parlor will yield to baldness (3:24). Poured out upon the heads of mankind, in a series of divine acts that are in some respects "beyond history" rather than within history, the day of the Lord will establish justice and give meaning to history. "In that day," the mood will once more be that of divine rescue. Zion's daughters will be cleansed, not through their own efforts, but by the work of the Lord who will provide "a shelter from the storm and rain" (4:6).

Second Day	**Read Isaiah 5-9**

Once he has been overpowered by his vision of the Lord "high and lifted up" (6-1), Isaiah is no longer his own master. He belongs to the Lord, for whom he is a spokesman— a mouthpiece, in the literal sense. In this role, the prophet himself runs the gamut of religious experience, from despair to exultation. Partly for this reason, and partly because all his messages fall upon the ears of a people too dull to hear God speaking directly to them, Isaiah's prophecies are not arranged in orderly sequence.

Yet, in spite of the fact that his messages spill out in almost chaotic fashion, all of them revolve about a few central ideas. These ideas are repeated over and over in a variety of ways, somewhat like the theme of a symphony.

Almost any segment of his book, selected as arbitrarily as today's five chapters, will yield many of the same emphases.

Faithlessness of the Chosen People must be punished, Isaiah repeats. Israel must be led out of her new Egyptian captivity, which consists of bowing down to "idols" of materialism. In order that these rebellious people shall turn their hearts to repentance, they must be chastened.

So far, there is nothing radically new. But now the prophet's message takes a strange turn—one that is frequently anticipated earlier but nowhere clearly spelled out. GOD WILL USE A NATIONAL FOE AS HIS INSTRUMENT. MILITARY DEFEAT WILL RE-ESTABLISH CONDITIONS IN WHICH THE PEOPLE OF THE COVENANT WILL CEASE TRUSTING IN THEIR OWN STRENGTH AND TURN TO THEIR CREATOR FOR RESCUE. This radical interpretation, according to which national calamity is a dramatic message or "sign" from God, is so basic to Isaiah's prophecy that it is repeated over and over—appearing in these chapters in such passages as 5:26; 7:18-20; 8:7-8; 9:8-11.

Because God's dramatic signs can be viewed from many perspectives, they are even harder to interpret than are verbal messages. What one sees in a divinely-ordered event (such as the birth of a child, 8:1-4, or invasion by Assyrian armies, 8:7-8) depends upon where he stands and with what eyes he looks. It is the role of the prophet to ponder such signs, soak himself in them until they are part of him, and then "translate" these divine messages into words with which to challenge other men too dull or too busy to notice the signs that abound everywhere.

One such sign of which Isaiah makes a great deal is that of the coming of a child, through whom God will once more provide rescue for his people (7:10-17, 9:6-7). For Christian thought, it is inevitable that this should be taken as a new milestone in *salvation history*. Here is a finger pointing forward to the grandest of all acts of rescue: the climax of the drama, the birth of the child for whom the divine-human

128

marriage was consummated . . . he who was at one and the same time Son of God and son of man, the pivotal figure in the drama of Creator and creative.

Third Day   **Read Isaiah 10-13**

Viewed from one perspective, any occasion on which God pours out his wrath constitutes "the day of the Lord." Punishment is a major ingredient in the compound constituting that day, and God can use any circumstance or event whatever as his agent in effecting such punishment.

But there is also an element of glory in the day of the Lord. Once Assyria has served God's purposes, functioning as the rod with which he chastens godless Israel (10:5-6), Assyria herself will be laid low (10:12, 25). When Babylon has executed God's anger (13:3), the Lord of Hosts will march against that great nation and turn its cities into waste places (13:19-22).

So far as *salvation history* is concerned, therefore, it may be concluded that all the movements of men and of nations play their special roles in the implementation of God's purpose. What seems to be a national calamity, actually can be the stimulus to re-dedication of the Chosen People. Having grown lax in their performance of Covenant vows, they will be stirred to fresh zeal by onslaughts of Assyrian and Babylonian armies.

That is to say, the Covenant is never canceled. God never withdraws his promise, no matter how flagrantly man abuses his confidence. Consequently, there is no possibility that the ultimate triumph of God shall be threatened. Out of what seems calamity, there always comes a fresh appetite for rescue. When the oak is cut level with the ground, "there shall come forth a shoot from the stump of Jesse" (11:1). God's punishment is never total; he always preserves a remnant, and always that remnant will turn back to him, reaffirming the Covenant to write another page in the book of *salvation history* (10:21).

Fourth Day   **Read Isaiah 14-18**

There are two overwhelming impressions offered by these chapters.

First, many of the places and powers of which Isaiah talks are so thoroughly forgotten that their names mean nothing to us. Moab and Babylon may sound faintly familiar, but who has ever heard of Heshbon and Elealeh, of the road to Horonaim or the waters of Nimrim?

When we focus our fears and yearnings upon the powerful of earth, we tend to regard them as holding life's meaning in their hands. But, the truth is, God so overshadows kings and generals that, by comparison with him, the most exalted of rulers is a bit of new growth on a vine, soon to be chopped off with a pruning hook (18:5). Whether they be our friends or our foes, the nations of earth are like chaff on the mountains (17:13). No man or nation has more than fleeting significance. God alone is powerful. God alone is everlasting. God alone commands our awe, our fear, our loyalty, and our worship.

Fifth Day   **Read Isaiah 19-24**

"Tumult and trampling and confusion" (22-5) pervade these pages. "In that day," nature herself is turned topsy-turvy: the mighty Nile becomes "parched and dry" (19:5). From fishermen and weavers of Egypt to merchant princes of Tyre, men find their affairs suddenly thrown into chaos. Archers of Kedar and horsemen of Babylon are alike dashed to the ground. Egypt's fabulous City of the Sun, stronghold of idolatry, becomes tributary to the Lord of Hosts (19:18).

130

Here is a definitive repudiation of the plea, "Peace, peace." Let the soul who enters into Covenant with God recognize that, in this state, there can never be an armistice. No culture, no society, no nation can long escape divine wrath. No institution, no stronghold, no monument will endure beyond the life of a puff of smoke; "the earth shall be utterly laid waste and utterly despoiled" (24:3). In this uncertain and insecure life, the only way any man can find certainty and security is to throw himself upon the Lord of Hosts, whose glory outshines the moon and sun (24:23).

Sixth Day   **Read Isaiah 25-29**

God's offer of rescue is made to mankind in general; indeed, it is potentially universal and unlimited. But in order to be accepted by individual men, rescue must be introduced into history. This, in turn, requires a specific and not a general place—particular men, and not "mankind." It is the function of Jerusalem, the holy mountain, to serve as the valve or spigot through which salvation flows.

In the same fashion, it is the role of the Chosen People to serve as a channel through which God may move to encounter all the far nations. But this chosen vessel is a vessel of clay. Jacob continually falls and fails, so must be scourged and reawakened. That is what happens in time of national and international turmoil. Never lose sight of the fact that God's hand is involved in calamities and disasters. God is the keeper of the vineyard, and he will not turn his back upon it even for an instant. By using her proud foes to chasten the Chosen People, God revives the sense of Covenant and guarantees the continuing movement of *salvation history*.

Seventh Day   **Read Isaiah 30-34**

God is terrible! Oh, how terrible he is! (30:13-14, 27-33; 32:14-15; 34:1-17)

But the wrath of God is poured out for the healing of the nations. He strikes fear into the hearts of men in order to cause us to bow down before him (30:18), to cease trusting in some "Egyptian alliance," to turn away from our idols of silver and gold made with our own hands. The day of the Lord is a day of reckoning, the role of which is to awaken us out of our complacency (32:9-11).

Because of its awakening role, the day of the Lord is not only a day whose terrors no tongue can describe; it is also a time of joy and exaltation (30:19, 26). When the land mourns, then God is known in his glory (33:9). Then and only then do the eyes of men succeed in seeing that Zion alone is fixed and eternal (33:20)—the one source of stability in an unstable universe.

Eighth Day   **Read Isaiah 35-39**

Much that is reported in these chapters falls into the realm of what we have come to describe as "history." National and international events are dramatic and stirring. Sennacherib, the powerful and ambitious King of Assyria, brings armies and lays siege against Jerusalem—reduced to such weakness that the city does not have enough warriors to mount the spare horses of their foes (36:8). Sudden death strikes the encamped Assyrians, who abandon the siege and flee in panic (37:36-37). King Hezekiah falls gravely ill, but recovers to reign over Judah for another fifteen years (38:1-6). Babylonian diplomats make their appearance, presaging the rise to power of that great Eastern empire whose expansion will bring an end to the Hebrew monarchy (39:1-7).

It is against such a background that Isaiah the prophet gives his unique interpretation of history. God is in history, using men and events, he declares. Whatever comes must be interpreted in the light of a faith that cannot waver. Regardless of how absolute defeat may seem, God always preserves a remnant (37:31-32) through whom the Covenant is maintained and to whom ultimate victory will come (35:10; 38:20).

Ninth Day   Read Isaiah 40-42

The flail has threshed out the grain; the razor from beyond the river has shaved off every hair. Rebellious children of the Covenant have come through the years of the Babylonian Captivity predicted in chapters 1-39, and now are chastened.

What is the outcome?

A new movement in the cyclical unrolling of *salvation history!* Now that his chosen ones are panting with thirst, the Lord is ready to open up fountains (41:17-18). Prostrate, Abraham's descendants no longer trust in their own strength, but throw themselves upon God alone. Now Jerusalem sees with new clarity that even mighty Babylon is like grass that withers—while "the word of our God will stand forever" (40:8).

Here is Good News, indeed!

Out of despair, there comes a new kind of joy. From the ashes of defeat, there springs a totally unexpected kind of victory. Out of captivity, there emerges freedom in God. Israel has been made new through suffering.

But that is not the end of the story. This reborn people, transformed through acceptance of rescue, have a role to play in history. The new servant of God (sometimes the nation, sometimes Jerusalem, sometimes an individual "suffering servant") is the divine instrument through which healing will come to the nations.

Rejoice! Rejoice! Rejoice! Through his servant, God will

level mountains and make rough places smooth, turning darkness into light, so that instead of having forsaken man as hopeless, God has established his Covenant anew!

Tenth Day **Read Isaiah 43-46**

"Don't be afraid," God soothes Israel through the lips of the prophet. "You are my son. You belong to me. You were born of my covenant with Abraham. Come what may, my blood flows through your veins. Nothing can change that fact. Nothing can sever our relationship."

Basic to the divine-human bond is the quality of emerging novelty (43:19). God, the Creator, continues his work and brings it to a cosmic climax in the Covenant. Something utterly new is forever emerging! Divine forgiveness makes guilty sinners into new persons (43:25; 44:22). Divine mercy brings water out of dry ground (44:3). *God is all in all.* "I am the first and I am the last" (44:6) . . . "and there is none like me" (46:9). In the Covenant relationship, God continues his work as Maker.

God is utterly unlike the impotent idols we humans make with our hands. God uses us and all things as his instruments. Why, in his hand, mighty Cyrus and the hosts of Persia are but pawns (45:4). This powerful Maker, this Creator of all that is and of *all that is to be,* pours out upon man a stream of "everlasting salvation" (45:17). His deliverance, always potent to transform the whole of existence, is perpetually near! (46:13)

Eleventh Day **Read Isaiah 47-50**

Babylon the great, daughter of the Chaldeans, rules the world. But she did not reach these heights by her own strength alone. She is an instrument of God, who deliberately gave Israel into her hands (47:6)—sold Israel into slavery for her sins (50:1).

Basking for a moment in the sun, Babylon has dared to think herself almighty and everlasting (47:10). It is therefore time for her to learn who really is in control. Both to punish rebellious Babylon and to restore the people of the Covenant to their glory, Israel is about to be redeemed once more (48:20).

What glorious fruit God has caused to grow upon the tree of Babylonian Captivity!

Made prostrate in order to be eager to accept the helping hand of God, Israel will rise up stronger than ever. She sat down by the waters of Babylon to weep (Ps. 137), but now rises up to rejoice that in such a situation she succeeded in hearing a new message from on high (48:6). Worship of Jehovah, so long tribal and national, has become international. God's suffering servant will not only bow before him in Jerusalem, but will also be "a light to the nations" in order that salvation may bathe the whole earth (49:6).

Twelfth Day   Read Isaiah 51-55

Songs of triumphant praise abound here. No passages in Scripture are more eloquent and moving. Commentary upon them is superfluous, if not presumptuous.

Here is the climax of the Covenant. Here is Calvary foreshadowed. Out of the marriage between Israel and the Lord, there comes the Suffering Servant—the Redeemer. It is for this that the world was created.

Thirteenth Day   Read Isaiah 56-59

Almost immediately there is a distinct change in the mood and style of the writer. Even before a side remark reveals

that the outcasts are now back home (56:8), we sense that
the conditions of the Babylonian Captivity no longer prevail. Instead of comforting promises about the redemptive
work of the Suffering Servant, we encounter a volley of
stinging rebukes.

Restored to their homeland, the people of God have fallen and failed once more. Immorality and idolatry flourish.
God is forgotten, and his holy day is profaned. Injustice
and wickedness prevail. Even the solemn religious ceremonies dedicated to God are futile, for they are empty and
pretentious (58:4).

In this situation, the prophet takes yet another giant
stride in the human pilgrimage whose goal is a glimpse of
the height and the depth of God's redemptive love. God will
restore the penitent, he exults. The sins of his people do
not cause the Covenant to be canceled. BUT INSTEAD OF RE-
JOICING AT THE REDEMPTION OF ABRAHAM'S SEED OR THE SONS
OF DAVID, THE PROPHET SINGS HIS PRAISE THAT "those in Jacob
who turn from transgression" WILL BE VISITED BY THE RE-
DEEMER (59:20-21).

No longer regarded as transmitted through biological
processes or by a select nation into which one enters by
birth, the Covenant is now seen to be spiritual in nature.
Once this startling leap of understanding has been made,
we are not far below the pinnacle from which a few sensitive ones will grasp the fact that God offers salvation to
THOSE WHO BELIEVE IN HIS SON.

Fourteenth Day   **Read Isaiah 60-63**

God's free salvation, poured out for all persons, necessarily
enters history at a particular place as well as through a
special agent. That place is the city of God—Jerusalem. Because the light of the world shines in her streets, she will

enlighten nations (60:3). Foreigners will rebuild her shattered walls (60:10), and those who are in captivity will be set free (61:1). Jerusalem's people will become recognized as God's earthly representatives (61:5-6), and divine righteousness will spread over the earth (61:11). This new instance of the divine-human marriage, in which the Holy City becomes the bride of the Lord (62:4-5), promises utter transformation.

But that transformation is temporary. The mighty promises of God have hardly been sounded before he begins once more to shout his anger that the Chosen People have not responded (63:1-6). Man perpetually rebels and arouses divine enmity. No matter how mightily saved or how wonderfully restored to some Jerusalem, God's own people perpetually backslide and become like strangers who have never bowed before him as king (63:15-19).

Fifteenth Day   **Read Isaiah 64-66**

Small wonder that any man who really looks about him yields to despair—until he looks again and sees that the human race is the handiwork of God. Such recognition, leading to hope in hopelessness, evokes a mighty groan (64:9-12).

God replies, reciting a group of grievances (65:1-7) whose punishment will contribute to formation of "new heavens and a new earth" (65:17). In the end, God's Chosen People will participate in victory rather than defeat. Regardless of struggle and failure in the past and defeat in the present, God will establish a glorious and triumphant reign in the future. No matter what the conditions of his earthly life, anyone who really believes in God has such radiant optimism that nothing can dispel his joy.

137

Jeremiah

It hardly seems possible that we have reached the twenty-fourth Book of the Old Testament. With half our year of reading to be completed in just two weeks, the age of the patriarchs is behind us and the coming of the Saviour is ahead of us.

That is precisely where Jeremiah found himself. From the past he inherited a rich legacy of law, history, songs, and ceremonies. He recognized himself and his contemporaries to be on the receiving end of a stream of divine revelation and guidance that began with Abraham. And to a degree seldom matched in *salvation history*, Jeremiah found messages from God in the events of secular life.

Jeremiah lived through one of the most chaotic periods in Jewish history. Three world powers were struggling for supremacy, and little Judah lay in the path that their armies naturally took in meeting one another. Egypt, Assyria, and Babylonia alternately offered threats and protection, after a fashion. Judah's leaders turned first to one, then to another of these pagan nations. Jerusalem entered a series of futile treaties; she was first made a tributary, then captured outright, and finally destroyed about 587 B.C.

Throughout this tumultuous epoch, Jeremiah tried to persuade the people of the Covenant to rely upon God instead of their own strength or the promises of foreign kings. He never succeeded more than briefly and partially. But no event or circumstance could silence this man!

To a degree unmatched in the Old Testament, he offers dramatic as well as verbal messages. It seems that he is perpetually *doing* something as well as saying something to attract attention and persuade men to bow down before God. Failure never daunts him. Reverberating as they do with the voices of diplomats, the noises of battle, and the groans of prisoners, these pages are yet exuberant and triumphant. Nothing can defeat our great God!

138

Sixteenth Day   **Read Jeremiah 1-3**

It is a basic affirmation of Scripture that God speaks to men without ceasing. He uses not only words, but every kind of experience and object—from almond rod to boiling pot. But there is no flow of communication (or revelation) unless some sensitive one sees or hears in order to understand and act. Hence the stream of divine-human dialogue is not continuous, but broken. It comes in spurts, and is poured out in history through men like Jeremiah.

In these opening chapters, the prophet's message is as blunt as it is damning. Israel has fallen into idolatry, he asserts. She not only engages in all kinds of pagan worship, but tries to preserve herself through alliances with sinful nations rather than by dependence upon Jehovah. She has violated the marriage contract between God and man. She has turned her back upon the Ark of the Covenant. But the situation is not hopeless. God calls for repentance in order that he may show mercy. In a future era of divine victory that the prophet labels simply "in those days," rebellious Judah and wanton Israel will be joined together and all nations will flock to Jerusalem to bow before the Lord!

Seventeenth Day   **Read Jeremiah 4-6**

Spiritually regarded, there are no impossible situations. All men (and most of all, those especially favored by God) do fall and fail. They wallow in sin, and enjoy it. But the possibility of a return to God—no, the certainty that a remnant will return—is never challenged.

It is in order to reawaken sleepers and to make restless the comfortable that a merciful God uses national disasters as tools. His judgment is within history, as well as beyond history. When priest and prophet alike have become corrupt (5:30-31; 6:13-14), when both great and small have turned their backs upon God, he uses other nations to punish his Chosen People.

No matter how far they may have wandered from the path to life, once men are brought to a state of despair they are ready to find strength in God.

Therefore, the ray of hope always shines. It may become very dim, but it is never extinguished. Man's follies and failures cause his Lord to sow desolation, not once but over and over. But God "will not make a full end" (4:27; 5:18; 6:9). However hard it may be to order one's life by a promise that is almost totally obscured in a given historical situation, nevertheless, the assurance of meaning and of victory gleams through the mists of our chaotic existence. Hope, and not despair, is the final word.

Eighteenth Day   **Read Jeremiah 7-9**

It is part of the paradox of the Hebrew-Christian faith that though hope in God is ultimate and decisive, the happy verdict does not necessarily apply to a particular person or epoch. We have almost a spiritual counterpart of the statistical principle that is the foundation of modern science. Given large numbers of cases over a long period, the scientist can predict in advance a cumulative result. But, confronted by a specific instance, his laws of probability give him no answers.

God's ceaseless Covenant with mankind is conditional in about the same sense. Individuals and epochs may depart from the Covenant; indeed, many are certain to do so. Ultimate triumph of the divine purpose does not for an instant relieve anyone of freedom and responsibility. Indeed, part of the plight of Jerusalem in the time of Jeremiah is the tendency to rely upon the fact that God has chosen Israel as his bride. This gives a false sense of security, leads to a new low in social degradation and a new high in pagan practices, and hence causes God's heart to break. No lines in Scripture exceed the power and pathos of those which describe the grief of God at the waywardness of his people (8:18; 9:2). Lovingly though the punishment is administered, God's judgment upon Israel is so fearful that words can hardly describe it (9:11-16).

Nineteenth Day   **Read Jeremiah 10-13**

I cannot today resist noting that these chapters confirm the judgment that tendencies toward idolatry are never eliminated. Man, simply because he is man, is prone to bow down before less than God. With half an eye, one can look about our own land today and see modern counterparts of the idols whom Jeremiah's people displayed in their solemn processions.

Man, being man but wanting to be a god, fails most utterly when his efforts are directed toward scaling the heights. No failure is like spiritual failure. Jerusalem, chosen from heaven to be the bride and beloved of her Maker (11:15; 12:7), has become more vile and filthy than her neighbors who have not yet made an effort to rise above their wallowings.

As you read these gripping chapters, are you beginning to feel a sense of revulsion? Do you abandon hope in man's capacity to live up to the best that he knows? Are you spiritually seasick at the waverings and failings of the Chosen People who so badly muffed the most glorious of opportunities?

If so, you are again entering the mood that makes spiritual victory rest upon divine rescue rather than human achievement. Jeremiah's scintillating description of the way finite goals transform the best of men into the worst, begins

141

by indirection to lift up the distant vision of a man upon a cross who will die in order to accomplish for mankind what our race cannot do for itself.

Twentieth Day   **Read Jeremiah 14-17**

Throughout this vivid book, and especially in today's chapters, we are confronted by a paradox. In all its forms, organized religion is prone to fail and to fall—yet, when such instances of human depravity are most abundant, God raises up some amateur through whom the Covenant is revived.

Jerusalem's respected religious leaders have sold out. Instead of offering yeasty and transforming messages from on high, they wink at the sins of their people and support the status quo (see 5:30-31; 6:13-14). Priest and prophet alike "ply their trade" (14:18) in utter blindness. That is, they act the part of the professional religionist instead of the spokesman for God. They are being well paid to speak soothing words of peace, when they ought to be shouting warnings that would shake the foundations of society.

It is in this apparently hopeless situation that God raises up men like Jeremiah. It is when the institution fails most completely that individuals respond to the divine call most grandly. It is when conduct of religious officials seems to question the validity of religion itself that some layman steps forward so thoroughly surrendered that God uses his lips to pour out authentic new warnings and promises.

Twenty-first Day   **Read Jeremiah 18-21**

Anyone who thinks the lot of a genuinely God-inspired prophet to be soft and easy will revise his judgment after reading these chapters!

142

Jeremiah is so attuned to the still, small voice that he hears God speak in every situation of life. For example, he gains a vivid message from on high while watching a potter at work (18:1-11). Not only does he receive messages through a great variety of media; he also uses unconventional methods in making public what he hears from God. Unable to persuade men by use of words alone, he arranges a dramatic setting in which to smash a flask to symbolize divine punishment (19:1-2, 10-11).

Just how popular this makes the prophet, we learn in such passages as 20:1-2. Convinced that he is a voice crying in a wilderness of idolatry and degradation, Jeremiah runs the emotional gamut. At one moment, he sings with delight (20:13); the next moment, he is overcome by despair (20:14-18). He hears God in a time when nearly every ear is dull. He speaks with power and passion—and nobody responds.

Dare we draw a tentative and hesitant conclusion?

Is it possible for any prophet who presents an authentic message from God to be universally popular?

What does this suggest concerning the programs of today's middle-class churches, hardly to be distinguished from other segments of the culture, that seek to serve God by means of pleasing all and offending none?

Twenty-second Day　　　　**Read Jeremiah 22-24**

Jeremiah's denunciation of false prophets and priests continues, interspersed with warnings about fearful judgments certain to come upon the heads of those who follow such leaders.

In hopelessness, however, there is hope. Echoing Isaiah's verdict that "a remnant will return," Jeremiah catches a glimpse of light in the darkest hour of Israel's history. Both

143

in the last climactic months before the nation falls (23:1-8) and in the aftermath of Babylon's victory (24:1-7), Jeremiah sees hope. God, who punishes sin wherever he finds it, will never give up. Always, he will woo and pursue. Though a new deluge comes in our day, tomorrow at least a few repentant ones will thrive in the sunshine of God's love.

Twenty-third Day   **Read Jeremiah 25-29**

Were it not for the dramatic incidents that punctuate his message, Jeremiah's prophecy would seem repetitious to the point of monotony. During a period of more than twenty-three years (25:3), he has said about the same thing, over and over. Public reaction remains uniformly unfavorable, varying from indifference to indignation. Opposition of the religious institution remains firm; "false prophets" continue to be satisfied with the status quo and to resist reform. Under such circumstances, why bother continuing to seek new ways to make public a message through drama (25:15-17; 27:2; 28:12-13) as well as speech?

Simply because Jeremiah is not a free agent. The choice is not his to make. He is a tool in the hand of God. Though playing a very different role from that of the king of Babylon, the prophet is like the ruler in being an instrument of Providence (25:9). Jeremiah is voicing a system of crisis theology; in a time when it seems that God has deserted his Chosen People, God is using Jeremiah to offer a re-interpretation of the Covenant. So the prophet has no choice. Even at the risk of life and limb (26:11), he must speak. He is a mouthpiece for a message bigger than he.

Seldom achieved even by the most dedicated of God-seekers, this is the ideal state of the religious leader. This is the goal toward which every preacher and teacher and church officer should aim: surrender so complete that he becomes a spokesman for God rather than for himself.

Twenty-fourth Day   Read Jeremiah 30-31

There are woes, calamities, and punishments. Precisely because we are human, we shall never escape these conditions
of our manhood. But neither present nor future signs of
doom represent God's final word.

Always, that word is positive. God is perpetually saving
his people (30:10), binding up our wounds (30:17), and
establishing conditions for rebuilding (31:4). This is true
of history in general, and of every period and epoch in particular. That is to say, the divine-human Covenant is a basic
factor in creation—as characteristic of it as are those forces
which regulate the sun, moon, and stars (31:35). Consequently, the verdict of Jeremiah (like that of Scripture in
general) is in the end one of unqualified optimism. The
Covenant itself is perpetually being made new (31:31),
and the final outcome was assured before the world began:
". . . you shall be my people, and I will be your God."
(30:22)

Twenty-fifth Day   Read Jeremiah 32-35

Regardless of the holy zeal that moves his lips, and the
social evils that stir him to speak, we have to confess that
Jeremiah almost seems to enjoy his role! Reading such
passages as 34:17-22, the wonder is not that the prophet
spent time in the guardhouse (33:1), but that he survived
his first frontal assault upon entrenched evil.

That the king and his officers tolerated Jeremiah is solid
ground for hope. Things never get altogether bad. Man is
perpetually involved in the cyclical movements that grow
out of the Covenant, of course. The succession of events is
monotonously sure: in every generation, men will fail and
fall about as their fathers did; God will cleanse (33:8),
restore (32:38), and accept his children into a new Cov-

145

enant relationship (32:40). This pattern is as much a part
of the life situation as the day-night cycle (33:20).

Yet something more is involved. There is an element of
what we moderns tend to call "progress." Though the rolling
of the wheel takes it in perpetual circles, it is also moving
forward. Absolute and not simply relative gains are promised through a Branch from the tree of David (33:15).
Individuals and cultures really do continue to call upon
God, even though sin and evil never vanish. Answering
such calls, God does not simply repeat the old answers. He
gives new ones from time to time: "I will answer you, and
will tell you great and hidden things which you have not
known" (33:3).

Twenty-sixth Day   Read Jeremiah 36-39

Anyone who thinks of God's prophets as men withdrawn
from the world and shielded from ordinary problems in
order to meditate and pray will gain a fresh outlook from
the fast-moving Chapter 36. Few passages in the entire
Bible exceed this chapter in emotional impact.

Having survived his frontal assault upon the king of
Judah and having prepared a revised edition of his scroll,
the much-imprisoned Jeremiah sees, firsthand, many of the
woes he has predicted. Egyptian control of Judah is followed by Babylonian. No matter what puppet ruler happens
to be on the throne, Jeremiah gets about the same treatment. A climax is reached in the episode of the cistern
(Chapter 38), but the prophet lives to see his king blinded
and led away in chains (39:7).

Fresh messages from God, in such a time as this!

Twenty-seventh Day   **Read Jeremiah 40-45**

Writing style employed by a historian is quite different from that used by a prophet. That is the case even when both write prose or both write poetry. Here, the use of prose in historical sections helps to emphasize differences between reporting political events and "speaking for God."

Even in historical sections, however, the religious viewpoint is dominant. All the woes and disasters that come upon God's people stem from one cause: wanton idolatry (44:23). Egypt and Babylon are instruments of God in working out the divine purpose: so chastening the Chosen People that they will turn away from idols and prostrate themselves before God.

Egypt has both historical and symbolic meaning, here and elsewhere in Scripture. Groaning under Babylonian rule, Judah's "remnant" turns hopefully to Egypt. They prefer the service of the queen of heaven (44:17) to remaining in Judah and wearing the yoke of captivity. It is part of the basic message of Jeremiah that every choice of an "Egypt" is futile and self-defeating. All who elect what seems an easy life in some Egypt or other enter a new idolatry that will launch a fresh cycle of war, famine, and pestilence (42:11-17).

Twenty-eighth Day   **Read Jeremiah 46-48**

In their pride, men continually engage in a subtle form of idolatry. They pay homage to the state, bow down before a symbol of human power that may range all the way from an ancient monarchy to a modern Fascist or Communist regime.

God has spoken very plainly to Jeremiah, reminding him that such aggregations of power are finite. Seen against the backdrop of ongoing divine creation, no nation is of sig-

147

nificant duration. Egypt and her sacred bull will pass away, along with Philistia and her great mercantile cities. Moab's wealth and fortresses are futile to protect her.

Just now, the prophet asserts, it pleases God to use Babylon as his sword. Every battle that helps reveal the futility of human pride serves as a day of the Lord (46:10). For the more clearly men recognize that nations—all nations—come and go, the more likely we are to see that the only genuine source of strength is trust in "the King, whose name is the Lord of hosts" (48:15).

Twenty-ninth Day   **Read Jeremiah 49-50**

Intoxicated, as it were, by the glory of the Lord, Jeremiah continues to call the roll of great cities and mighty nations. One by one, they shall go to their doom. As his chastening rod, God is presently using Babylon. But when her invincible armies have served their purpose, Babylon herself will go down in such defeat that the very earth will shake.

Is there no security in this insecure life?

Yes! God overthrows the proud and topples the strong in order to show that man's one sure source of strength and comfort is trust in his Maker. He himself is our Redeemer and our advocate (50:34). No matter how dreadful the present moment may appear, the Covenant stands. Always we have the assurance that a remnant will return (50:4-20; *compare* 46:27-28).

Here is a major paradox of *salvation history:* it is the downfall of the proudest human institutions that serves to awaken us and point us to the God who alone is eternal and omnipotent.

Thirtieth Day   **Read Jeremiah 51-52**

War is the apex of human conflict. All the factors that affect struggles of lower order are involved in war, so that, in a sense, it is the definitive example of our human dilemma. Simply because of the conditions of manhood, we can never find tranquility. Struggle is an ingredient in existence.

Though he does not set out his conclusions in 1-2-3 order, Jeremiah here and everywhere implies that God is the author of the factors that produce conflict. When men vie with one another and someone gets hurt, that does not mean that God has turned his back upon the world. Even in time of utter desolation, such as the sack of Jerusalem described in Chapter 52, the believer must hold fast to his conviction that God is intimately involved in what happens.

Here is a faith that cannot be shaken.

How strangely modern the Book of Jeremiah sounds, now that we have reached its end! Though the arena is today occupied by different gladiators, and though the weapons with which they fight have little in common with the war implements of Babylon and Judah, today's mood is the same as yesterday's. Use modern names instead of ancient ones, and Jeremiah might almost be writing in the twentieth century.

Can we reach the citadel from which he looked down on the affairs of men and nations? Is it possible for us, too, so to fear the God of Jeremiah that neither man nor beast nor engine of war holds any terrors? Can we make the Covenant so binding upon our own lives that it becomes increasingly sure under test? If so, with Jeremiah we become invincible—not through anything we are or do, but through the God in whom we trust absolutely.

SEVENTH MONTH:

From Lamentations through Malachi

Lamentations

If we could read these exquisite verses in their original Hebrew, we should more readily grasp the prophet's literary power. In the first two chapters, all three lines of each verse begin with one of the twenty-two successive letters of the Hebrew alphabet. Chapter 3 has sixty-six verses, with each letter of the alphabet used for three successive verses. Chapter 4 is similar, but has a pattern of two rather than three verses beginning with each letter.

Lamentations of the poet-prophet center in the destruction of Jerusalem in 587 B.C. But in present-day Hebrew worship, this book is also used to lament the sack of the city by Romans in A.D. 70. In this sense, therefore, the book is oriented forward as well as backward. The lament over Jerusalem, and by the city herself, speaks for all men everywhere in time of overwhelming disaster.

First Day **Read Lamentations 1-5**

Here are the outpourings of a sensitive and gifted seeker after God, who is all but overwhelmed by tragedy. Sometimes he seems to speak for himself (3:1-20); more often, the

150

lips of the prophet are instruments for Jerusalem's outpourings.

There are no really new elements here. We have met all the ingredients over and over: flagrant violations of the Covenant, a state of spiritual decay so advanced that priests and prophets stand for evil rather than for good, fearful divine punishment, despair, repentance, and new hope in God.

Rooted as it is in a specific place at a particular time, this message is none the less universal. Substitute any city you please: Babylon, Karnak, Constantinople, Rome, Berlin, Pearl Harbor, Hiroshima, Moscow, Chicago. Read these lamentations as though written over the ashes of your own city, allow enough time, and she that was powerful in the land will become like a widow sobbing in the night.

Here, then, is a timeless warning.

It is balanced and completed with a ceaseless promise. Every individual, every city, every nation can, through war and desolation, be stirred to turn back to God (3:40). All alike can glory that, though nothing that man builds is permanent, God reigns forever, and his throne endures for all time (5:19). That being the case, the potential for restoration is as ceaseless as the certainty of destruction.

Ezekiel

The writings of this prophet-poet, living in exile during the sixth century B.C., form one of the longest and most difficult books of the Bible. Present-day Christians tend to take one of two attitudes toward Ezekiel's visions, warnings, entreaties, and sublime messages of hope.

Most church folk, I fear, ignore the book altogether. Because it is hard to read and harder to understand, the temptation simply to stay out of its pages is hard to resist.

But a minority of Bible readers spend much time with Ezekiel. I wish I could honestly say that I think their time is well spent. Perhaps it is in some cases. For the most part, however, I fear that the fire-breathing evangelist who centers much of his attention upon this book misses the real point of Ezekiel's message. Abstract ideas and high-level poetic imagery abound here. Such material naturally lends itself to almost any interpretation one may wish to read into it. Therefore, for some readers, Ezekiel is a book of detailed prophetic statements about national and international events in the twentieth century.

If I seem blunt and stubborn at this point, forgive me. But this most recent re-reading of Ezekiel's sublimely dark visions has convinced me that his message is not intended for the twentieth or any other one century. Rather, it is directed to all men in every century. His truths are not centered in the doings of a few Western nations at one period of time. Rather, they are universal. They reveal God in his timeless and unchanging glory, his ceaseless and ever-hopeful courtship of mankind in general and of every man in particular.

Our hasty schedule requires that you go through this book rapidly; in any case, to dwell on minor details is to miss its grand message. Read with eagerness, though with speed, listening for the voice of God as he tells you, through Ezekiel's lips, the meaning of life and of salvation.

Second Day   **Skim Ezekiel 1-10**

To read Ezekiel's account of his visions, filled as they are with strange wheels and stranger creatures, is almost to have one's head swim. The dizziness that comes from trying to follow the prophet's imagery is a tribute to his poetic power. For he employs symbols and metaphors that are so vivid you and I recoil, bewildered, and *knowing* that we are bewildered.

Ezekiel's visions "say" that God is above and beyond

seeing or describing. At its most exalted level, the human imagination cannot dimly perceive the Creator in his totality. When we strain most fervently to see God, we are most completely overwhelmed by a sense of divine wonders, mysteries, and marvels.

Yet the invisible and inscrutable Creator can communicate with the creature, man. Revelation is real! Man can feed upon the word of God (2:8; 3:3). It is the special role of the prophet to do just that: accept divine truth, then share it with his fellow men. The fearful burden of the prophet, son of man, foreshadows the sufferings of the Saviour. For the prophet bears the sins of mankind upon his own back (3:16-21).

Here, the heart of Ezekiel's God-given message is:

All idols are futile. God alone is great. All that is human is limited. Men forget this and, in their pride, rebel against God. Such sin is fearfully punished (7:15-20) in order once more to convince men—through sword, famine, and pestilence—that Jehovah, and not man, is supreme (6:13-14; 7:15-27).

Third Day   Skim Ezekiel 11-17

It is useless, or worse, to pore over the imagery of these chapters in order to treat them as predictions of twentieth-century history. The prophet, at times almost intoxicated by his passion for Jehovah, is a poet of the highest order. He uses high-level imagery as naturally as you and I use everyday nouns and verbs.

Breathtaking imagery of Chapter 16 gives new depth to metaphors of the Song of Solomon. Jehovah's beloved having become wanton, God ceases to whisper sweet promises through the lips of his prophet, and thunders warnings. "Thus says the Lord . . ." echoes and reverberates through these pages like the roll of celestial cannon (13:8; 13:20; 14:6; 14:21; 16:2; etc.)

Reduced to its simplest elements, the divine warning is also a promise: wanton Israel, the bride of the Lord, has played the harlot and must undergo fearful punishment; this, however, is simply a prelude to renewal of the Covenant (11:14-20; 14:11; 16:60).

Fourth Day   Skim Ezekiel 18-23

Responsibility for sin and failure is individual as well as social. Though every person is shaped by his society and his family, in a special sense he also stands before God upon his own two feet alone (Chapter 18).

So for individual men as well as the Chosen People in general, the divine-human drama throbs with promises and warnings. God is perpetually rescuing; mankind in general and individual men are perpetually falling and failing. Thus 20:28 becomes a kind of capsule summary of human history. Always, without exception, God's own people drift into idolatry.

If you can succeed in centering upon grand movements of the divine-human drama, and not upon gross details, these chapters will become soul-stirring. Nowhere else in Scripture is there a more vivid description of the faithlessness of Jehovah's chosen bride, Israel. God's own has so thoroughly played the harlot that princes, priests, prophets, and people are alike in their total failure. Not one clean, upright man remains in all the land (22:30).

Always, without exception, the wages of spiritual immorality—idolatry in one form or another—is death (23:46-49).

Fifth Day   Skim Ezekiel 24-30

God is perpetually engaged in revealing himself to mankind. He uses the lips of devout men as his instruments, in order to pour out his words in such fashion that multitudes will hear and understand.

But revelation is by no means limited to processes that employ words.

Much of Ezekiel's work of proclaiming truth is centered in actions, rather than speeches or sermons. His boiling of meat, melting of the pot, and disregard for death (Chapter 24) are divinely-inspired actions, whose role is to communicate things of God to the sons of men. In this respect, the work of this prophet, who is so often called "son of man," is strangely prophetic. It points to the work of the Son of Man, whose Gospel is communicated not only through what he says but also through what he does and Who he is.

When secular history is viewed through eyes made sharp by faith, all the tumultuous risings and fallings of nations also serve to communicate. Indeed, they repeat over and over the single message: "God is the Lord" (25:7, 11, 17; 26:6; 28:23, 24, 26; 29:6, 9, 16, 21; 30:26).

Sixth Day   **Skim Ezekiel 31-36**

Some of the stirring passages in these chapters have a sweep and grandeur seldom matched even in Scripture. It is a pity that the impassioned and sometimes obscure language of the prophet has caused his book to be neglected by so many modern Christians, and distorted by some fiery ones eager to pour their own meanings through his metaphors.

Ezekiel's visions are so vivid and overpowering that they are often keyed to the year, month, and day of God's outpouring to this sensitive listener. For his part, he continues to use every possible vehicle of communication in order to make public what he hears. His reports are in both prose and poetry; earlier we saw that he frequently dramatized his messages. That is, revelation is so potent and overpowering that it can flow through any and all channels open to man.

One of the breathtaking revelations of this section centers in the nature of divine justice and grace (33:10-20). Ezekiel has not arrived at his understanding of these matters by logical analysis; truth towers over logic. It is *given*—not won by striving. Gloriously, incredibly, and victoriously, "the existential now" that is this present moment is the definitive point in the divine-human relationship! Justice and grace center in this moment—not the past or the future.

To proclaim so incredible and difficult a message is to play the role of true prophet. And that is to invite popular misunderstanding (33:30-33). Even the paid officers of the religious institution—the shepherds—are likely to be deaf to fresh word from the Lord (34:1-10), so that (incredibly) God must actually rescue the sheep from the shepherds (34:11-17)!

God alone, acting personally and not through agents, is ultimate. He alone judges both nations and individuals.

This is a source of absolute, unquenchable hope (34:24-30). Such hope is not rooted in ideas about man or the flow of some impersonal kind of "progress." Rather, it is founded upon the nature of God (34:22, 31)!

Seventh Day   **Read Ezekiel 37-39**

Chapters 40-48 are all but meaningless to most modern readers, though providing a happy hunting ground for persons who go to the Bible looking for obscure "proof" of some pet idea. We shall skim through these chapters very rapidly—tomorrow.

Today we are dealing with material of entirely different nature. These radiant prophecies deserve to be read and re-read. For, in language suitable to the Babylonian Captivity of Israel, the prophet underscores many central warnings and promises later offered to mankind through Jesus Christ, in whom divinity was in history.

When a human agent so yields himself that God really speaks to him, Ezekiel sings, all concepts such as "dead" and "impossible" vanish. Graves of whatever kind—physical, intellectual, spiritual—are opened and dead men spring to life (37:1-4).

That is, God's Covenant is never annulled. It stands forever. Regardless of how frequently men fail and fall, the divine promise is not withdrawn. God's grace is the definitive pigment in the entire canvas that we call human history (37:26-27).

Because the eyes of men are often dull, we perpetually and perennially lose sight of this central core of meaning and hope. Thwarted in his attempt to love us into creative union with him, God is not defeated. Over and over, he uses tragedy to open our eyes and force us to see—sometimes almost against our own wills, as it were—that he really is the one decisive center of meaning and of hope for creatures made in his image (38:23; 39:6; 39:21).

Eighth Day   **Skim Ezekiel 40-48**

It is difficult for a modern Westerner to find a point of contact here. To dwell upon minute details of these visions, attempting to use them as keys to national and international events of our time, is worse than useless.

St. John must have pored over this material until it became meaningful to him, for it clearly influenced many sections of the Revelation.

For most of us, the most we can hope to get here is a distant glimpse of the near-ecstasy in which a man lives after he has been given a vision of the New Jerusalem. Details of the city and its Temple aside, one who really sees it is thereby made invincible. He lives in the light of the all-powerful God of heaven and of earth, protector of those who have entered into the Covenant relationship.

Whether it be Ezekiel or St. John or a very ordinary twentieth-century follower of the Christ, the person bathed in that heavenly light shakes off some limitations of his humanity.

Daniel

This strange and fascinating book deals with a man who was at one and the same time the Hebrew prophet, Daniel, and the Babylonian officer, Belteshazzar. His turbulent life hints that every true servant of Jehovah is going to spend a lot of time in hot water—or worse! Whether in modern times or ancient, the notion that piety guarantees a happy and tranquil life is utterly false, if not heretical.

But it is equally false to be gloomy, even in the face of world catastrophe. Whatever we may see when we scan the horizon, it will not be there very long. Our changeless God wove change into his created world partly, perhaps, to persuade a few sensitive ones that tangible prizes are not worth winning.

All that counts is the divine verdict in the Judgment. There, princes and kings will loom no larger than other mortals. Regardless of what foes threaten us, we ordinary folk really can win—by throwing ourselves upon the mercy of our all-powerful God.

Ninth Day   Read Daniel 1-3

These familiar stories are so vivid and colorful that we may be in danger of treating them simply as stories. Here, as everywhere in Scripture, we need to focus upon *salvation history* rather than upon external factors, however exciting they may be.

Daniel and his three friends, symbolizing all who bow to God rather than to a power less than God, deliberately set themselves apart. By so simple and so basic a choice as that of food and drink, they dramatize the fact that they are different from other persons.

It is this profound difference that accounts for Daniel's ability to see the truth that is hidden from magicians, enchanters, sorcerers, and Chaldeans. Because the Hebrew youth will not yield his allegiance to any idol, he finds Kingdom messages in troubled dreams of a king. God's Kingdom is alone enduring, he declares. Using the same figure of speech that Jesus later applied to himself, Daniel asserts that a stone "cut from a mountain by no human hand" (2:45) will shatter all the kingdoms men can fashion.

As though to test that point of view, Nebuchadnezzar—"the golden king"—throws Daniel's three friends into the fiery furnace. They are delivered by a more-than-mortal hand, giving a specific illustration of the principle that God indeed sets all the schemes and devices and destructive instruments of man to naught.

Tenth Day   **Read Daniel 4-5**

In our day, we are sometimes prone to be a bit impatient of the mysterious. We may even fall into the error of wanting a religious faith that is wholly logical, having no halo of the holy unknown about it.

Daniel's experiences here remind us that interpretation of mysteries actually is a central function of religion. He who succeeds in catching whispers from the lips of God will arrive at meanings that are hidden from the wisest men of the kingdom. Not infrequently, such messages from on high serve to put the prophet of God into the role of an attacker.

With two kings in succession, Daniel fathoms mysteries

159

to persuade them that God alone is great. If not actually "original sin," pride comes very close to being the source of basic human guilt. In all its forms, pride is idolatry—the creature's rebellion against the Creator.

A king with endless dominions (4:22) learned humility through tragedy, and as a result extolled God as his Lord (4:1-3, 34-35). If mighty Nebuchadnezzar could change so greatly, you and I are left convicted without an excuse when we refuse to bend our own haughty necks.

Eleventh Day   **Read Daniel 6-8**

It is easy to get one's feet tangled in the symbolism of these chapters, and trip over he-goats and horns, beasts and wheels. This danger is not easily avoided. Yet it can be met.

Remember always, here and everywhere, that the true role of Scripture is to communicate things of God to the sons of men. That being the case, it is always the central message for which we must look. To focus upon incidental details—garments in which that message is clothed—is to misuse the sacred word.

If the motif of these chapters had to be reduced to one word, I think that word would be *victory*.

Human and superhuman forces are at war here. Lions faced by Daniel are of trifling significance by comparison with the "beasts" of nations at war. These, in turn, lose all their terrors when viewed alongside Satan and his legions of demons. Yet Daniel (and mankind) is not overwhelmed! Gloriously, all the terrors of the planet and the cosmos fail to conquer God's man.

Jehovah, the Ancient of Days, rules over all! There is no defeat for him or for those who trust in him through his supreme agent, "one like a son of man" (7:13). All the goings and comings of men and of kingdoms are brief and limited. But God's dominion is everlasting, and his kingdom is one

160

that no force or power in the universe can destroy. To know this with unshakable certainty is to enter into victory!

Twelfth Day   Read Daniel 9-12

Whether they be prophets like Daniel or simply readers of the Bible like us, all who ponder the meaning of God and of man must deal both with history and beyond history.

Within history, humans are prone to exalt themselves and thereby rebel against God. That is the case with us common folk as well as with princes and kings. But, however splendid it may seem in man's eyes, such a rebellion is always brief. Princes and powers are perpetually rising. But all quickly fall. None lasts; no, not one. Grandeur is fleeting. Power is a vapor that vanishes overnight (11:45).

There is nothing permanent on the finite, created scale. Princes of Persia and of Greece, like ordinary men, must face divine Judgment. But to recognize that God's absolute rule will bring final Judgment is not to gain skill to analyze it in detail. Absolute, complete, neatly-wrapped-up analyses of the Judgment are not given to men (12:8).

Hosea

This little book deserves to be read slowly. Frequently you will wish to mark a passage that catches your attention, and turn to it several times during a day in order to find its deeper meanings.

A stark note of personal tragedy runs through the whole prophecy. Out of a broken marriage, Hosea has come to glimpse the feelings of God at the faithlessness of his own bride, Israel. Sometimes pleading, frequently condemning, and at last hoping, Hosea pours out messages so fervently personal that they are seldom matched even in Scripture.

161

Thirteenth Day   **Read Hosea 1-4**

Moral and spiritual decay, such as described in Chapter 4, represent a crisis in any society. But in the society of the divine-human Covenant, such a state of affairs seems to threaten the very meaning of creation.

What is God to do?

Certainly, it will be useless for him to rely upon the officials of the religious institution; they have helped create this crisis. Only an outsider—a religious amateur—can possibly yield himself sufficiently to hear and repeat the divine message.

Then and now, any man who plays the role of Hosea is likely to be scorned by "bad" people and condemned by "good" ones. For this God-intoxicated fellow enacts in his personal life the drama of Jehovah's marriage with Israel. He enters into union with a harlot, gives his children symbolic names, and, through the tragedy of his family, dramatizes the fact that the bride of God has forsaken her husband for the couch of Baal.

Fourteenth Day   **Read Hosea 5-8**

Woe unto the faithless bride!

Not only must God punish; for the present, he is altogether hidden. It is useless for Israel to go through the motions of seeking him, so long as her heart is wanton. This is the one state in which the search for God is defeated before it begins (5:3-6).

For the present, therefore, there is no light and no hope. Whatever hope there may be is rooted not in history but beyond history. Matters have become so bad, viewed from the human perspective, that sowers of the wind can only reap the whirlwind (8:7).

Fifteenth Day   **Read Hosea 9-11**

To pay homage to anyone or anything except God is to
engage in immorality (9:1), to tarnish the divine imprint
stamped upon men made in God's image. Such failure is
universal and inescapable. When Israel (and all mankind)
is not trusting in pagan idols, she is bowing her knee to
powerful nations that promise her rescue.

The sin of Adam—striving for a way to gain the qualities
of God by an avenue other than total surrender to him—is
universal and inescapable (10:1). Israel must fail and fall,
not once but over and over. All men must yield to their
manhood by seeking to provide their own rescue through
their cunning, their strength, foreign alliances, or some
other form of rebellion against God.

Sixteenth Day   **Read Hosea 12-14**

Perpetually, not simply the worst of men but the best of
men make the fatal mistake of seeking a saviour other than
God. To make that mistake is to erase all meaning and significance. A person who bows down before idols (whether
hand-carved long ago or mass-produced on the modern as-
sembly line), cancels out his capacity to endure beyond
time and space. Because everyone worships some idol or
other for some period, it would seem that all is hopeless.

That would be the case, were not God able to do more
than we can expect or imagine! Regardless of one's shame
and infamy, if he will repent and bow down before God
alone, he will be restored to the Covenant relationship. Such
a reunion is a state of ecstatic bliss so wonderful that the
tongue can describe it only through metaphors and figures
of speech (14:4-7). It is this state of healing, not that of
rebellion and idolatry, that is ultimate and finally triumphant.

163

Joel

Seventeenth Day   **Read Joel 1-3**

No ingredient in this brief prophecy is new. Its pages ring with echoes of many voices from the past. In a sense, this is just one more interpretation of the Covenant's unfolding and a fresh rephrasing of the old recognition that divine-human relationships produce a cyclical pattern: God's wooing brings about marriage, but the bride proves inconstant so must be punished in order to be restored and blessed afresh.

Old as the story is, Joel manages to make it new and vivid. For he stresses the idea that the day of the Lord is terrible in order to produce joy; it is a day of blackness, which is a prelude to new and glorious light. Regardless of how many times the wheel has turned in the past, in spite of the many repetitions of about the same cycle, this time the triumph of God and his people will be absolute and final! This time, failure and punishment will cease: "And my people shall never again be put to shame" (2:26, 27).

Amos

Much of the Old Testament rings with "official" voices. It is the religious institution that has produced and preserved most of the books about the law and its applications, as well as Psalms and other worship materials.

For the most part, the prophets are lonely outsiders who challenge and attack the religious establishment. Their contact with God has been personal and direct. It is their role to denounce evil in high places and to awaken society permitted or encouraged to doze, because religious officials can be comfortable only when their constituents are less than fully awake.

Amos, crying with the harsh voice of a shepherd from Tekoa, offers a definitive case history of criticism of the household of God by one who knows himself to be included in the Covenant, but who cannot tolerate the way the Chosen People have failed to keep their part of the divine-human bargain.

Eighteenth Day   Read Amos 1-3

Joel was almost exclusively concerned with the day of the Lord—that set of movements, on the part of God, by which history is given its meaning, and the Covenant is completed beyond history. Amos is almost exclusively concerned with moral and social ills of his society.

Surely one of these prophets must be wrong!

Reflection persuades us that in the placement of these two emphases side-by-side, we discover a chief paradox of *salvation history*. God is absolutely and entirely concerned with BOTH "now" and "then." It is not a case of either/or, but of both/and. It is equally false and equally pernicious to focus on heaven to the exclusion of earth, or to so concentrate upon reform and progress on earth that heaven loses its absolute significance.

Nineteenth Day   Read Amos 4-6

Official religion flourishes—but is rotten to the core. Instead of bringing delight to God, pious exercises offend him. That is because the people who burn sacrifices and go through ceremonies are not actually conscious of guilt and of need. They are not presenting themselves to God for forgiveness and rescue, but, in their pride, they strut to the altar as though they were doing God a favor by coming.

165

All such going through the motions is futile, but no one who is deeply involved in the fate of the religious institution can see this truth. It takes an outsider, a man with nothing to lose, to demand that men begin to practice love of their fellows before they can expect God to be pleased with their ceremonies and offerings.

Twentieth Day   Read Amos 7-9

Amos is so intoxicated with God that he finds divine messages everywhere: in a swarm of locusts, a fire, a workman with plumb line in hand. Interspersed with brief visions growing out of everyday experiences, there are longer divine revelations. Because the people of the Covenant have grown deaf and blind, God can no longer speak to society. He must pour his warnings and promises into the ear of "a herdsman, and a dresser of sycamore trees" (7:14) with the hope that this unofficial spokesman can—somehow—attract the attention of Israel and gain a new hearing for the word of the Covenant.

Once more, we find the now-familiar pattern: fearful punishments are coming. But these are not final and decisive. They constitute a prelude to a restoration that will be decisive and final (9:13-15). Like the strange and illogical pairing of time/eternity in *salvation history*, this wedding between judgment and blessing is basic. To emphasize either at the expense of the other is to distort the message of Scripture. To enter into the Covenant, to become the bride of Jehovah, is to enter into that state of judgment/ blessing, and wrath/grace which constitutes the Kingdom of God.

Obadiah

Twenty-first Day Read Obadiah

This brief prophetic message hardly deserves to be called a "book." Yet a second or third reading will confirm the judgment of the ancients who considered it important enough to be revered as Scripture in spite of its small bulk.

For the prophecy is both specific and universal.

It proclaims the fearful doom of proud Edom, a land perennially at war with Israel. But at the same time, it depicts in brilliant colors the downfall of every nation and culture whose trust has been in power, wealth, and allies—and not in Jehovah. Verses 15-16, in particular, speak to our own age as clearly as to that of Obadiah himself. Throughout the vision, substitute present-day names for ancient ones, and the whole is fearfully contemporary. This remarkable double focus is a distinguishing trait of great Biblical prophecy.

Jonah

Twenty-second Day Read Jonah

What a fearful thing it is, to attempt to get away from God! Jonah discovered that it could not be done. Even in the belly of a whale, he could cry out to God, and he heard in order to be answered and rescued.

That his rescue did not make him perfect is clearly indicated by the cycle of events in Nineveh. Judgment belongs to God, not to man—no matter how dramatic that man's experience of divine transformation may be!

Like certain classical books outside the Bible, this brief and strange message can be read on two or more levels. Children get one set of meanings from *Gulliver's Travels,* while adults get an entirely different message from that

167

book. In the same fashion, babes in the faith will not find
in Jonah the transcendent and transforming truths that
emerge when the book is read by a long-time faithful servant of the all-powerful Lord.

Micah

Twenty-third Day   **Read Micah 1-4**

Official religion is silent and impotent (3:5-7). But an unofficial voice speaks with authority that can stem only from
personal encounter with God (1:2; 3:8).

The message of Amos is not new. After having entered
into the marriage Covenant with Jehovah, Israel has become
a faithless bride. Her playing of the harlot centers in that
camouflaged kind of idolatry which consists of worshiping
money and power. Therefore God has punished her, and
will continue to pour out his wrath upon her. But, in the
end, a remnant will be gloriously saved (4:7-8).

Can there be a subtle high-level message for us in the
fact that it is necessary for one prophet after another to
shout the same warning/promise heard so many times before? Are there any really new truths about God's relationship with mankind? Since failure has always marked man's
striving to keep the Covenant, why bother shouting of
judgment and of grace from generation to generation of
men who are also sure to fail and fall?

Twenty-fourth Day   **Read Micah 5-7**

Socially speaking, human failure is absolute (7:1-6).

So long as one's eyes focus upon his fellow men and their
total inability to deserve God's goodness or respond faithfully to it, it is hard to see anything but evidence leading to

168

despair. Yet, the very fact that at least one inspired individual is capable of reacting to this situation with despair instead of complacency gives a glimmer of light. God has not deserted his own. The end is not yet.

That end involves both history and beyond history, of course. For the punishing, cleansing, and restoring day of the Lord gives life a dimension that is beyond time and space. This day is somehow linked with the coming of a strange and unique ruler, born of travail and coming out of Bethlehem (5:2-3). Therefore, even in the most hopeless of situations, hope flourishes. God's absolute victory, turning upon forgiveness as a hinge, is the most assured of all certainties (7:18-20).

However different they may be in other respects, practically all the brief books beginning with Hosea are alike in a central characteristic. Though they stress failure, evil, and woe, each of them ends upon a note of victory. Whatever the evidence to the contrary at a given moment in history, the unfolding of *salvation history* is more certain than the movements of the earth and stars. Meaning will triumph over meaninglessness; hope is victorious over despair; frail man, incapable of achieving godlikeness by striving, will receive it as an unearned gift!

Nahum

Twenty-fifth Day   Read Nahum

Looking back at that part of the Biblical story we have already surveyed, it is a bit startling to see how many of its chapters echo with war and violence. From the days of Abraham until the time of Nahum, there have been few decades when the people of the Covenant were at peace. Some dreadful foe or other was always crouching on the horizon, ready to pounce and kill. Time after time, the

Chosen of Jehovah were actually attacked, defeated, plundered, and made captive.

Nahum is intimately aware of this aspect of *salvation history.*

Yet, he is convinced, without a shadow of a doubt, that the most recent of enemies will meet the same fate as all the others. Nineveh, too, will fall—and great will be the fall thereof! In poetic imagery seldom surpassed even in the Psalms, this obscure prophet praises the awe-full God who is bringing his heavenly hosts to fight for his own. Confronted by such an army as only Jehovah can muster, the idol-worshiping culture is BOUND to fall.

One solemn question confronts the modern reader. Precisely what nation or nations could we identify as "modern Nineveh?" Are you absolutely sure your selection is right?

Habakkuk

Twenty-sixth Day   **Read Habakkuk**

This little "book" is actually a series of dialogues between the prophet and God. Habakkuk raises searching questions, then listens, and hears God's answers. Here, then, are illuminating case histories in answered prayer!

Why do the wicked prosper? Their prosperity is apparent rather than real, for it is contained within time. Sooner or later, every wicked one will fail—but the servant of God will *live* (conquer time and space) as a fruit of his faith (2:4). There is no question whatever about God's ultimate victory (2:14); present material triumph on the part of "nations" is meaningless. They will win the prize, of course; but the prize is empty.

Such a point of view as that which the prophet reaches through struggle and prayer provides a vantage point from which to see more clearly. Regardless of defeat and despair within our time-linked human lives, faith produces timeless victory within the context of God's all-inclusive Providence (3:17-19).

Zephaniah and Haggai

Twenty-seventh Day   Read Zephaniah and Haggai

These two brief messages are utterly different—yet they have a common point of reference. Both of them focus upon the day of the Lord, though in quite different fashion.

Earlier, we saw that this paradoxical day is both within history and beyond history. Haggai stresses the divine acts of judgment, wrath, and reward that shape the destinies of individual nations; Zephaniah is more largely concerned with universal aspects of the day.

Both prophets fall back in fear and trembling before the terrible wrath of God. Both insist that, regardless of overwhelming evidence to the contrary, God's Chosen will somehow be preserved.

Indeed, this paradoxical day which is the cause of so much horrified shuddering, actually becomes a source of victorious joy for all who know and serve the Lord!

So much, we cannot escape recognizing here and at many other points along the trail of *salvation history*. But to attempt to press beyond the record of the Biblical text is quickly to get into trouble. Just when the day will come upon us in its varied forms, we dare not try to guess. Precisely what its specific details will be, only God knows.

Zechariah

Twenty-eighth Day   Read Zechariah 1-8

"Strange" or "weird" is likely to be the first adjective that comes to mind when one takes a quick look at collected

171

messages of Zechariah. This fervent seeker after God has so poetic an imagination that he can hardly speak in ordinary, literal fashion. He is so filled with a sense of awful and wonderful things that he snatches metaphors and images from every hand: a red horse here and four horns there, seven lamps each with seven lips, an enormous flying scroll, and women with wings of storks!

How is one to make heads or tails of this?

Certainly, not by trying to interpret each individual bit of symbolism. It is the over-all effect that we are seeking—not the many-sided set of ideas that Zechariah uses as building blocks for his mansion of thought.

Clearly, he is asserting that God rules, the divine Covenant stands, and a remnant of the faithful will enter into glory. This conviction is voiced with great fervor and attention-catching figures of speech, partly because it is wholly unbelievable. Nothing in the present situation supports the prophet's conclusions. Viewed from the perspective of common sense, the international scene seems to prove that all God's promises are empty. But Zechariah is looking through faith-oriented eyes, so shouts his convictions through impassioned lips!

Twenty-ninth Day   Read Zechariah 9-14

This present epoch is not final. Life's meaning is not to be decided on the basis of what can be seen and touched, bought, sold, and captured. History gives some clues to the riddle of our existence, but the past is not a mold into which the future will be poured. Because God is an active agent in ongoing life, the meaning of life is pregnant with capacity for the absolutely new.

Whatever else he may do, Zechariah clearly looks forward and not backward. He is sure, beyond doubt or argument, that God really will do unbelievably great wonders for the people whom he has chosen. As a result of new outpourings of divine compassion, it will be as though faithless ones never had been rejected (10:6)!

Malachi

Thirtieth Day   Read Malachi

Everything has been said that can be said. Malachi's messages from on high include the same basic strains that have distinguished poetic and prophetic voices of the past. Institutional religion is rotten to the core: the people chosen and rescued and nurtured by God have failed.

Anybody but God would have given up long before now. But he not only holds firmly to the Covenant and continues to insist that men accept rescue from their manhood; in this darkest of hours he promises a new messenger (3:1-4; 4:5-6).

The stage is set! Out of the centuries-long marriage between Jehovah and Israel, a son is about to be born! The new Elijah, so long anticipated, will turn the world upside down, and, from the barren soil of rebellious human hearts, he will prepare fallow ground ready to receive divine seed with which to produce a magnificent harvest!

EIGHTH MONTH:

Matthew and Mark

The New Testament

Long ago, God entered into a Covenant with Abraham and his descendants. Though active partners in the contractual relationship, these people "set apart" from the rest of mankind did not initiate the Covenant. Unfolding of their verbal agreement (testament) over a period of centuries forms Act 1 of *salvation history*. As recorded and interpreted from the viewpoint of inspired lawgivers and kings, priests of the institution and prophets outside it, the unfolding pattern of developments in this special divine-human compact forms the literary body we have inherited as The Old Testament.

Without an Act I, there never can be an Act II. Act I reaches its climax in the making ready of Israel to bear fruit. For the Covenant is a marriage contract between God and the people whom he called to be his bride. In due time, a Son will be born—incorporating in one flesh both divinity and humanity, thereby bridging the absolute gap between Creator and creatures. It is in order that such a Son may be born that the marriage Covenant was drawn up by God in the first place.

Actual coming of the long-anticipated Son radically changes the total situation, which includes men in general plus particular ones in Covenant with God. For the Son who issues from the Covenant becomes a dynamic—better, *the* dynamic—factor in the situation, which now includes

174

Almighty God, fallen man, and the God-man whom history knows as Jesus Christ.

Born of a virgin's womb through agency of God's Holy Spirit, Jesus partakes fully of the qualities of man. In his role as man, he voluntarily gives his life for all men. Each man who accepts the gift so offered is "made new"—that is, enters a radically altered relationship with God the Father.

The challenge to strive for godliness through keeping the law of Moses is withdrawn. Rather, it is superseded. From now on, men may accept the substitutionary death of Christ as a way of "dying" to their own sins. The role of the law shifts to that of an awakener and a convicter—serving to convince men that they need to accept divine rescue.

That rescue is offered and conferred through the paradox, the mystery, and the miracle of the Cross. Though Jesus Christ died upon it, every man may make that death his own, so that he and the world of natural men are "crucified" to one another (Gal. 6:14). Such a severing of ties between a man and the world is a particular instance of the general cosmic victory won on Calvary, in which the God-man "disarmed the principalities and powers and made a public example of them" (Col. 2:15). Freed from sin through participation in the death of Jesus Christ (Rom. 6:6), his follower becomes literally and not simply figuratively a *new person.*

It is for the production of such new persons that the Good News is proclaimed. The story of the coming into the world of the Son of the Covenant, together with witness about the meaning of that coming by a few who were close to it in history, forms the literary amplification of the New Covenant that is commonly called The New Testament of our Lord and Saviour Jesus Christ.

Abraham's blood descendants are human partners of God in the original Covenant, or Testament. The new one radically alters terms, so that belief in Jesus Christ is the con-

175

dition for human participation—"all believers" now playing the role that was formerly reserved for Abraham's seed. Precisely what tangible human system is formed by all believers is a vexatious central question of the faith. Clearly, the ideal spiritual Church is not identical with any visible Church or body of churches. Yet these finite systems are the guardians, transmitters, and interpreters of The New Testament, just as the failable historic Israel was the guardian, transmitter, and interpreter of the original Covenant.

To read the New Testament as literature is instructive but not necessarily fruitful in more than a surface fashion. Faith, in the inclusive sense of recognized spiritual guilt blended with eagerness to accept unearned divine rescue, is essential to meeting the Saviour in the pages of the Book that centers in him. Hence, the Book that is for all mankind is also, in another sense, private and secret. Each reader will engage in dialogue whose depth and duration depend partly upon what he brings to the meeting—the self whom he presents for encounter with the Saviour to whom the entire Old Testament points and of whom the entire New Testament witnesses.

Though the New Testament contains only a small fraction of as many words as the Old Testament, we shall devote five of our twelve months to it. Many days, you will wish to turn back to Old Testament passages and re-read them in order to get an entirely new message; again, you will wish to discover fresh relationships between the message of a day's passage and other portions of the New Testament. Comparatively brief readings in the Biblical text itself, therefore, invite you to look far and wide for vivid correlations, fresh revelations, and absolutely novel interpretations of passages upon which you center for a day.

The Gospel According to Saint Matthew

For this gospel writer, Jesus of Nazareth is supremely and superbly the King, before whom all believers prostrate themselves. Though born in obscurity, Mary's son is also the Son of David. This title, established by Matthew's elaborate genealogy, is used more frequently in his Gospel than in any other. From the cradle to the grave, literally and not figuratively, persons and circumstances proclaim the royalty of Jesus. He is revered as King by wise men from the East. He deliberately uses the language of authority to assert his own supremacy over the law of Moses. His triumphal entry into Jerusalem is that of a conqueror. Even though it is bestowed in mockery, he accepts the title of King in his encounter with the representative of Roman power. And it is as King that he dies upon the Cross.

Matthew's special interpretation is cast in the framework of an appeal to the Jews that they hail Jesus of Nazareth as their King. More than any other, this Gospel deserves to be subtitled "An Appeal to the People of the Covenant." For the Jewishness of Matthew's report is basic to its structure and content. More than a dozen times, the evangelist specifies ties between prophetic voices from Israel's past and events or emphases in the proclaiming through Jesus.

Faithfully reporting the total rejection of Jesus by leaders of Israel's religious institution, Matthew yet believes that Abraham's descendants can be persuaded to see and to know. Therefore, his account is more closely related to the approach of a teacher than an evangelist. More than any other Gospel writer, Matthew has organized large bodies of instruction by Jesus, so that they come to us in the form of lengthy sermons and messages: The Sermon on the Mount (Chapters 5-7); Responsibilities of Apostles (10); Parables of the Kingdom (13); Qualities of the New Life (18); and a foreshadowing of Act III of the divine-human drama—The Coming of the Kingdom (24-25).

To be most effectively prepared for response to Matthew's outpouring of the Good News of the New Covenant, readers must approach it in precisely our present mood—satiated, almost, with the story of God's dealing with his Chosen People and almost bursting with impatience for the

177

coming of the long-promised Son who will unite, in one person, the spirit of God the Father and the flesh of all mankind.

First Day   **Read Matthew 1-2**

Though some modern persons find it hard to accept, ancient thought saw no difficulty in using numbers as well as words to convey meaning. More than any other Gospel writer, Matthew is skilled in such ways of expressing complex ideas. He reports three messages to Joseph, three temptations of Jesus, three denials of Peter, three prayers in Gethsemane, and three questions of Pilate. There are three crosses, three hours of darkness, and three days of guarding the tomb. Though each expresses other ideas as well, every such occurrence of "three" also points to the Holy Trinity— God in three persons.

In addition to the number three, Matthew makes great use of the perfect number, seven. He reports Jesus' warning that an evicted evil spirit will bring seven others back with him (12:45) and specifies his Master's use of seven loaves (15:34) to yield seven baskets of fragments (15:37). Chapter 13 gives seven parables of the Kingdom, while Chapter 23 lists seven woes. So whether the twentieth-century interpreter can find it there or not, there is a hidden message in the fact that the genealogy of Jesus is reported in three sections, each of which includes twice seven generations.

Lacking written vowels and employing letters of the alphabet for numerals, the Hebrew language indicated "David" by DWD. Taken as numerals rather than letters, this cluster of symbols has the meaning "14." So, in order perfectly to express the hidden truth that Jesus of Nazareth is Son of David, Matthew lists ancestors in groups of fourteen—divided to form a trinity of witnesses!

178

That the materials of Matthew's history should lend themselves to such testimony about his King is to be accepted rather than explained. Anything that is explained is thereby reduced to human dimensions—so it is faith rather than logic that rejoices, because everything in Israel's history testifies that Mary's son is also the Son of David.

Jesus Christ, entirely divine and altogether human, is a fruit of the Covenant. Biologically, however, he is generated by the Holy Spirit. That such would be the case, Isaiah announced long ago (Isa. 7:14). Full understanding of the prophet's message did not come until after believers made a radical reorganization of their total belief and understanding, in the transforming light shed by Calvary and the empty tomb.

Yet it is not simply a genealogy (history) that identifies Jesus of Nazareth as the King. Men from a distance—wise ones from the East—have keener vision than most close at hand. Jerusalem's very dedication to the Covenant, the absorption of her wise and good ones in minutiae of interpretation, clouds her eyes with a cataract. It is a perpetual source of wonder that those most adept in handling an inherited system may be slowest to find in it radical new patterns of meaning. Fulfillment of numerous Old Testament prophecies shouted, "This is the long-promised Saviour!" Yet functionaries of the established religious institution looked and looked, and saw only a carpenter's baby.

Second Day   **Read Matthew 3-4**

One or two announcements (genealogy and wise men) of God's supreme work are not enough. There must be proclamations through every medium likely to convince or persuade some men that Jesus of Nazareth and the Christ of God are one and the same.

Chapters 1 and 2 make that identification through: gene-

179

alogy, visitation by divine messengers (angels), fulfillment of prophecy, and recognition by wise men. Almost, it would seem that God has done more than we could reasonably expect. But no avenue can be neglected.

Accordingly, God sends a special herald, John the Baptizer, whose great central role is to arouse public interest, then point to Jesus. His announcement, sealed by baptism, is confirmed by still another supernatural messenger—the Spirit of God who appears to human eyes to be in the form of a dove.

Identification of the Saviour completed so that even the dullest of men can hardly fail to recognize and venerate their King, the drama of his work for men is interrupted by brash intrusion of the chief antagonist: Satan himself. This is his last chance. Unless he can inveigle or persuade Jesus to turn aside from the path that leads to Calvary, evil will be defeated, and the battle for the souls of men will be permanently decided. So here Satan exerts his supreme effort (in a trinity of temptations). He appeals to the human needs and wants of the God-man—and fails absolutely to sway him.

This hurdle passed, the work of the Jesus of history is formally launched by the calling of disciples and the start of a visible crusade.

Third Day   **Read Matthew 5-6**

The Sermon on the Mount, as here reported, is the largest organized body of formal teaching by Jesus. Because it seems sensibly practical, by comparison with visions and angels and miracles, it has been especially elevated in recent centuries of common-sense religious faith. Many have treated the Sermon as "the heart of the Gospel," and from it have extracted a "social gospel" of change on the human level designed (however disguised) to enable men to build the Kingdom here on earth with their own hands.

Viewed from some perspectives, the Sermon actually seems to present a sensible pattern of moral and ethical conduct, conformity to which makes it possible for men to live up to the requirements of Jesus. That is to say, the new code of conduct here defined by Jesus is adopted as a substitute for the law of Moses. Though the two patterns differ greatly, they are alike in that each is viewed as offering a way to spiritual victory through discipline and regulated conduct.

Beautiful and instructive though it is, in the context of Matthew's account of the King's coming, the Sermon on the Mount is not offered as an amended version of the law of Moses. No substitute for the requirement that sinful men surrender as a prelude to acceptance of divine rescue, the Sermon itself echoes throughout with impossible demands. Instead of comforting, it convicts—persuading us that we cannot possibly meet its terms, so must accept grace rather than achieve goodness.

Murder, adultery, divorce, profanity, justice, and love are radically re-defined here. The demand is for perfection, and that according to a divine rather than a human standard. Total commitment to God, with absolute exclusion of loyalty to less than God, is required. Here is no call to imitate an ideal man, but a challenge to measure one's self by a divine and hence utterly impossible standard. Every man who sees himself in the light of that standard can only kneel before his King and cry, "Have mercy on me, a sinner!"

Fourth Day   **Read Matthew 7-8**

It is not pious mouthing of "Lord, Lord," that opens the door to heaven—but a surrendered life. Always, the direction of that surrender must be toward a high and holy God who demands the impossible.

181

So paradoxical and astonishing is the demand/promise of the Sermon on the Mount that "insiders" are likely to reject it automatically. So Matthew describes a series of "outsiders" who act in surrendered obedience, and thereby become recipients of supernatural power. These outsiders are: a leper, a fisherman's mother-in-law, a Roman centurion, and a pair of Gadarene demoniacs. Meanwhile, scribes and disciples alike betray their lack of capacity to accept the highest and best gifts of the King. This perpetual failure on the part of those whom human logic judges as the best of men, is part of the *scandal* of the Good News proclaimed in the life and through the words of Jesus Christ.

Fifth Day	Read Matthew 9

Mighty and unexplainable demonstrations continue. All distinctions between physical and spiritual healing (making whole) vanish. Jesus demonstrates his capacity to rescue any part-person and restore him to wholeness. Recipients continue to be "common folk" and outsiders such as tax collectors and rank sinners, while upright and devout leaders of the community and the religious institution stand back, challenging Jesus and rejecting his offer of mighty works.

Surveying the evidence and unable to refute popular claims that wonders are being worked, Pharisees reject Jesus' claim that he represents God. They are therefore left with but one alternative: this worker of wonders must be a representative of Satan.

"Who is this man?" remains a central question to which everyone who encounters Jesus of Nazareth must give his personal answer.

Sixth Day   **Read Matthew 10-11**

From an informal beginning, the Jesus movement has become an organized campaign. Universal elements are prominent: there are no qualifications to Jesus' promises or their recipients. At first look, this seems strangely inconsistent with a clearly-defined mission to the Jews. In spite of the fact that Jewish scholarship and piety are offended by Jesus' claims and performances, it yet remains true that Israel constitutes the fertile soil that was cultivated for centuries in order that it might be ready to receive the new and definitive divine revelation embodied in the flesh of Jesus Christ.

All these things—and all events whatever—are included in the context of Providence, not chance or blind fate. For a disciple to recognize this, is to enter a state of absolute confidence. Defeat is not even an alternative; whatever may occur, the will of the Father is actively at work, moving forward. Victory is guaranteed, and can sometimes be seen dimly from a distance even through feeble eyes of mortal men.

Thus, the imprisonment of John and the rejection of Jesus by scribes and Pharisees and entire cities are no causes for despair. Of course, only those wise with the wisdom of God can hear the truths proclaimed through voices of mockers and challengers. But, to listen with the inner ear is to hear promises of the Covenant with Abraham repeated and reinterpreted in every aspect of the human life of the divine-human Son, whose coming marks the drawing up of a New Covenant.

Seventh Day   **Read Matthew 12**

Christians find it easy to become self-righteous in condemning Jewish legalism. Laws of the Temple and customs of the synagogue, seen from the perspective of a Christian

183

culture, are obviously man-shaped even though adopted in obedience to divine directives. Jesus' creative and spontaneous reshaping of customs and laws, seen from our point of view, is so laudable that it is hard to discover how any man could fail to applaud.

But matters are not quite the same when *our* laws, *our* traditions, and *our* institutions are involved. Authorities today are no more eager for disruptive and threatening change than were authorities then. We ourselves—you and I—are prone to cry "Beelzebub!" when it is our system of values, our set of standards, that is challenged.

This chapter uses specific practices rooted in a particular culture (no less than that one shaped by a centuries-old sense of Covenant) to illustrate the universal principle that encounter between the human and the divine is always *necessarily* disruptive. Whenever individual men or their social institutions really and not theoretically meet God, the alternatives are clear: traumatic change, or rejection of the divine revelation.

Eighth Day	**Read Matthew 13**

As a method of putting the truth of God into channels that can be used by men, the parable illustrates the paradox it always presents. That is, the parable is uniquely fluid. Meaning conveyed through it is not automatic and constant. Rather, it is a variable, shaped largely by the human recipient—the personality that constitutes soil into which seeds of divine revelation are tossed.

Hidden things uttered through parables or other media of communication are revealed only to those few persons whose eyes are prepared to receive highest truth. That is why misunderstanding is a recurrent Gospel motif. Recipients of bread from heaven fail to understand the meaning of the miracle (16:5-12). Disciples themselves completely disregard the message of the children (18:1-6; 19: 13-15). Zebedee's wife asks rewards for her sons on the heels of Jesus' statement about ensuing crucifixion (20:20-21). Inherited Scriptural messages about resurrection are meaningless until after Jesus has demonstrated victory over death (22:29).

Truth proclaimed, in any fashion whatever, may become truth distorted by the recipients. It is a high-level message of this sort, perpetually proclaimed in public but often widely misunderstood, that is offered through Jesus' private instruction of members of the inner circle. Discipleship *is* a continuous program of discipline calculated to increase capacity to receive the messages of God.

We modern Americans are prone to think of discipleship in terms of *doing*. But here (and everywhere in the New Testament) it is *being* that comes first. The chief work of the disciple is to seek eagerly and obey joyfully, in order to grow in capacity to produce a crop from seeds that are scattered upon him from above, without his doing anything to initiate the shower.

Ninth Day   Read Matthew 14-15

Events in the career of Jesus the Teacher, absolute revealer of God the Father, move forward with the relentlessness of a Greek tragedy. Whatever may happen must contribute to the climax. That is, every incident reported in the Gospels is keyed to the announcement and interpretation of the New Covenant. From the womb, Jesus Christ is headed for self-sacrifice. He came in order to give himself as a divine-human sacrifice, providing rescue for all men who will participate in the marvelous feeding that he provides in the wilderness of society.

185

It is futile, therefore, to speculate what the outcome might have been had events been ordered otherwise. What if Herod had not been so weak a king? What if John had lived to head a movement whose growth might have kept Jesus in obscurity? What if Jesus' move into the spotlight made empty by John's death had resulted in acceptance by authorities instead of rejection?

All such speculations are empty. Every development and each encounter underscores the basic message that God was in Christ, come into the stream of humanity in order to effect reconciliation between the Creator and creatures made in the divine image. Always, such reconciliation is accepted only by the consciously alienated: "the lame, the maimed, the blind, the dumb" (15:30).

Tenth Day   **Read Matthew 16-17**

Whether he be a scribe, a Pharisee, a teacher of the Men's Bible Class, or an executive of a denomination, any man who sets out to "test" Jesus Christ is restricted to a single result. By the very conditions of the test he precludes recognition and acceptance of transforming truth from God. It is in this sense that a vigorous (and not a passive) faith is essential to grasping the Good News. Not simply skepticism but absence of vital faith renders soil of the personality sterile and incapable of multiplying the seeds scattered on it by God's perennial messengers.

Every "sign" is fluid and paradoxical, conveying one set of meanings to the skeptic and various sets of other meanings to believers of various levels of faith and experience.

Jesus' most intimate ones, so close to him, are so much of the time so far from understanding! Even the great confession of Peter represents a momentary interlude of fertility; there will be future periods in which the Rock will be

186

sterile—incapable of nurturing seeds and causing them to sprout. Indeed, his moment of illumination is followed by what (to us) seems almost unbelievable blindness.

Let every seeker beware of adopting a patronizing attitude toward Peter. Here he represents not the worst but the best of which humanity is capable. To reduce the New Covenant to a system that is wholly understandable, so that it "makes sense" by our human standards, is to repudiate it —voluntarily to be counted among "this faithless and perverse generation." God chose to offer salvation in an utterly incredible fashion; failure to register distress (17:23), to act as though the self-giving of the God-man is reasonable, is to substitute our own system of achievement for the divine rescue that gives life to the New Covenant.

Eleventh Day   Read Matthew 18-19

Jesus the King offers citizenship in a realm so alien to any human system that direct description of it is impossible. Its nature is dimly hinted by the fact that, in it, values and conditions of human existence are "turned inside out," in complete reversal of the established order among men. In the Kingdom, it is not princes and rulers who are great— but those who are as humble as children.

Because the Kingdom defies human power to analyze and master, candidates for citizenship must meet conditions that are demanding to the point of utter absurdity. For example, instead of exhibiting "perfect forgiveness" through seven instances of it, the seeker for the Kingdom must forgive "seventy times seven." Instead of meeting the letter of the law concerning divorce, he must go to the radical extreme of regarding a perfectly routine divorce action as adultery— punishable by stoning. Instead of striving for goodness through living up to the commandments inherited from old, the pilgrim toward the eternal city must exhibit *absolute* love in all of his relationships.

It is this basic factor of the *impossible* in Jesus' call that upsets everything reasonable and causes the (seemingly) last to be (actually) first, while those whom men regard as first are really last in the Kingdom. That is, no system of values that men can devise is exalted enough to remain stable in the utter transformation that characterizes the society of the redeemed.

Twelfth Day   Read Matthew 20

To say what the Kingdom of heaven *is*, puts upon language a strain it cannot bear. The most that can be done is to suggest what the Kingdom *is like*. As reported by Matthew, Jesus consistently teaches that the Kingdom is so absolutely different from human society that many conditions will be totally reversed: "the last will be first, and the first last" (Verses 16, 26-27).

Some of the many similar "reversals" reported elsewhere in this Gospel are those that involve substitutions between destitute and prosperous (5:3), mourners and comfortable (5:4), things hidden and things revealed (10:26), prosperity and want (25:29).

It is precisely this kind of scandalous logic that is involved in the Crucifixion of the King. Everything in that idea jars us. It may so repel us that we refuse to accept such a notion, repeating the conduct of Zebedee's wife who listened to Jesus' description of his glory ("to be mocked and scourged and crucified," Verse 19) and promptly begged him to give her sons temporal power in the Kingdom. She who had so many opportunities to hear and understand fails utterly. Reversing that situation, two blind men seized upon a chance encounter to succeed absolutely in accepting the most sublime gift Jesus can confer: divine mercy.

Thirteenth Day   **Read Matthew 21**

Paradox, contradiction, and scandal continue.

For a King to ride on an ass is a contradiction in terms; the horse is the animal of royalty. Hence the very triumphal entry itself witnesses that the King of whom Matthew writes is no ordinary one—but a King whose sovereignty will be demonstrated to all the world through his death as a malefactor.

Hailed by the masses and rejected by religious leaders, Jesus demonstrates his authority to exceed that of the Temple. Verbally, he underscores the paradox by which "babes and sucklings" can speak more wisely than learned men. (*Compare* Ps. 8.) Dramatically blasting a barren fig tree that stands for fruitless official religion, he underscores the vital role of faith as a factor in human dialogue with God.

Through every conceivable medium—direct words, parables, and dramatic lessons—he underscores the warning that those in the best position to recognize God's supreme messenger are likely to be last to identify and revere him. It is this basic human blindness (inherent in our status as creatures and no more potent in ancient Israel than any other era including our own) that once more vividly demonstrates our need for a *Saviour*. We cannot by any means save ourselves; the very institutions and processes that we develop in our zeal to know and serve God always become stumbling blocks.

Fourteenth Day   **Read Matthew 22**

The Kingdom of Heaven, that spiritual realm in which the Lordship of Christ is definitive, is the goal toward which all creation moves. This is the destination of every Christian pilgrim. Yet, even our Master himself cannot directly communicate its nature to us because of our limitations. Even the basic human institution, the family, does not carry over into the Kingdom in anything like its present form.

No wonder the religious institution perpetually plays the role of arch foe and bitter critic of God's supreme messenger! By nature, the institution (of whatever type—not simply the religious one) is conservative. It exists in order to develop and perpetuate structure and system. Society could not continue for one generation without the conserving and directing influence of its institutions. In some form or other, men must pay taxes to some Caesar; that is one of the prices of manhood.

Nowhere is the basic dualism—the dividedness—of man more vividly demonstrated. Man, made in the divine image, has feet of clay. His head is lifted toward the clouds, but his feet are firmly planted on earth.

We cannot get along without religious systems that include the law of Moses or some equivalent. We cannot function as corporate seekers for God without a Temple or its equivalent. Scribes and Pharisees and Sadducees of some variety or other are absolutely essential. But, whenever and wherever the divine stirs and yeasts in the souls of men, religious experience comes into conflict with institutions and authorities whose work is vital to the engendering of such experience.

Whether by means of the Temple or revival meetings, we cannot save ourselves. All the avenues and bridges that we build partake of the limitedness of the builder. Ideally, the Church is of God—but in all its concrete manifestations, absolutely essential though they are, the institution is finite and limited. Each of us is a creature; our most sublime religious systems partake of our creaturehood. If we are to reach the Kingdom, it will not be along any highway of our construction—but through divine *salvation* that makes of us what we can never become through striving.

190

Fifteenth Day   **Read Matthew 23**

Pride in its many forms is an inescapable human weakness; indeed, it may be that, if original sin can be named at all, it is best entitled pride. Not "even in the highest and best religious circles," but especially there, pride takes root and flourishes. Men who ought to be fully occupied prostrating themselves before God inevitably take their eyes off divinity long enough to compare themselves (favorably) with humanity—ceasing, in the blindness of pride, to become candidates for *rescue* and elevating themselves as having achieved righteousness.

This unparalleled chapter of woes pronounced upon the most godly men of Jesus' day is among the most misunderstood of Matthew's record. For you and I are prone to commit the very error Jesus condemns. We find it dreadfully easy to measure ourselves by these ancient blind ones and congratulate ourselves on our keener eyes. Arrogant in our certainty of 20-20 spiritual vision, we are ready to kill and crucify once more—in the name of Christ.

Until we center our attention upon the Father, whose glory reveals us to be spotted and tarnished, we lack that eager humility which is prerequisite to recognizing the Son when he is met face to face.

Sixteenth Day   **Read Matthew 24-25**

In the drama of *salvation history*, Act I is the period of the marriage Covenant through which a particular people, Israel, becomes the bride of Jehovah. Act II deals with the coming of the Son of that union—combining divinity and humanity in one person in order to effect reconciliation between the Creator and fallen creatures. Act III centers in the spiritual Kingdom where God rules supreme over a society of redeemed souls.

191

Though this climax of the process for which the world was created has its roots in history, it cannot be contained here. Because it is spiritual and not material, heavenly and not earthly, the most that mortals can do is dimly to grasp a few vague outlines. We know from such passages as these something of the principles that will prevail—but we are here repeatedly warned against too great concern with details of the Kingdom. We know that justice will be done, but not how. We know that there will be rewards and punishments, but we cannot even imagine what specific ones God has prepared for souls without bodies.

Nevertheless, a cardinal aspect of the Good News emerges precisely here: THE MOST IMPORTANT BUSINESS OF THIS LIFE IS TO PREPARE FOR THE LIFE TO COME. Nothing that one can win or do or achieve on this earth is of more than fleeting consequence—while, through the work of our Saviour, the eternity for which this life is a prelude offers meaning and glory and enduringness to once-finite creatures.

Seventeenth Day   **Read Matthew 26**

It is at the most sacred season of our planet's most devout people that outraged religious leaders press their demand for blood. Here is a supreme paradox of the Good News—so incredibly creative that it necessarily scandalizes and offends all who have status and authority to defend. The natural man cannot long be at peace with the divine Saviour; confronted by his challenge/demand, man must either accept transforming grace, or he must help send the God-man to his death. Even the most intimate and ardent disciple cannot, in his own strength, go for even a day without some kind of denial.

All these factors, and the specific events that reveal them, are "necessary and inevitable" in the sense that they are basic to the divine-human situation. *Salvation history,* clearly delineated in the scriptures that form the Christian's Old Testament, treats of man alienated from God, but moving toward reunion. In order that the Scriptures should be fulfilled (Verse 54)—i.e., their essential message revealed in such fashion that men can see and understand—it was necessary ("written into the stars") that divinity should suffer and die for the sake of humanity.

Eighteenth Day   **Read Matthew 27-28**

It is the son of Mary—flesh of her flesh, bone of her bone, and therefore brother of every mortal—who is sold into death. But, at the same time, it is the King of the Jews—the Son of God, wholly and absolutely divine—who mounts the Cross on Calvary. If the incredible story of Matthew had to be condensed into a single phrase, it would be the charge on which his Lord was executed: "This is Jesus the King of the Jews" (27:37).

Divinity incarnate in humanity suffered and died in order to accomplish for mortal creatures those results open only to the Creator. This is the glory, the mystery, the paradox, and the miracle of events that produced the New Covenant between God and man.

In the fearful events of the day that ushered in the new epoch for all humanity and not simply the Israel of the blood, one outsider suddenly saw that Jesus of Nazareth was truly God's Son (27:54). But, for most, including intimates of his bosom, it took the empty tomb to reveal that their Master actually could not be restrained by that absolute master of mortality, death. Even dimly seen from a distance, this central fact of existence literally ushers each believer across the threshold into a new age—a radically altered order of existence, prepared before the foundation of the

193

world to receive and shelter those who dare let God do the impossible for them through Christ.

The Gospel According to St. Mark

St. Mark's account of the establishment and meaning of the New Covenant is often regarded as the simplest and least difficult of the Gospels.

It is true that this evangelist uses a vocabulary which, in translation, yields an account made up of short words and brief sentences. This actually is the shortest of the Gospels, and employs fewer technical symbols than any other. It is far less "Jewish" than Matthew's account, for example.

But any notion of "simplicity" in ideas will vanish as soon as a reader ceases jumping over familiar words without noticing them. For the very first sentence announces Mark's high purpose: putting into human words and thought forms an account of incredible circumstances through which the Son of God entered history in order to proclaim the Good News.

As truly as any other, Mark's Gospel deals with the God-man who at one and the same time was Jesus of Nazareth and the ever-lasting Christ. Thoroughly Gentile in outlook and manner of expressing himself, Mark tells precisely the same story as Matthew, Luke, and John. Precisely because his telling tends to be less obviously poetic than the others, somewhat more plain and direct, it will stir us and awaken us in a fashion different from that of the other Gospels, even though the rescue we are here offered is identical with that of each other account.

Nineteenth Day **Read Mark 1**

Jesus of Nazareth, whom a few clear-sighted ones recognized and hailed as the long-awaited Christ of God, served as an inlet through which the Spirit of God could pour into human society. Nothing that the Son does is apart from the will of the Father. It is the Holy Spirit who serves as active agent in the baptism that identifies a man as God; it is the same Spirit who launches the temptation in the wilderness.

Action and urgency are basic in this account; there is no time to lose. Centuries of preparation are at stake; the meaning of human existence must crystalize, not simply in the life of one man, but in a few years of his life. Everything moves forward in almost relentless fashion. "Immediately" occurs nine times in this brief opening chapter; notice the occasions, and what they mean.

Urgency is the keynote because "The time is fulfilled, and the kingdom of God is at hand" (Verse 15). Men must immediately act upon the challenge of John—or forever bypass the opportunity to repent and believe. Neither individual men nor societies have "all the time there is"; *now* is a cutting edge that moves forward through time in such fashion that none can believe and be made whole yesterday or tomorrow. The meaning of my life—and the significance of the whole creation—trembles in the balance *now*. In the moment of my encounter with Jesus Christ, I can be freed from tyranny of evil spirits and cleansed of the spiritual leprosy that makes me loathsome to myself as well as other men. But the time of decision cannot be prolonged at my pleasure; Jesus is moving swiftly toward a predetermined goal. Nothing can persuade him to stop or even to pause longer than the Spirit prescribes; I must act in the light that I have now, if I expect ever to act at all.

Twentieth Day   **Read Mark 2-3**

Jesus' mighty works, of which forgiveness of sins is chief, are absolutely without parallel. No one—then or now—has ever seen the like. As clearly as any section of any Gospel, these chapters challenge the whole concept of "growing more like Jesus." The absolute gulf between the Son of Man and all men requires the believer to accept rescue rather than simply strive to be Christ-like. Yet this central truth of the Good News is not acceptable to all who hear it; only the spiritually sick, who know they are sick, are capable of responding.

For those who represent established patterns of piety, the mighty works of Jesus offend and disrupt. No hardened wineskin can expand enough to keep from bursting; we are quick enough to see that Sabbath customs of ancient Pharisees restrict rather than liberate—but slow to apply this conclusion to ourselves and our codes.

Given the totally creative and necessarily disruptive impact of divinity upon humanity, small wonder that friends and foes alike should be aghast. Confronted by Jesus Christ, but unable to see him as Son of God, the kindest possible response is to conclude that the poor fellow must be out of his mind.

Twenty-first Day   Read Mark 4-5

All men are potential citizens of the Kingdom over which Jesus Christ reigns. But it is not easy for any man to want citizenship so eagerly that he will meet the terms. Chapter 5 consists of case histories which have only one feature in common. Each underscores the paradox by which it is the unlikely candidate, humanly speaking, who has the best chance of acceptance. It is the outsider—conscious of his alienation from God—who is most likely to understand and act upon the divine offer of rescue.

Chapter 4 has made it abundantly clear that states we call "understanding" and "misunderstanding" (acceptance and rejection) are not automatic or constant. Instead, the organized system of experiences, values, beliefs, and hopes that makes up a human individual is variable and fluid. Even when a message comes directly from the lips of Jesus Christ (perhaps *especially* when this is the case), meaning found by the hearer will depend upon his total outlook. The most likely candidates for great gifts (intimate disciples) center attention on the riddle of who their wonder-working Master can possibly be, while a master of the synagogue (whom logic would label a foe of the Good News) seeks in such eager belief that he finds the gift of new life.

Twenty-second Day   **Read Mark 6**

Urgency and mighty works mark the witness not simply of Jesus but also of his disciples. Confident expectation that great things are going to be done by God for His glory, right now, is a necessary condition for driving out demons, healing souls and bodies.

John the Baptist, mighty co-worker and herald of the Messiah, was sometimes regarded as the long-anticipated deliverer. His death heightened the climate of crisis, made it imperative that Jesus plainly announce himself as the new Moses. He did so both in the dramatic feeding that re-enacted the ancient feeding in the wilderness and in his demonstration of mastery over the sea—that ancient and relentless symbol of chaos and death.

As a result of these two spectacular acts of declaration through deeds rather than words, multitudes of common folk understood the message. In mingled joy and expectancy, they rushed to accept divine power made tangible through marvelous healings.

Twenty-third Day   **Read Mark 7-8**

Official religion always finds it hard to continue paying homage to God the Creator. Instead of seeking enlargement and transformation (for self, the institution, and society) it is easy for the priest—whatever the title by which he is called—to center upon guarding and transmitting good things from the past. Many a Christian group falls into precisely this error—glorifying the first century (as seen darkly through the glasses of time) and making *it,* rather than Christ, the goal of religious experience.

Regardless of how much heavenly bread may be offered by Jesus Christ, all the proud who have status to defend will continue to test and question. Signs from heaven do not communicate divine truth to persons who see themselves as inheritors and guardians of all truth. Such "leaven of the Pharisees" (8:15) bubbles and yeasts through the whole personality, creating the only incurable kind of spiritual blindness—that variety which persuades the afflicted one that his vision is keener than that of other folk.

Twenty-fourth Day   **Read Mark 9**

Mighty portents continue. Elijah and Moses add their voices to those of men and events witnessing about Jesus. Still the intimate disciples do not dimly grasp the meaning of the forthcoming victory over death. To make matters worse, they hesitate to ask for more explanations.

Tongue-tied disciples are in sharp contrast with the father of a demon-possessed boy. This man wavers, too. But his wavering is positive, and that of the disciples is negative. Their reluctance to ask questions seems to stem from pride rather than devotion, since Jesus gives them (and us) an indirect rebuke by elevating the importance of childlike dependence and trust.

198

Twenty-fifth Day   Read Mark 10

Laws are given, not as standards of righteousness, but as points of departure in striving for righteousness. Measured by the higher standard of Jesus, those who succeed in keeping the letter of Moses' law are yet dismal failures.

Even warned of this, disciples themselves once more fail the test of ambition. They remain greedy and blind.

The healing of a blind man, in the aftermath of this repetition of warning against materialism, shouts that spiritual blindness is not cured by striving but by believing in Jesus as Christ, in order to accept the great gifts he offers.

Twenty-sixth Day   Read Mark 11

Eagerness for Messiah's coming, as a prelude to an earthly state of peace and prosperity, is a guarantee of disappointment. For Christ came into the world to bring a sword rather than peace. Both by word and example, he demonstrated that prayer is explosive, working transformations in men and, through them, in society and all its institutions.

By nature, the Saviour confronts and challenges. He requires men to take a stand for him or against him. Neutrality, complacency, satisfaction with the status quo, all are human defenses against the disruptive, traumatic, and growth-inducing effects of encounter with the Saviour, recognized in his creatively saving role.

Twenty-seventh Day   Read Mark 12

Part of the paradox of the Incarnation centers in differences between personal reactions and judgments about reactions of others. Always, it is easy to see the blindness and folly—

199

of others. Surveying the actions of first-century leaders, it seems impossible that these tenants should have failed to recognize and revere their divine Landlord's Son. But the scandal and glory of the Gospel focus partly in the fact that as tenants instead of observers of other tenants, we are prone to engage in the very rejection that we so readily denounce—in others.

Because God rules a realm where *life* is basic, and not death, it is the spirit—the living principle—of the law that we must seek. This precludes any fixed and final interpretations, any ethical and moral standards that are absolute for all times and conditions. We must perpetually welcome re-evaluation of values, creative transformation of attitudes and practices as a fruit of encounter with our Creator.

Twenty-eighth Day   **Read Mark 13**

"Accomplishment" of God's purpose for mankind, in such fashion that finite creatures can perceive and understand this fruition of creation, is necessarily a source of marvel and bewilderment. No aspect of Jesus' message is more important than the proclamation that human existence is meaningful and not meaningless, because it is rooted in a heavenly Kingdom. No phase of his promise lends itself to greater diversity of interpretation.

Watch is the key word here. By cultivating the mood of attuned expectancy, the believing seeker prepares himself to receive whatever it may please God to send, whenever it is God's will to send it. This is the most that any man can do to "hasten the coming of the Kingdom"—personally, or in society.

Twenty-ninth Day   **Read Mark 14**

By her dramatic action at dinner, Mary of Bethany proclaims Jesus of Nazareth to be the long-expected Anointed
One—the Messiah. In some respects this marks the end of
the series of events through which Jesus Christ is announced to the people whose Covenant served to prepare
them to receive him.

Yet lack of understanding—or partial understanding—continues even among the disciples. With the supper that is to
stand in relation to the Passover meal as the New Covenant
stands to the Old still fresh in experience, Peter and James
and John fail and fall.

That is to say, at the very height of the dramatic interlude
that leads up to divine self-giving by which salvation is
offered to all men, the chief apostles demonstrate that they
still need rescue. They are mortals, prone to all mistakes of
mortality. After walking with the Saviour for months, they
remain incapable of saving themselves. Mercy, and not justice, is essential if any expect to hear, "Well done, thou good
and faithful servant."

Thirtieth Day   **Read Mark 15-16**

Chief priests, who are chief among mockers, succeed, by a
perverse kind of genius, in putting great emphasis upon a
central aspect of events that lead up to the New Covenant.
For they offer to believe in Jesus of Nazareth as the Christ,
provided that he come down from the Cross and save himself. And this is precisely what the Saviour could not do,
and still be true to his saving role.

Far from comprehending that the voluntary death of
Jesus Christ has made the new age not simply potential, but
actual, a handful of faithful ones remain to pay a last tribute of love. At the empty tomb, scales fall off their eyes, as

201

it were. Not simply the tomb and their Master look different —but everything under the sun. For these new persons, there is a new universe whose most incredible feature is that the Saviour does for them what they never could do for themselves. To accept the conditions of citizenship, and enter the Kingdom by faith, is to become a co-signer of the New Covenant.

NINTH MONTH:

Luke and John

The Gospel According to Saint Luke

Luke, a Gentile physician writing for Gentile readers, has a style and an approach that are all his own. He tells the same story as Matthew, Mark, and John. But, because the man through whom the story bubbles is distinctly different from other Gospel writers, his report differs from theirs.

Ancient preachers and evangelists used the calf to symbolize Luke's Gospel. For the calf is the animal used in major sacrifices—and for Luke, the supreme fact about Jesus Christ is that he voluntarily gave himself as a sacrifice for every man.

This Gospel is, in a special sense, "the book of Jesus' parables." Luke not only reports many more of them than does Matthew or Mark; he gives every evidence of having deliberately emphasized this special medium through which deep spiritual truth can be offered to men. As you follow his vivid account, notice that Luke repeatedly stresses the vital role of the listener. The precise message that one gets from a parable, Luke shows us over and over, depends upon the framework from which that parable is approached.

Jesus Christ himself, truth incarnate, meant many things to many men. Part of the work of the witness—whether New Testament writer, medieval singer, or twentieth-century evangelist—is to select and shape the vehicles through which he attempts to pour the truth that is inside him, but which must be translated into words (or musical notes, or formulas, or visual patterns) before it can haltingly be made public.

In his ardor to pour out for mankind the universal message that Jesus Christ, Lamb of the World, offers salvation to all who will accept it, Luke makes prodigal use of symbols. To be sure, his literary style is not so scintillating as that of John, and his metaphors are not so blinding as those of the Fourth Gospel. Yet it takes but a few hours with him to see the grandeur of the fashion in which he uses words on two or three levels of meaning.

I am not sure that any modern reader can ever grasp the whole range of meanings which Luke attached to symbols such as: water, light, fire, marriage, bread, Jerusalem, the Sabbath, stone, and the like. The very least that you and I can do, therefore, is to read in meditative fashion—expecting, in each fresh encounter with a familiar sentence or phrase, suddenly to get a flash of light that reveals totally new meaning.

Whatever the vehicle used—history, parable, symbol—the end purpose is the same. Everything in the account is included because, for Luke, it serves to point the eyes of men to the central Cross on Calvary and persuade each viewer that God proposes to let him see (in a spiritual sense) . . . himself. It is to foster the *sympathetic identification* between Christ and man, between Saviour and saved, that Luke writes.

First Day   **Read Luke 1**

Luke, the physician, whose experience with childbirth makes him especially tender in his interpretations of womanhood and childhood, here preserves some of the most lofty poetry of the human race. Like the marvels and portents which they accompany, the Magnificat of Mary (Verses 46-

55) and the song of Zechariah (Verses 68-79) express messages over and above those conveyed through their literal words.

For, like marriage and childbirth, the very existence of poetry "says" a great deal about God and man. Made in the divine image, man is co-creator of his own world. True religion involves not monologue, but dialogue. Man's thrust upward matches and meets God's thrust downward. So, the Gospel story is the climax of the centuries-old romance between God and man. Supremely and superbly, the child, who is flesh of Mary's flesh while generated by the Holy Spirit, unites God and man in one person. It is this that enables him, in dying as a substitute for man, to "make amends" in a fashion that no mortal could do.

However good the intentions of an interpreter, every attempt to tone down the fervor of Luke's report in order to make it reasonable and rational is an exercise in futility. For he has set out on a wholly irrational task—none other than that of persuading his fellow men that the limitations of mortality disappear when we so believe in Jesus Christ that we "identify ourselves with him." That being the case, the only suitable prelude to the heavenly symphony is precisely the one Luke gives us: beautiful stories of utterly incredible events working together to produce a God-man.

Second Day   **Read Luke 2**

God has given man a physical body that requires tangible things: air, water, food, a narrow range of temperature, and so on. But, to be human in the full sense, a social as well as a physical environment is required.

That is to say, even God could not send his own Son without a context into which he could be received. Existence of some kind of civilization, and preparation on the part of some Chosen People, were necessary before a Christ

205

Child could enter the stream of human history. So it is both appropriate and suggestive that Luke, the Gentile physician, should go to great pains in stressing the "Jewishness" of his Saviour's human background. Lacking a prepared and expectant people, the actual coming of God's Son would have gone completely unnoticed.

Both in this literal sense and in figurative ones, the bursting forth of the Saviour from the womb attracts the attention and commands the reverence of a select company—precisely those who ardently seek encounter with a Saviour and are attuned to wave lengths conveying evidence about him.

Third Day   Read Luke 3-4

The word of God offers solace to the troubled and distressed. It is balm for the wounded heart, and it gives strength to the weary. But stress upon its soothing and healing functions must not blind us to the fact that the divine word is also a weapon with which God attacks the Evil One and all who support his cause or give him shelter.

Vivid metaphors of the Old Testament make the word of truth function as a weapon: "the sword of the Lord." Now slashing, now stabbing, it is a disturbing and disruptive influence in society and the lives of individual men. This is the sense in which Jesus came to bring a sword rather than peace. Yet precisely here, by a shining paradox of the Gospel, lies Good News (3:18)!

It was the role of John the Baptist to wield the sword of the Lord in such fashion that men, made aware of their danger, would instinctively seek a protector. His divinity attested not only by marvels attending his birth but also by visible and audible witness of the Holy Spirit, Jesus steps forward to champion the cause of doomed mankind. Demonstrating his power to function as Saviour, he disarms and humiliates Satan at the very outset of his public ministry.

Yet many who hear him persuade themselves that they can fight their own battles and do not need a divine substitute. Such persons, vividly portrayed through the rejection at Nazareth, are the only ones for whom the Saviour can do nothing. The hands of God himself are tied, so long as mortal man takes the attitude that he is able to stand on his own feet and meet every foe that threatens his (spiritual) life in this world and the world to come.

Fourth Day   **Read Luke 5-6**

Nothing can withstand the power of God's supreme agent, come into the world in order to strike the word "impossible" from the vocabulary of believers. All limitations vanish before the power of his presence. The sea, ancient and relentless symbol of the frontier man cannot conquer, gives up its treasures. Leprosy is overcome, paralysis is vanquished, and the heart of a tax collector is warmed!

Why does the story not come to a quick climax, right here? Why is it that men, confronted by such evidence, scan it and remain unmoved? How could these ancient ones deceive themselves into thinking they could win God's approval by their own efforts, directed toward following the highway of obedience to the law of Moses?

Viewed from the perspective of twenty centuries, it seems incredible that men who were good and holy by the highest of human standards should have been the chief opponents of Jesus. But, now as well as then, the tendency to resist and rebel is basic. We, too, want to work out our own salvation. We, too, are prone to demonstrate by our lives that we feel we must hack our own way to some destination that will give meaning to our lives. So we, too, need the spiritual slap-in-the-face that is offered by messages Luke preserves as the Sermon on the Plain (6:20-49). Instead of being the spiritual soothing syrup we often try to make it, this collection of Jesus' sayings offers an opportunity for genuine encounter with the living word. Here, every reader is first confronted and then convicted: persuaded that he is unable to achieve the approval of God, so he must have divine help if he is to be acquitted in the Judgment.

Fifth Day   **Read Luke 7**

Part of the recurrent note of scandal in the Good News stems from the fact that while salvation is offered to all men, there are those who cannot be saved: namely, any and all who fail to see themselves as desperate men for whom no human help will avail.

Were it not so fearfully tragic, I think there would be an almost comical note in the fact that elders of the Jews serve as emissaries on behalf of a Roman centurion—but themselves reject Jesus' offer to confer new life!

It is not particularly difficult to see that this chapter centers upon eager acceptance of God's good gifts through Christ, on the part of "outsiders." It is much harder to survey the contemporary scene, in which I am included, and decide just what persons and what groups are sufficiently conscious of their alienation to be eager and receptive.

My real business in reading Luke's account of the watershed of *salvation history* is to make personal application of his challenge and promise. Are there respects in which I am a modern Pharisee, blind to my own nakedness and indignant at the suggestion that I should accept God's offer to clothe me? Have I been busy serving causes which, however pious they appear on the surface, represent camouflaged instances of idolatry? How can I become more vividly aware that I am blind, lame, unclean, deaf, and dead, in order that—recognizing my poverty—I may become rich (Verses 21-22)?

Sixth Day   Read Luke 8

Luke not only reports the Parable of the Soils; he is careful to include Jesus' own interpretation of it, and to set it in a context of incidents that illustrate central truths of the parable. In this respect, his seventh chapter is without parallel in the New Testament. Here we have, in effect, a capsule delineation of the central role that is played by the hearer of the word.

It is not from "witnessing" as such but from vital encounter between a body of witness and recipients of it that transformation stems. Even when the person offering his witness is the Son of God—divinity lodged in flesh—no "automatic" or sure results can be expected. Always, the harvest is radically affected by the nature of the human soil upon which the seed of the word falls.

Having preserved the parable through which this high-level truth is offered, Luke reports that bewilderment of Jesus' own disciples. Their verbal reaction is simply a mirror of the dramatic reaction of "the world" when confronted by the enigmatic promise that constitutes the offer of salvation. For, in quick succession, we see negative principles of the parable illustrated by reactions of: Jesus' mother and brothers, fearful disciples, and the people of the Gerasenes. In sharp contrast, positive principles are illustrated by reactions of an outcast woman and (incredibly!) an important official of a religious institution.

Seventh Day   Read Luke 9

It is one of the openly proclaimed secrets of the Gospel that there can be no salvation without a Saviour. Because of the limitations of humanity, we mortals are incapable of recognizing and accepting divine bounty in wholly spiritual form. We must have something—better, Someone—tangible. However difficult it may be to achieve encounter with the source of salvation, we could not so much as attempt that encounter were we not aided by divinity having become incarnate, in order that, through Christ, God might appeal to our eyes and ears and not simply our capacity to think abstract thoughts.

Consequently, a vital aspect of the New Testament story is the recognition of Jesus as Saviour. Of the multitudes who see and hear him, a few succeed in brief and halting identification between Jesus of Nazareth and the Christ of God. For them, and for all others who manage to stand where these stood, "salvation is real," because it is an item of personal experience.

We must not get discouraged if we are puzzled by this aspect of the Good News. Peter did not leap to his "great confession" at one bound. And even after other disciples heard it with their own ears, they continued to misunderstand the work of their Master. Whether on a personal Mount of Transfiguration or among hostile Samaritans of our own time, we are prone to fall and fail! *Were this not the case, we might need a guide and helper—but not a Saviour.* It is our limited-ness, our failability, our feet of clay, that require the Gospel of rescue through the divine-human son of the Covenant.

Eighth Day   Read Luke 10

Kingdom truths are both openly revealed and hidden, at one and the same time. For no amount of proclamation will serve to convey the Good News to any person who is incapable of recognizing and accepting it. Perennially, the pride of "wisdom" leads to failure, while the humility of "ignorance" is likely to be a prelude to success.

Yet the Gospel must be proclaimed—not only by the Son in whom the Word of God is incarnate, but also by his disciples and messengers. It is the real function of the Church (and perhaps the only real function of it) to "propagate the

210

faith" by multiplying opportunities for encounter between men and the Gospel. Measure results, witnesses cannot. Whether dealing with some astute "lawyer" who is master of inherited codes and interpretations, with a modern Sodom, or some counterpart of Capernaum, disciples must be true to their mission—and leave the results to God.

Ninth Day   Read Luke 11

It comes as a shock to realize that the chief "formula" Jesus offered his disciples is a pattern of prayer. The entire history of the Covenant relationship points to two-way flow between God and man, it is true. In a sense, the Bible, which is the most sublime verbal fruit of divine-human dialogue, also exists in order to foster such exchange. But we are not really prepared to see prayer as *the* religious life.

Note the sequence here. Jesus provides a pattern of prayer—very brief to be sure. Then he exhorts his disciples to be urgent in thir seeking, and, by casting out a demon, gives a dramatic illustration of the power that stems from relationship with the Father. All these things are wasted on the Pharisees and lawyers (standard character types in every form of organized religion). These men do not know how to pray, in any vital sense. Their yearnings and longings turn inward upon themselves, so to speak. Instead of being involved in dialogue with God, accepting all the dreadful risks and glorious opportunities that dialogue includes, for all practical purposes these holy men spend their lives talking to themselves and to one another.

I cannot think that the consistent blindness and failure of "Pharisees and lawyers" is underscored in order to condemn first-century Jewish leaders, only. Rather, these unredeemed ones are symbols of those men in every age who trust themselves in lieu of seeking salvation so urgently that they demand it of God.

Tenth Day   **Read Luke 12**

How dumb can you get?

Jesus devotes a whole sermonette to the dangers of concern with material goals—and a listener immediately pipes up asking for divine help in gaining an inheritance!

You and I frown indignantly or smile in patronizing fashion. Then we proceed to urge upon Jesus our own yearnings for tangible blessings! To enter the mood symbolized by care-less lilies, is not simply desirable, but essential. This involves centering upon the Kingdom in such fashion that eagerness to greet the Master causes all other goals and concerns to fade into the background.

Eleventh Day   **Read Luke 13-14**

Repentance is a turning inside-out of the self. Through it "the natural man" becomes spiritual, his surrender enabling God to work such a transformation that he is literally no longer the same person. It was to call men to such repentance, and to provide avenues along which we may move toward it, that Jesus Christ came into the world.

Through repentance, in its inclusive sense, barren trees begin to bear fruit, and bent persons become straight. It would seem that any man in his senses would want this transformation so eagerly that he would "assault the gates of heaven" to get it. But that is not the case. Many—perhaps most—are willing to settle for a degree of satisfaction and status within the context of human society.

It is for this reason that the altogether positive Good News becomes threatening and negative when rejected. To eliminate the element of dread from the encounter with God is to reduce him to human dimensions. The fearful prospect of being shut out from the banquet is as live an alternative as any vision of ecstasy. Here trembles the meaning of human existence: acceptance or rejection of God's overtures has not simply personal, but also cosmic consequences.

Twelfth Day   **Read Luke 15-16**

Chapter 15, with its three parables of the lost, is among the most radiant of the New Testament. God is eternally on the offensive, these stories say. There are no impossible situations—except those centering upon lost men who are comfortable and satisfied in their lost-ness, and do not wish to respond to divine overtures.

This is not to say, however, that the pilgrimage to the New Jerusalem is easy. For if God is perpetually bidding for surrender, so is the world. Our space- and time-bound physical selves easily fall prey to that all-pervasive kind of idolatry which consists of making "riches" of some type the goal of life. In a special sense, this captivity to the material is the "far country" to which each of us flees but in which no prodigal (whether Pharisee or rich man or ordinary church member) need stay long enough to die and be buried in a lonely grave.

Thirteenth Day   **Read Luke 17-18**

Though "salvation is free," there is another sense in which it is very costly. Including as they do warnings about the terrible day of the Lord, these chapters also stress that the price of rescue is a totally dedicated life in which belief in Jesus Christ is dominant. The fact that of ten lepers cleansed, only the Samaritan gave thanks is enough to warn us; the realization that a Pharisee whom his fellow men considered holy was rejected while a wretched tax collector was approved, is enough to frighten the wits out of

213

us—if we will apply the warning to ourselves. Once more, we are confronted by the fearful announcement that salvation is impossible (humanly speaking). To be proud or casual or complacent is to create a mood encouraging rejection of God's offer to do for us what we cannot do for ourselves.

Fourteenth Day   **Read Luke 19-20**

Paradoxes are strewn through these pages like boulders along a mountain road. It is the man conscious of being lost who is likely to be saved. That person who has much (spiritually speaking) is sure to gain more, while the poor fellow with nothing will surely lose what he has. Escorted into Jerusalem in triumph, Jesus does not exult—but weeps. Entering the Temple, chief holy place of God's Chosen People, the Son of God does not soothe and commend; instead, he condemns. The rejected stone, he says, becomes the foundation on which an edifice rests.

Surely this clustering together of (apparent) contradictions on the eve of Calvary is not accidental or incidental. It challenges all notions of an easy or "simple" Gospel. We expect too much if we hope to grasp all the subtleties and nuances of the Good News as a result of giving it part of our attention during a single proclamation. Here is a soul-absorbing quest that demands undivided attention throughout life!

Fifteenth Day   **Read Luke 21-22**

Overturning and actual "reversal" of accepted conditions and ideas is as characteristic of the Kingdom as is paradox of the Good News. The day of the Lord is so transforming that no established conditions will prevail. Man's great task is to "watch at all times" (21:36), to avoid being entangled in worldly pursuits, so that the explosive impact of the Kingdom will not destroy anything regarded as important or valuable.

Judas' betrayal illustrates and symbolizes results of failure in this respect. For the sake of a tangible trifle, a disciple disposes of his own soul. In a special sense, it is really himself and not Jesus whom he sells for thirty pieces of silver.

Through that act, Judas unwittingly implements the flow of *salvation history*. For it is on the day of unleavened bread that the new sacrifice, God's Son, plays the role of Paschal Lamb.

Sixteenth Day   Read Luke 23-24

It is as a man condemned by due process of law (however barbaric that law may seem, viewed through twentieth-century eyes) that the Son of Man goes to Calvary. He is guilty of the offense charged—i.e., being King of the Jews. Punishment is absolute, not simply severe. Jesus of Nazareth "pays the price" for his offense against the society of his day.

In a special sense, just such a sequence of events is "necessary." For the grand theme of Luke is Jesus' taking upon himself the sins of mankind and meeting for mankind the demands of the law. So the working-out of human justice is a prototype of the working-out of divine justice, under which every man is sentenced and must receive the death penalty.

Only the condemned man who succeeds in seeing himself as condemned and who, in faith, accepts Jesus Christ as Saviour is released from claims of the law. He is already "dead," already "punished," because the Saviour mounted the Cross for him. This wholly incredible series of events is

215

true, being proclaimed and authenticated by the empty tomb.

Salvation history reached its climax on Calvary, but the feeble eyes of men required "the impossible met face to face" (resurrection of an executed lawbreaker), in order to be simultaneously blinded and wholly enlightened by recognizing Jesus of Nazareth to be the Christ of God—divinity come into flesh in order to rescue mankind from the sentence of death.

The Gospel According to Saint John

Even a first-time reader senses the change of pace and the new mood when he turns from the last chapter of Luke to the first chapter of John. Because there are many types of men—varied kinds of soil, if you please—the likelihood of a maximum harvest is increased by using a variety of methods to sow seed. John's sowing, altogether different from that of any other Gospel witness, has dynamic impact upon some persons who are left unmoved and unconvinced by Matthew, Mark, and Luke. He conveys precisely the same message they offer, but transmits it through a different channel: his unduplicated self.

It is commonplace to speak of John's Gospel as "poetic." That label is valid, but does not convey the depth and height of his message. Essentially, it is an impassioned personal testimony: a confession of faith.

Consequently, John is all but unconcerned with things that interest the historian. Not only does he by-pass every single incident of Jesus' first thirty or thirty-three years; he also ignores the whole matter of his Saviour's human lineage. For John, the fact above every fact is that God the Creator is totally incarnate in Jesus Christ.

Hence, for him, the supreme vehicle through which the Saviour teaches is action. John reports many miracles, but not one parable. Every act and deed is communicative.

Each mighty work is a divine proclamation! As a result, the Gospel of John is both easy and difficult. More than any other body of Christian witness, it has power to stir men into belief-powered surrender. Yet, the testimony that makes converts of novices never ceases to yield fresh insight and to heighten conviction of veteran readers. Here is a book not so much to be read, as to be encountered—growing more powerful and more intriguing with each meeting.

Seventeenth Day   Read John 1

Jesus Christ is wholly communicative. It is his work to reveal God to man in such fashion that man gains power to throw off limitations of his finite nature. Hence, the experience of knowing God through Christ is the most creative event into which a human can enter. In "listening to the incarnate Word," man becomes co-creator with God. It is this for which the world was created, and in it the divine work of creation is as vital as that described in Genesis. Notice that, in Gen. 1, God the Father *speaks* the world into existence. Speaking "in these latter days" through the Word made flesh, God fosters the coming into being of transformed persons—each instance of such transformation being a cosmic event, on the scale of the creation of the world.

John the Baptist raises his voice in order to catch the attention of men, to help them make ready to hear the divine Word in all the deeds as well as all the words of Jesus Christ. In his work as Saviour, Jesus serves as the Lamb sent down from heaven in order to be offered up by men (who do not know the import of their action) in a once-for-all sacrificial ceremony, the effect of which is to atone for the sins of all men who succeed in believing that this unbelievable thing has been done for them.

Eighteenth Day   **Read John 2-3**

At the outset of Jesus' public ministry, we discover that he is going to use dramatic action as a means of communication. Through his turning water into wine he not only demonstrates divine power; he also announces the marriage feast celebrating the union of God and man in the New Covenant.

This message was not fully understood by those who heard it; they were puzzled and uncertain. Precisely the same reaction followed his verbal message announcing the coming demonstration of victory over death (2:19-21). Much later, disciples came into encounter with divine truth through nonverbal messages proclaimed by the empty tomb. So transforming was this encounter that their total systems of understanding and believing were reorganized. In the light of that reorganization, they looked back on past events and re-interpreted them—finding deep meanings they had overlooked at the time (2:22).

Such a pattern of religious experience can mark the life of every believer. It is partly because John's Gospel so clearly exhibits this process in action, and "yields itself" to it, that this account both appeals to the beginning Christian and continues to enlighten the developing one. Nicodemus' experience is an example of apparent failure to see light when confronted by the Light. Yet John is careful to show (19:39) that this man, too, was led to re-evaluate and reorder his house of belief in the Light shed by events of Passion Week.

Nineteenth Day   **Read John 4-5**

Persons outside the Covenant relationship, lacking Nicodemus' disadvantage of seeming to have gained spiritual security by birth, do not have to make so radical a readjustment as he. So a Samaritan woman and her fellow villagers join a Roman official in recognizing divinity incarnate, without the necessity of the Cross and the empty tomb as proof.

In Jerusalem, center of true worship, it would seem that everyone would be ready and eager for the healing power offered by the Saviour. But that was not the case; only those really wanting to be made whole were capable of receiving the gift freely offered to them, thereby passing from death to life (5:24).

Once more, the danger of considering one's self spiritually secure is underscored. For experts in the interpretation of the written law so trusted in their superior virtue that they felt no need for rescue, and they lacked capacity for transforming belief in the new law proclaimed by God through the Son himself.

Twentieth Day   Read John 6

Remember that deeds as well as words serve as agents of the Word made flesh. In the light of this fact, it is not hard to see that the feeding of the five thousand is communicative and revelatory. Here is a re-enactment and re-interpretation of the ancient feeding in the wilderness provided for children of the Covenant as they moved from Egypt to the land of promise. Jesus of Nazareth, the second Moses, delivers from captivity to sin and self.

His absolute and unqualified lordship is demonstrated in his mastery of the sea. Still multitudes do not understand. They look and look, but fail to see. Stumbling over literal meanings of symbolic formulas, "the Jews" scoff at the notion that the son of Joseph should be regarded as "the new manna"—or bread from heaven. Even intimate disciples find sayings of this sort to be hard. But in the moment that many once-ardent followers withdraw their allegiance, Peter is inspired to witness in sublime fashion. Not simply

219

in our own day, but also in first-century Palestine, the disciple who demands a neatly-ordered man-sized set of understandings thereby makes all the doors of his house too small to admit a Saviour.

Twenty-first Day   **Read John 7**

Though Jesus exhibits power and confers healing, he also brings about divisions among men. Many causes and interests are challenged by the Good News; incredibly, the religious institution and its functionaries are high on the list, if not actually at the top of the list, of opponents. That is because pride, status, self-interest, and materialism take root in organized religion as readily as in any other soil.

In your community today, as truly as in first-century Jerusalem, men disagree about who Jesus is. And no human system of classification is adequate to separate sheep from goats. Men with positions and background that make them seem logical candidates for recognition of God in the moment of encounter with his power, may prove proud and blind. But it is equally true that, at any moment, any counterpart of Nicodemus may enter into that blending of surrender and seeing which leads one past the religious institution to its divine object.

Twenty-second Day   **Read John 8**

When one is incapable of accepting evidence, it is as though that evidence did not exist. No power on earth can serve to stuff proof into a person in the fashion that sausage is packed into a casing.

Much of the New Testament deals with the nature of knowledge, meaning, and communication. Few chapters, however, face these issues so directly and continuously as does John's eighth. For here, "the Jews" flounder and thresh about; almost, they seem to wallow in their attempt to find a point of contact between their ordered systems of belief and this disturbing one who demands that belief be oriented toward him.

During several centuries of our era, religious thought became hardened and distorted in such fashion that Jews were regarded as natural enemies of Christians. This identification was made on the basis of the very kind of verbal literalism here demonstrated to be sterile. For, though Jews actually were Jesus' opponents in the historic situation, Jews also provided the cultural seed-bed necessary for the coming of the God-man in the flesh. Lacking a people with the sense of Covenant, which we traced so laboriously through the Old Testament, there could have been no Incarnation.

So, it is precisely here that the self-styled Christian needs to make a leap of faith and recognize that any person secure in his own sense of righteousness actually is a "Jew" in the sense of this chapter. Pursued to its depths, this issue becomes very personal. I have no business standing in judgment of other men; judgment belongs to God alone. My sole business is to "continue in the word" with such ardor that I am constantly increasing my capacity to receive and nurture seeds sown in my life by God.

Twenty-third Day   Read John 9-10

All men are blind from birth, but only those who know it are subjects for healing.

Like many other mighty works that took place on the Sabbath, the opening of the blind man's eyes created a new occasion for bickering. The Sabbath controversy itself has deep symbolic meaning; for, on the day intended to point men toward God's work as Creator, guardians of the religi-

221

ous system insisted that an outburst of creative power constituted an offense against God! Which raises the question
(now as well as then): Who is it—really—that is blind?

Ask such a question, and seriously seek an answer, and
you also will either take a trembling step toward transformation—or else will pick up stones to hurl at Jesus Christ.

Twenty-fourth Day   **Read John 11**

I think this is the longest of all New Testament accounts of
a miracle, with its antecedents and aftermath. Here is a
chapter to be read, re-read, and then read once again. It
could be used for a month's pilgrimage, rather than that of
a day.

Surface meanings center in Jesus' demonstration that he
has power over death. Exhibition of this power, however, is
utterly unconvincing to his opponents, who go right ahead
with their plans to seize him—at the very season when, in
ancient Egypt, the angel of death passed over the firstborn
of God's people.

Like all the other mighty works of Jesus, this one is performed in order to convey messages calculated to attract,
and to convince in a fashion that words alone cannot. Fully
to plumb the depths of meaning here, it is necessary for us
continually to seek to enter into the experience of Lazarus—
over and over being raised "from the dead" (spiritually, intellectually, physically) through the power of the divine
word as uttered in the words and deeds of the Son of God.

Twenty-fifth Day   **Read John 12**

Though subsequent events challenged tributes paid during
the triumphal entry, the fact is that Jesus, who died as a

malefactor, really is a King. Like so many other high-level truths, this one is too sublime for any disciple (ancient or modern) to incorporate into his system of experience, until that system has been transformed by encounter with the glorified Saviour.

God trumpets from heaven—and bystanders nod to one another in agreement that it has only thundered.

How, then, can any man hope to gain capacity to hear?

Every pilgrim must use what light he has, be it bright or dim, to be in the process of moving forward. It is in this state of poised and oriented moving toward the goal, not in arrival at some terminus, that a disciple magnifies his capacity to be a seed-bed in which belief can flourish. He who waits for total illumination in order to run with all his might will never start. "While you have the light, believe in the light, that you may become sons of light" (Verse 36).

Twenty-sixth Day   **Read John 13-14**

One of the "secrets" of the Kingdom, proclaimed so loudly that we often tune the message out, centers in the relative importance of men and of Providence. Especially in modern times, we deceive ourselves into thinking it is our job to "bring the Kingdom in." When we talk of that, we actually claim ability to use our minds and our muscles and our time in such fashion that we achieve results God could not accomplish, left to himself.

Strictly speaking, this view trembles very close to the edge of heresy. For the truth is that the yeasting and fermenting divine work proceeds, whether a single human being responds to it or not. It is my job and yours to try to make ourselves fertile soil in which divine seeds may flourish; but we may be sure that God will scatter seeds in society and his harvest will come to maturity if individuals do nothing whatever to help him.

223

These chapters, like so many others, reiterate the promise/warning that "likely candidates" (humanly considered) are poor risks in the sight of God. For it is the humble ones who are receptive enough to receive seeds and nurture them. Bent old women, along with "the poor and maimed and blind and lame" (Luke 14:21), can only hobble—yet, in the end, they always outdistance "Pharisees" and "rulers" who run at top speed!

Twenty-seventh Day   Read John 15-16

Bonds between Saviour and saved are organic. There is continuous two-way flow: a spiritual dialogue, as it were. Precisely such a relationship is basic to that "identification" between the two, by which the suffering and death of Christ serve to wipe out the guilt of his disciple. That is to say, when the vine-branch relationship is taken seriously, we begin to see how it is possible to say that you and I suffered and died on Calvary.

Jesus' invitation into the role of friend rather than of servant, plus his unsolicited promise of the Counselor's coming, serve as sources of strength and comfort. They will be sorely needed, he warns, in time of conflict and apparent failure.

Of course, much that he is saying is falling upon deaf ears. Never mind. Listen and treasure and remember in spite of lack of understanding, he urges. There will come a climactic moment of spiritual-emotional-intellectual experience in which the crucible of experience will reach such a temperature that everything in it will melt—assuming new and undreamed structure when it crystallizes upon cooling. This aspect of knowledge and faith, already stressed so strongly in John's report, is basic to man's entering into a life of discipleship. However comprehensive it may be, religious education is not enough. It must be extended and transformed by religious experience. Then and now, the definitive ingredient in vital religious experience is encounter with a personal Saviour, recognized as God in human flesh. When the disciple experiences such an encounter, all his accumulated meanings and values and beliefs are reorganized. It is the empty tomb that will catapult disciples into the hour of encounter whose dramatic results might be called "spiritual travail." (*See* 16:16-23.)

Twenty-eighth Day   **Read John 17-18**

Jesus' long "priestly prayer" of Chapter 17 is totally oriented toward that select company which makes up his true followers. It is the destiny of these persons, "given to him by the Father," with which he is concerned. Though the actual moment of physical self-giving has not yet come, Jesus here gives himself as absolutely as upon Calvary.

How vivid the contrast, therefore, when Chapter 18 is read.

For the concern of the Saviour is totally directed outward, while the motives and actions of the men described in Chapter 18 make them totally self-centered. Notice that the whole spectrum of humanity is involved. From Judas the traitor to Peter the rock, we are confronted by rejection of the Saviour because of selfish motives. The best of men, as well as the worst, fails and falls.

Nowhere in the Gospel record is there a sharper and more dramatic piece of evidence helping to convince us that all men need not merely help, but *salvation*. Our nature is such that we cannot long focus upon the highest and best. Even in religious service (sometimes especially here), it is easy to become self-centered, concerned with what rewards are in prospect. Before the Master's utterly unforgetful prayer has ceased to echo, the chief apostle finds himself concerned only with saving his own life.

225

If the Good News invites you and me so to identify ourselves with the Christ that we are "crucified with him on Calvary," it also warns that we cannot escape running the gamut of denial that extends from Peter to Judas. In the hour when we should rise to sublime heights in the strength of Jesus' complete love for us, we stumble and fall. Try as we may, we can never long follow our Master's good example; we must turn to him for rescue.

Twenty-ninth Day   **Read John 19**

For the fulfillment of the unfolding New Covenant, it was necessary that the Son of God pay the supreme penalty. Moreover, for the New Covenant to come into being, he had to be executed as a felon. Guilt (humanly speaking) was a necessary ingredient. For only through his own entering into a state of guilt was it possible for Jesus Christ to become a substitute for guilty men (spiritually speaking).

We are prone to get sentimental about the indignities heaped upon our Lord. It certainly is true that the events of Passion Week stir us and convict us. And it is equally true that the condemnation and death of Jesus Christ can be viewed in more than one light. But, in spite of these factors, it yet remains a paradox (and a stumbling block) of the Good News that no agent of God who lived and died as a hero could have played the role of Saviour. In order to provide a way by which mankind could be offered rescue from the inevitable consequences of mortal deeds, divinity had to be condemned to death.

Thirtieth Day   **Read John 20-21**

High-level Christian principles could hardly have been grasped by even a few, had not the fact of the Resurrection served to reorganize their thoughts and beliefs. Disciples themselves, in spite of months spent with their Master, did not grasp the mystery and miracle of the Incarnation until the first Easter demonstrated him to be fully divine as well as so completely human that he had died as an executed felon.

Such sets of meanings cannot be seized intellectually. They must be encountered in the crucible of experience. For them to "come alive" in a more than academic approach to Christian thought, it is necessary that they *become a part of the believer.* There is a fusion, as it were, between the self and the Good News, in such fashion that, in its scandalous and paradoxical and glorious and transforming role, it leads to *identification with Christ.* Such a state, in which the disciple so surrenders that he cannot clearly determine boundaries between his organized self and his divine Saviour, constitutes redemption. It was for this to come into being that God entered history in the person of his Son.

TENTH MONTH:

Acts and Romans

The Acts of the Apostles

As the title clearly indicates, this throbbing book deals more largely with deeds than with ideas. Yet even a hasty reading cannot fail to show that beliefs and loyalties are the foundations on which the outward actions rest. This is indeed an account of the tangible actions of the Apostles, obedient to an inner compulsion that makes them do strange and powerful things. But, precisely because it is an incredible story, dealing with accomplishments that any sensible person would consider impossible, it is also a book about Jesus Christ.

His indwelling power, conveyed through the Holy Spirit, literally transforms those men whose "acts" fill this book. From a bewildered and defeated group of obscure followers of a village visionary, they are suddenly welded into a band of dynamic witnesses, who will be satisfied with nothing less than the conquest of the whole world!

Read in isolation, the Book of Acts can be seen as almost "ordinary" (in spite of the incredible impact of a single disciple, who has to be guarded by Roman hosts). Read in context—not simply as a follow-up to the four Gospels, but also as standing in organic connection with the entire Old Testament—the Book of Acts suddenly emerges as one of the strangest and most explosive documents ever penned. For it deals with nothing less than World Revolution.

Though men are deeply involved in that revolution, and are essential instruments of it, this is unlike political or social upheaval; it is the continuing work of God the Father among men made in his image, in whom the yeasting and fermenting impact of the Good News, that Jesus Christ offers rescue *now*, serves to work absolute transformation. Not simply individuals, but also institutions and cultures—eventually nations and ideologies as well—are affected.

Even to skim through these pages hastily is to recognize that God-oriented change (often unpleasantly disruptive) is absolutely basic to ongoing Christian development. God does not want or expect the flow of creative enlargement in our day to be a re-enactment of that in the first century. He does not call us to imitate or duplicate the precise outward effects of the day of Pentecost or the great church conference in Jerusalem. But, through his Son, who entered death in order that men might live on a new level, the Creator does expect (better—*demand*) creative enlargement on the part of those who call themselves his own.

It is death for any individual or group, any class or congregation, to reach an intellectual-spiritual peak, however high, that permits ease and complacency. Struggle and growth and God-oriented enlargement are the most precious gifts that can be conferred on a soul still enmeshed in a physical body. With the soul as with that body, life retreats and death reigns the instant two-way interaction with the environment ceases.

First Day   **Read Acts 1-2**

For Luke the historian, Jesus' death and resurrection mark not the end, but the midpoint of history. Though it is approximately the same band of followers with whom he deals throughout, his account whose first half is the Gospel bearing his name depicts men and women who are noticeably "different" in the second half of the story. All their values and ideals are in the process of being re-interpreted in the light of the absolutely system-shattering recognition that Jesus of Nazareth was the Son of God.

Notice that their re-interpretation extends not simply to personal experiences, but also to Scripture. In the light of receiving the Good News as communicated in Jesus' total life and words, familiar passages take on radical new meaning. A case in point is the long passage from the book of Joel, which Peter quotes on the day of Pentecost (2:17-21; *see also* 2:25-28, quoted from Ps. 16:8-11).

Not simply familiar Scripture, but *everything*, is new—for personal transformation of disciples is so great that they are literally, and not figuratively, *new persons*.

A major aspect of the transformation centers in the strange and potent "gift of the Holy Spirit." These disciples do not pay homage to their old goals; they are now so dominated by zeal for the Kingdom that they are "possessed"— dominated, controlled, and owned—by the indwelling divine personality. Necessarily and inevitably, social structures are as radically affected as are individual lives.

Second Day   **Read Acts 3-4**

Not simply holy boldness, but marvelous new power, marks the daily life of the transformed disciples. Even the most casual reading persuades us that these are not the same men as those who floundered and misunderstood and hesitated so recently. Something tremendous has happened to them, and it has come to a climax in the period between the Crucifixion and Pentecost. Before, these quite ordinary men and women would have made little impact upon society. Now, they are so potent that they quickly begin—almost in spite of themselves, as it were—such mighty works that they "turn the world upside down."

For faith today, these tumultuous events have a vexatious set of questions. Shall we try to recover first-century Christianity, seeking to duplicate experiences and patterns of the emerging Church? Or shall we seek new outpourings of the Holy Spirit, calculated to bring new Pentecostal experiences whose fruits will be appropriate to conditions of the present age?

The crux of the question is the direction of creative transformation by divine power; does the first century exhaust its potential, so that the Christian ideal is re-enactment of events in the Book of Acts? Or is the ideal, rather, divine-human encounter, calculated to have such creative impact that no man can predict or channel the explosive results? If the Holy Spirit takes possession of lives today, will men spontaneously return to practices and patterns of Peter and Paul—or find totally new ones whose shape cannot be predicted in advance, but simply accepted as they emerge in mighty works of continuing divine creation?

Third Day   Read Acts 5

You may take this as a basic principle: whenever the power of God is actively at work, strange and fearful things will take place in the lives of individuals and in the corporate life of the Church. Today, we who name the name of Jesus Christ tend to commit, I think, one of two grave errors.

Frequently we approach our faith as though we could be in a transforming relationship with God through Christ; yet we live in a fashion calculated to win social acceptance as good and upright men who are "normal" by prevailing secular standards. This fearful error, by which the utterly transforming impact of being in the stream of salvation is rejected, is balanced by an opposite one. For if we regard the Christian pilgrimage as the focal point of continuing divine creation, so that radical transformation is expected,

231

we are likely to insist upon guiding the flow of that transformation. That is, we may expect neither more nor less than the outward effects which are described in the Acts of the Apostles.

Actually, it may inhibit God's creative power to expect him to strike down a new Ananias and a fresh Sapphira every time men and women seriously seek the Holy Spirit. Authenticating "signs and wonders" (Verse 12) there will be aplenty, when men and groups really put God first. But precisely what these will be we cannot possibly know in advance. Nor can we measure any group or movement by the degree to which it conforms to accepted patterns. Like Gamaliel, we must insist upon open-mindedness and willingness to let time and events challenge or support validity of all claims that God is presently working in mighty ways among men who believe themselves to be guided by him.

Fourth Day   **Read Acts 6-7**

Is it inevitable that mighty outpourings of divine power should create divisions and arouse opposition? Probably so. As a rule of thumb (dangerous to adopt for its own sake), it may be proposed that when no opposition is being aroused, little creative work of God is taking place. Notice especially the near-automatic factor of antagonism to Jesus' own message and ministry. (*See,* for example, practically every instance of encounter between Jesus and officials of religious institutions.)

Martyrdom of Stephen, viewed in this light, is an index to the explosive impact of divine power, released through Peter and his comrades. It is a perennial fallacy, however, for God-seekers to pursue "martyrdom" on some scale, for its own sake.

Stephen's great defense, in Chapter 7, is among the most

illuminating of all New Testament passages in its power to show the absolute interdependence of Old Testament and New. While it is true that the New Testament (or individual books of it) can be read in isolation with profit, it is also true that some familiarity with the Old Testament will serve to give new dimensions to the New Testament and each of its parts. Stephen here summarizes *salvation history* in its entirety, and shows the organic bond that stretches (through the Chosen People) from Abraham to Jesus Christ.

Confronted by so great a challenge, Stephen's hearers could not be neutral or passive. In a sense, their unwillingness to accept his invitation, to bow at the feet of Jesus Christ, required them to stone Jesus' messenger. No middle ground was possible.

Fifth Day   **Read Acts 8-9**

In its solemn unfolding, *salvation history* requires continuous creative encounter between God and man. Humanly speaking, the plot thickens when we recognize that the creature who moves toward the Creator must participate both socially and individually. That is to say, both an Israel and a Saul of Tarsus are essential factors. There is a unique human group, the Chosen People, whose marriage contract with the Creator leads to birth of the God-man, our Saviour. But the fruition of the Covenant does not eliminate the need for new human partners of God. On the contrary, the New Covenant involves both a social group (the Church) and hosts of individual men and women willing to surrender in such fashion that they become agents of God.

Chief among such individuals in the emerging Church is Saul, who becomes Paul. In somewhat the same sense that a betrayer was *necessary*, so that, had Judas not functioned, God would have had to raise up a substitute for him, so a

233

theological spokesman—a man of the keen mind—was needed in order to put the new faith into systematic form. Had the versatile and disciplined Saul not responded to the divine call for a theologian, God would have had to provide another.

Peter's vision and Saul's conversion are two sides of the same coin; both men were instruments of the divine purpose, by which the Good News would burst out of Judaism and offer new life, in Jesus Christ, to the whole world.

Sixth Day   **Read Acts 10-11**

Whether in a biological organism, the spiritual-intellectual realm of an individual, or the structured group that constitutes a human institution, life is a state of continuous traumatic change. That individual pilgrim toward the City of God who ceases to engage in conscious struggle has forfeited his opportunity to let the stream of divine creation use his life as a channel. That group or church or society which centers upon zealous preservation of what it has attained and received thereby says "no" to God's ceaseless invitation to grow toward him.

We applaud the decision to send the Good News to Gentiles—and are in danger of rejecting our own opportunities to engage in the transforming experience of letting God send us into virgin territory.

Even for Peter—especially for Peter—the "bursting out" into the Gentile world was fearfully demanding. He found himself in a state of dialogue with God, so attuned that events "spoke" to him with persuasive power. This served to erase the thin line between everyday sensory experience and divine revelation through an agent of God. So long as he remained in this exalted state, Peter actually found it hard to determine just when he was "seeing a vision," and when he was involved in mortal experience. (*See* 12:9.)

234

No man can make neat explanations and precise measurements of such phenomena. But any man can read of the utterly transforming events of these months and be very sure that—somehow—God's creative power was manifest in unusual fashion through the lives of a few dedicated men— very ordinary mortals.

Seventh Day   **Read Acts 12-13**

Peter's visions convey much the same message as Stephen's long defense (Chapter 7) and Paul's exhortation in the synagogue of Antioch (13:16-41).

In the intellectual-spiritual heat of his new personal authority, Paul re-interprets the whole history of the divine-human Covenant. His tremendous speech is a key passage in which to discover the organic bond between Israel and the Church, the essential connectedness of the Old Testament and the New. Here are early stirrings of the mind and spirit of a one-time Jewish scholar who, as Christian evangelist, is destined to write spirit-filled letters that will speak of salvation through Jesus Christ in such powerful fashion that he will communicate with men born two thousand years later.

It is significant for our pilgrimage through the Bible to find here underscored this warning: familiarity with words of Holy Writ is no guarantee of valid encounter with its spirit (13:27). This basic factor is a key to both acceptance and rejection of the Gospel; the outlook and goals of the hearer are vital ingredients in the compound: "message that is heard."

For a modern Christian (whatever the degree of his commitment to the Saviour), it is almost pitifully easy to congratulate one's self on capacity to hear with understanding in order to act with obedience. A crucial question here is: To what degree do I actually play the role of a "jealous" devotee of the Old Covenant (13:45), while persuading myself that I am listening with the eager ears of a Gentile hearing a first invitation to accept salvation and glory in the riches of the Kingdom?

Eighth Day   **Read Acts 14-16**

Suppose you were required to summarize these chapters in a few key words? It will be a tremendously fruitful exercise, by the way, to attempt just that.

For my part, I think I shall have to list (not necessarily in the order of their importance) these basic factors in the swift-moving events here described: action . . . power . . . marvels . . . struggle . . . division.

Looking through rose-colored glasses, as we usually do when we read about the doings of the Apostles, we tend to magnify the place of teaching, preaching, healing, and evangelism. At the same time, we tend to minimize opposition and defeat suffered in "the glorious first century."

Actually, these chapters suggest that, then as well as now, a fundamental "spiritual law of physics" can be seen at work. This principle might be expressed: "Every God-oriented flow of power creates a powerful contrary force." That is, to pour energy into service of God is *automatically* to arouse opposition on a proportional scale.

Whatever gives us modern Christians the notion that things are going well when nobody resists, nobody attacks? Perhaps because we have deceived ourselves into thinking we live in "a Christian society," we have too often equated piety with tranquility. Fearing the condemnation that may be an inevitable accompaniment of stirring up a commotion, we have (in practice if not in theory) valued the way of compromise, the route of least resistance. To read of Iconium and Lystra, Antioch and Jerusalem does not encourage any zealot to put a premium on controversy for its own sake. But it fortifies every disciple to know that any flow of divine power through him is likely to stir up the conventionally pious, and may even precipitate new stonings, beatings with rods, and imprisonment in the name of law and order.

Ninth Day   Read Acts 17-18

In the months that you and I have spent with the Scriptures, we have repeatedly seen that interpretation is not automatic, but variable. God's power to reveal himself (through the Bible or any other medium) is affected by man's willingness to accept divine truth. I suppose, therefore, it is both a consolation and a source of alarm to discover that Paul himself failed in his attempt to persuade devout men that Jesus Christ is offered through the Holy Books of Israel. Temporary success in Beroea is as notable as failure in Thessalonica—underscoring the realization that it is the work of the witness to sow in obedient faith, and leave the increase to God.

In all his encounters, whether with pagans in Athens or devout scholars of Israel in Corinth, Paul was concerned with pouring out a single impassioned and incredible message: Jesus of Nazareth, who died on the Cross, was the Saviour for whom God took a Chosen People as his bride and through whom God makes salvation possible.

Then as well as now, this "hard teaching" defied merely intellectual analysis. It was not especially difficult to accept "the Jesus of history" or to trust in "the Christ of God." Difficulties centered in achieving the leap of faith by which Jesus Christ may be encountered as the God-man: divinity joined with humanity, in order to offer unearned rescue to men made in the divine image. It is the Incarnation that serves as the enigmatic building piece of the Good News— a stumbling block that becomes a cornerstone for every man willing to use it so.

Tenth Day   **Read Acts 19-20**

Explain the events of these turbulent months, no man can. Accept them, every believer may.

Part of the intriguing riddle of Paul's life and witness lies in the fact that this man of keen mind was also subject to deep emotion. He clearly displayed charismatic gifts, himself experiencing ecstasy in various forms and, by his laying on of hands, inducing it in others (as 19:6). Yet this was no "Holy Roller" who elevated emotion above intelligence. He was not only one of the warmest hearts of Christendom; he was also one of the keenest minds.

In practice, you and I tend to emphasize one set of these gifts at the expense of the other. Some persons and groups give such emphasis to the intellectual side of Christianity that they tend to squeeze out emotion. Others make the opposite mistake, cultivating ecstatic states for the sake of ecstasy, rather than accepting them as an unsought side-effect of being captured by the Holy Spirit.

Somewhere between the two extremes (or in a synthesis of their divergent elements) lies what might be called "Pauline Christianity"—potent, transforming, and utterly unpredictable, yet utilizing every resource that is available to a trained and disciplined mind.

To the degree that you and I succeed in moving toward personal enhancement of a faith that demands "warm heart plus keen mind," our reading of the Acts of the Apostles will put us, with John Wesley, into the main stream of that salvation in which the divine work of creation is continued and completed. *Possessed* by so disturbing and enlarging a faith, small wonder that Paul created turmoil nearly everywhere he went, warned as he was by the Holy Spirit of impending "imprisonment and afflictions" (20:23).

Eleventh Day   **Read Acts 21-22**

Why on earth did not the Apostle settle down in Ephesus or some other fine city, and devote his life to making a long-term impact—instead of almost aimlessly wandering hither and thither and staying nowhere for any great length of time?

Because he felt himself under divine compulsion. Because a central aspect of his Christian experience was that of continuous change—participation in the flow of divine creation —that, for him, involved geographical moves. Because, being under compulsion to accept enlargement through Jesus Christ, he literally could not keep still!

To reach such a verdict concerning this footloose Apostle is not to say that every other disciple must follow his path. Response to encounter with God is as individual as the human soul whose surrender puts him in the process of being rescued. But transforming response there must be— a process as well as an act of commitment. This process requires change, flow, growth, enlargement, and movement: spiritual "unfolding" which is likely to have tangible and visible effects. These may center in one's prayer life, use of the Bible, relationship with neighbors, treatment of family, or any other aspect of experience.

One does not have to push restlessly from Cos to Rhodes, and from Patara to Ptolemais, in order to be a disciple. It is not always necessary to go back to Jerusalem against the dictates of common sense. But the very concept of *follower* of Jesus Christ implies spiritual-intellectual movement. When that ceases for any length of time, when there is such superb adjustment to life conditions that stirrings cease and no foes agitate the crowd, it is hard to think that any man can continue to be a pilgrim in the process of moving toward a destination. In this connection, re-read Paul's speech in self-defense (22:3-21) and notice how greatly it is dominated by verbs of action!

Twelfth Day   **Read Acts 23-24**

Talk about "turmoil in the Church!" Anyone who feels that "peace at any price" is the route to spiritual power, in an individual life or a congregation or a culture, needs to read and re-read these chapters.

Notice that the force of Paul's witness was so powerful that the "proportional and opposite force" created in reaction to him sent forty men into ambush, under oath. Notice that the Roman official called out 470 men to escort a little tentmaker from one jail to another. Notice the deep symbolism in the prisoner's transfer from Jerusalem (the city of David) to Caesarea (the city of Caesar).

Reading this stirring story from the perspective of twenty centuries, we see quite clearly that God was at work in and through the troubles that descended on Paul's head. Can we—dare we—make a great leap of faith to the conclusion that, if we honestly continue in the process of surrender to God through Christ, our own troubles and turmoil may be sanctified, in order to play vital roles in the ongoing flow of Providence?

Thirteenth Day   **Read Acts 25-26**

After two years, the foes of Paul still seek his life. Far from having turned aside to other interests, their hatred of the prisoner is such that they are eager to arrange an ambush, since legal machinery has not served to send him to death. One of the very early official acts of the new Roman governor is to reopen this sensational case.

If any additional evidence concerning the dialectical movement of the young Church is needed, here it is! Evangelistic success has engendered opposition on a life-and-death scale. And it is the strange back-and-forward alternation of direction, the emptiness and impotence of human justice, that sends the most eloquent of evangelists into the capital city of the world!

Once more, we are persuaded that nothing can defeat the purpose of God. Providence pervades every aspect of existence. Ultimate victory is guaranteed—"written into the stars." Nothing—not even the Roman Empire—can stop God in his ceaseless creative work of elevating reborn men to heights no natural man can attain.

Paul's impassioned evangelistic plea, hardly a "defense" in the accepted sense, is a reiteration of one claim and one only: in Jesus of Nazareth divinity entered the stream of humanity as a fulfillment of the Covenant whose unfolding constitutes *salvation history.*

Fourteenth Day   Read Acts 27-28

Characteristically, Paul is soon the dominant personality in the band of travelers! In a vivid exemplification of central paradoxes of the Christian pilgrimage, the prisoner of Christ directs men whose human status is that of power and authority.

Visions, providential care, mighty works, and radical transformations continue. Paul arrives in Rome imprisoned "for the hope of Israel" (28:20)—nearly everywhere being accepted by Gentiles "outside the old Covenant" in a fashion not matched by Jews conscious of their special blessings under that Covenant.

Always—to the very end—it is the outsider, the alien, the consciously outcast one, who accepts God's offer of rescue. Always, in Rome as in Jerusalem, it is the insider, the established one, the favored of God, who rejects salvation because he is offended at the suggestion he needs it.

Here dramatized as a central issue in the Jewish-Christian struggle, the paradox of salvation is destined to remain

241

vital, but to take new forms, as an ostensibly "Christian" culture establishes new categories of "insiders" and "outsiders."

The Letter of Paul to the Romans

Toward the close of his third missionary journey, sometime in the period A.D. 56 to A.D. 59, Paul paused for a period. Writing from Corinth or nearby Cenchreae, he addressed himself to a congregation he had never visited—those Christians who had gathered in the capital of the world. This letter, then, is a sort of "visit by proxy." Representing as it does what might well have been the evangelist's only contact with fellow Christians in Rome, it contains the distilled essence of his entire witness.

This letter, therefore, is not only the most important of Paul's writings. It is also the first and, by many standards, the greatest of Christian theological tracts.

If it stood alone, it would be insignificant if not actually unintelligible. To read it without continually linking it with the entire body of Scripture—not only the Four Gospels, but also the writings that make up our Old Testament—is to distort the nature and overlook the purpose of the letter. For it is written by a one-time Jew who wishes to show that in Christ was fulfilled the age-old promise of God to his Chosen People. In many respects, consequently, the letter is as intensely Jewish as it is ardently Christian. More than any other one document of Christendom, it provides a theological foundation for our total missionary and evangelistic enterprise.

Impact of this letter (buttressed by prior acquaintance with the rest of the Bible) has been without parallel. Space permits me to mention only a few all-time notables who linked their conversion or intellectual-spiritual awakening with passages from it. St. Augustine, Martin Luther, and John Wesley are among the hosts of immortal leaders who found Romans to be the torch that served to set their lives afire.

We shall spend a day with each chapter of this unequaled letter. Even so, we shall hardly do more than take a quick look at a few of its emphases. Many readers and interpreters have spent years with it. Donald Grey Barnhouse, for example, concentrated much of his life upon verse-by-verse and word-by-word study. His commentary on Chapter 1 occupies 301 pages, while that on Chapter 5 runs to 416 pages. I myself have an unpublished book, a running exposition of The Letter to the Romans, that extends to more than 200 pages.

Perhaps our quick passage through the entire Bible will persuade you, in future years, to devote long periods to meditative reading of special portions of Scripture. If that should be the case, you can do nothing better than to spend a year with this Epistle, and other years with each of the Gospels, the Psalms, Genesis, the Revelation of St. John, Acts, I and II Corinthians, and so on.

Fifteenth Day   Read Romans 1

In Jesus Christ two streams met. One of them was that biological stream whose flow constitutes the story of the Chosen People. The other was the direct spiritual encounter between God and man. Through the first stream, the Son of David entered history. In the power received from the second, Jesus Christ rose from the dead to display the unlimited and unqualified nature of effects resulting from impact of the Creator upon the creature made in his image.

Here, in the first sentences of Paul's letter, we discover a new clue to the significance and power of the name, Jesus Christ. Simply to breathe that name is, in faith, to link humanity with divinity, to witness that the God-man is the

243

pivot on which the whole of man's existence is bound to turn.

It is as a captive to this faith that Paul writes. He is not his own master. On the contrary, he has entered such a state of surrender that he cannot fully think his own thoughts or write his own words; using his life as a channel, God flows through him in such fashion that it is God's thoughts and God's words that are made public when God's Apostle writes and speaks. This is of course the ideal in all prophecy and evangelism; no new relationship, it is simply a fresh instance of that which prevailed with stalwarts whose messages make up much of what is now the Old Testament. On lower levels and for briefer periods, it is such a state of "impassioned surrender" that every preacher, teacher, evangelist, missionary, and witness tries to achieve. Partly because Paul exemplifies this relationship in its finest form, his letters are unique in capacity to help others move toward it.

Speaking through his servant Paul, God warns that there are two paths that men can follow—and only two. One of them leads to God and to life; the other leads to less than God and to death. Every man must choose one of these paths, and there is no middle ground. To vary from "true north" by even a fraction of a degree is to follow a course that will, over a period of years, take the pilgrim far from the one destination where abundant life may be accepted as a divine gift.

Whatever else it may do, this stirring chapter explodes the modern myth by which the comfortable road of compromise and easy conformity is the way to life on the part of the institutional Church, a local congregation, or an individual seeker after God. The religious quest is rigorous, demanding, exacting—and the tension never eases. Always, the creature who seeks his Creator is confronted by a cosmic choice, an either/or he cannot by any means escape for a single instant of his existence.

244

Sixteenth Day   Read Romans 2

Judgment is the prerogative of God, who will assess every soul. It is both rebellious and impious for any man to usurp the divine role and try to sit in judgment upon his fellow men. To survey one's own shortcomings and sins is to become involved in so absorbing an activity that there is no time left for criticizing or condemning others.

It is not life under the law of Moses, or outside it, that will determine the fate of the soul, but the individual's relationship with God. For, whether reared within the fellowship of the People of the Covenant or among pagans who never heard of that Covenant, one who sins (and everyone does) is sure to be condemned for that sin.

Once more we modern Christians discover, as we frequently did in reading the Four Gospels, that it is easier to make first-century applications than twentieth-century ones. We are prone to condemn the blind and rebellious Jews who trusted in an inherited status and so rejected the rescue offered by Jesus Christ. But we find it hard to see that one who has grown up in Sunday school and church, who may take an active part in the official life of a congregation, can be playing the role of the "Jew" whom Paul castigates here (especially Verses 17-29).

The heart of this chapter is a challenge to come into a personal relationship with God through Christ, rather than rely upon an inherited status or the favorable judgment of one's fellow men. Such is the nature of the religious institution, regardless of the name by which it may be called or the century in which it flourishes, that men are perpetually in danger of paying homage to "the Temple" or "the Church," instead of the God to whom both only point.

Seventeenth Day   **Read Romans 3**

If you have never examined a New Testament that indicates quotations from the sacred books of the Jews, this is a good time to do so. Verses 10-18 represent a mosaic of brief passages from the Old Testament, with the Book of Psalms being most heavily represented. Weymouth's modern-language translation of the New Testament shows such quotations in capital letters; with it, you can thumb through Gospels and Epistles and, at a glance, discover the basic interrelatedness of the Old Testament and the New.

Using the sacred writings of his people as a source of authority with which to support his arguments that are also rooted in dynamic personal encounter with God through Christ, Paul here presents the chief idea of the entire letter. Men are "justified" (acquitted in the sight of God the Judge) in only one fashion, he insists. It is futile to seek righteousness through keeping the law, however exalted that law may be. "Justification" comes as a gift, made available through the self-giving of God through Christ. No man can earn or achieve or win such a state of justification. He enters it only through the door of belief-powered participation in the cosmic sacrifice performed at Calvary.

"Justification by faith" became the battle cry of the Protestant Reformation. If you find it difficult to see why anyone should become excited about so abstract a theological idea, I must, in honesty, warn you that the indictment rests upon you and not Romans 3. For the unqualified verdict of the ages witnesses that here we have the distilled essence of Christianity. Neither Paul's letter nor his central doctrinal proposition is subject to serious challenge from the Christian perspective. Should you be inclined to object to the line of thought presented in today's reading, or if you find it dull or irrelevant, here is proof positive that you are in great need of deeper acquaintance with the Bible, and more transforming personal encounter with the God-man through whom men may enter a state of rescue and accept righteousness that cannot be achieved by any means whatever.

Eighteenth Day   Read Romans 4

Virtually the whole of first-century Jewish thought rested on the foundation of confidence in the law. It was through keeping the letter of the law, insisted the great religious teachers, that a man achieved righteousness. Since the law was regarded as the royal road to divine approval, it was natural that scholars should devote their lives to interpretation of it.

At least to his own satisfaction Paul did away with the whole legal structure with a single new interpretation. Abraham, symbol of the God-seeker who lived under law, had always been presumed to have gained his righteousness through the law. He did nothing of the sort, according to Paul. Rather, he became righteous through faith, before he acquired that legal righteousness symbolized by circumcision (marking him as a member of the Covenant people).

Viewed from the distance of centuries, Paul's argument is not especially strong. Nor is it easy for us to see why he, or anyone else, should become excited about so academic a question.

Rephrase the issue in modern terms, and it takes on a different character. Does a person become righteous by being born to churchgoing parents, who see that he is baptized, enrolled in a membership class, and eventually led to take the vows of the Church? Or is something less tangible required? Is church membership the royal road to heaven, or is it simply an outward process through which to seal and communicate inward changes? Cast in such terms, the issue of Abraham's claim to righteousness becomes strangely pertinent!

247

Nineteenth Day   **Read Romans 5**

It is faith and faith alone by which any seeker enters into the state of righteousness that makes him "just" in the sight of God, Paul asserts. But though this faith is spiritual and wholly intangible, it needs as substantial a channel as possible. Put in another fashion, man requires a handle he can grasp in his hand even though the door he seeks to open is spiritual.

Jesus Christ, wholly divine and entire human, is God's answer to human need. Because he was flesh of our flesh and bone of our bone, we can reach out our hands and touch him—grasp hold of the divinity incarnate in him. Because Jesus Christ was the creative agent of the Creator, "very God of very God," the Father himself was involved in the world-changing events of Calvary.

Every human can identify himself with Adam and, as it were, take part in his sin and its consequences. By the same token, every human can so believe in Jesus Christ that he "pours himself into the life of the Saviour" and *thereby himself suffers and pays the penalty of sin by death upon the Cross.*

Theologians refer to this line of reasoning as "a doctrine of redemption." It is only one of several historic ways of trying to put the mystery of redemption into words and thought-forms that seem "reasonable" to the human mind. Useful when employed as a tool, this doctrine (and all other theological systems) becomes barren or even pernicious if elevated to first place in the religious quest. Like the Jewish legal system, theology loses its power when treated as an end in itself instead of a means to the greater end of transforming personal encounter with the God to whom law and theology haltingly witness.

Twentieth Day   **Read Romans 6**

Belief-oriented "identification" with Jesus Christ extends to the special events of his life: his baptism, death, and resurrection. Provided that we surrender to him, his victories become our own—literally, not figuratively.

It is here that we catch a glimpse, from a fresh perspective, of the supreme significance of the empty tomb. For in his mastery over death, the Saviour, who was fully human as well as completely divine, "opened the door" for every man who will enter it. He proved himself victor over sin, and thereby invited all men to shed the limitations of humanity and enter the state of justification (righteousness in God's sight).

Of course, offer of rescue through Jesus Christ is not to be taken as an invitation to engage in flagrant sin! Precisely here we find one of the great danger zones of Christian thought. Many a zealous and eager person who has been transformed by encounter with God has been tempted to feel "safe for life." We could devote not simply this month, but an entire year to discussion of positive and negative aspects of ideas symbolized under such names as "sanctification," "the second blessing," and "the gift of the Holy Spirit." Whatever the language used, it is spiritually dangerous to conclude that one who has been rescued is thereby made invulnerable. It is some consolation to find that instead of being a modern heresy, the first century saw the rise of this persistent tendency toward error on the part of persons who had deep and genuine religious experiences and, as a result, distorted the whole idea of salvation.

Twenty-first Day   **Read Romans 7**

Capacity of the believer to "participate" in the life of Jesus Christ extends even to his relationship with the religious law. One who has died and been raised into new life, as is the case with all who truly yield themselves to their divine-human Saviour, is actually a new person. Old relationships have dissolved, and former bonds no longer restrain him. That being the case, it is foolish as well as dangerous to give too great a place to observance of the law. Every elevation of "good works" through the law is a way of reducing one's absolute trust in the redemptive work of Jesus Christ.

Paul's tangled and tortuous arguments at this point are not attractive to the modern mind. But his conclusion is as fresh and startling as the day it was penned. You and I, along with his first-century readers, know from experience that the religious quest actually is a warfare. We know, too, that neither our own strength nor the power of a socially-accepted set of approved practices is adequate for victory. In order to win, you and I must have help—divine help. We must accept rescue rather than work frenziedly for achievement. Once we accept that verdict and yearn for a gift of grace, in the act of yearning we gain it through our great deliverer: Jesus Christ.

Twenty-second Day   **Read Romans 8**

God is Creator and sustainer of all that is. In this sense, the universe and all its parts is a coherent whole. It is a *uni*-verse and not a *multi*-verse. But within the ordered system and many or all of its parts there is a state of tension such that a double or divided relationship may be seen. For example, man is both flesh and spirit at the same time. In the same fashion, the unified flow that constitutes "all time" may be seen as divided into "this present time" and "the time to come."

Part of the glory of Christianity, Paul asserts, lies in the fact that belief in Jesus Christ (both God and man, in spite of being one person) helps man tip the scales in every divided situation. In his own power, man is incapable of elevating spirit above flesh; through identifying himself with his divine-human Saviour, mortal man leaps the chasm and succeeds in centering his mind on the spirit. In precisely the same fashion, God's work of rescue serves to lift man out of "the sufferings of this present time" (Verse 18) and transport him into a realm of glory that, strictly speaking, is yet to come.

It is this strange and more-than-logical work of rescue through Christ that enables mere man to rise above all the stresses and tribulations of his mortal existence. Nothing in the world—no member of any pair of opposites, "neither death, nor life, . . . nor things present, nor things to come, . . . nor height, nor depth" (Verses 38-39)—can defeat or even hinder the man who lives "in Christ." Through Christ Jesus our Lord, we puny space- and time- and flesh-bound mortals burst all bonds and scale every barrier to become "more than conquerors"! (Verse 37). Here—right now—is the glorious reward for surrender!

Twenty-third Day   **Read Romans 9**

Chapter 9 represents Paul's radical re-interpretation of the idea of the Covenant. Grieving over the failure of his people to accept the long-awaited Saviour, he arrives at a startling conclusion. It is not the Israel of biology, but the Israel of the spirit to whom the promises of God pertain. This point of view lifts the whole Covenant relationship to a new level. It makes the divine-human bond potentially universal, rather than local and national.

Viewed from this perspective, neither the Covenant nor relationships deriving from it may be explained. Man's role is to accept what God has graciously established. That is to

251

say, faith and not works must be pursued in order to enter into righteousness. We come into a state of creative union with God by following the route of surrender, rather than that of clawing our way upward until, by virtue of our own effort, we stand shoulder-to-shoulder with him.

Twenty-fourth Day   **Read Romans 10**

All the age-old distinctions between Jew and Gentile have now faded away, Paul insists. Doubtless the sharp lines between the two groups were essential to God's purpose of sending his Son through a prepared people. But now that divinity and humanity have become one in Jesus Christ, every human is in precisely the same situation. Any and all who enter belief-oriented surrender and who call on God through the Saviour will be saved.

Now and always, God requires messengers and witnesses who will stir men into listening and responding. But no man has any excuse. Why, the very heavens are evangelists who shout the glory of their Creator day and night through all the ages! (*See* Ps. 19, whose total message is suggested by Paul's brief quotation in Verse 18.)

Twenty-fifth Day   **Read Romans 11**

Israel's failure, though real, is neither so absolute nor so lasting as it appears from a surface look. There are some from within the People of the Covenant who have accepted Jesus as the Christ. Indeed, without such a response, the divine breakthrough would have failed for lack of heralds.

Again, rejection of Jesus Christ by institutional Israel served as the lever with which God could thrust his Son into the Gentile world. Let Gentile converts take heed at this point, and guard against the fatal error of spiritual pride. Instead of boasting over their superiority to stubborn Jews, zealous adherents of the New Church must recognize that God is using them as instruments of his larger purposes.

Sublime movements of Providence are upon so large a scale that men cannot perceive them, and tend to get caught up in those few details they can distinguish. To avoid that idolatry which stems from making comparisons between ourselves and other men, we need to focus our attention upon the almighty and inscrutable Creator whom we can never fully know, but whom we can praise with all our hearts and minds!

Twenty-sixth Day   **Read Romans 12**

Paul's reasoning is upon a high level; this letter is intensely theological, in the sense that it deals largely with issues that men cannot resolve by experiment or logical analysis. But it is also very practical. For a man's beliefs will govern his actions, every time.

A person who thinks he can get to heaven by living a trifle better life than his neighbors will deal with them in the light of that belief. And one who is utterly convinced that both he and his neighbors must depend upon God's unearned grace cannot avoid conforming his daily life to his theological position!

In dealing with a document like Paul's Letter to the Romans, it is a temptation to center upon such "practical" passages as this chapter. But this chapter is a spontaneous by-product of Paul's primary message. It does not stand alone, but has organic bonds with earlier chapters. In order really to grasp his interpretation of "love in action," we must first glimpse the height and depth of his love for Jesus Christ as redeemer.

To begin with "good works" and move toward deeper surrender is to proceed along the spiritual highway in the wrong direction. Much of the emptiness of many modern Christian movements lies precisely here. We have tried to persuade men to love their neighbors for the sake of those neighbors, when surrender to God on the part of men and neighbors would automatically establish a new man-to-man relationship.

Twenty-seventh Day   **Read Romans 13**

The gulf between "the flesh" and "the spirit" is absolute, Paul insists. To place any value upon things of the flesh is thereby to reduce one's devotion to things of the spirit, and hence to fail in life's grand quest.

If this line of reasoning is accepted, it follows that the successes and failures, comforts and sufferings, of our material life are trifling and transient—not worth fighting over. Instead of agitating ourselves over such issues as conduct of masters, civil authorities, and tax collectors, we need to elevate the law of love into such prominence that everything else becomes unimportant.

Did Paul anticipate the long debates that would rage over this chapter? Perhaps he did. For he undoubtedly recognized that he was making impossible demands by insisting that Christians "make no provision for the flesh" (Verse 14). Once more, by a roundabout path, we are face to face with a trumpet call to justification by faith! For the man who tries to subdue the flesh completely is bound to fail; in his failure, he can look up and out and, in "a flash of intuition," recognize that righteousness cannot be won or achieved—and is reached by the road of surrender rather than striving!

Twenty-eighth Day   Read Romans 14

Tolerance of others' views and practices, like many other everyday attitudes, is not an end product but a by-product. Every person who sees himself standing under divine judgment will recognize that God is the judge who sits over every case. Conscious of being the accused and guilty one, he will not presume to pass judgment upon his fellow culprits—and "tolerance" will develop as a by-product.

Instead of condemning others in order to praise ourselves, we need to be spiritually sensitive, so that we may avoid doing things that cause others to fall. Even when I feel that no moral issue is involved, I need to abstain from any practice that raises moral problems for other persons. To guard my conduct in this respect is a full-time job that leaves no time for sitting in judgment of my fellow men.

Twenty-ninth Day   Read Romans 15

The pilgrimage toward the City of God is a lonely one. Every man must pursue it for himself, and no substitutes are permitted. Belief in the redemptive power of Jesus Christ and "identification" with him as Saviour is so highly personal that its deepest meanings cannot even be communicated.

Yet the pilgrimage is also as fully social as it is individual. (Here we discover one more instance of the "double nature," or dualism, that God has woven into his creation.)

No man, not even a St. Paul, makes his journey without contact with others. Some of them went before him. By their influence, and the legacy they left behind, they helped shape the course of his life. Other persons are fellow pilgrims to whom the Apostle gives a helping hand, gaining greater strength every time he assists some fallen one to his feet. Still others will come in other centuries, inspired and guided by the religious experience of a first-century tent-maker who excelled nearly all men in his capacity to make public the fruits of his quest for God.

Fully as much as they need him, Paul needs "the Gentiles" to whom he writes. Witnessing is the other side of hearing, and a rounded pattern of spiritual growth requires that the pilgrim be involved in both.

Thirtieth Day   Read Romans 16

Almost, one wonders why this chapter should be included in the New Testament. It deals with persons whose names are labels for compartments of ignorance. Except for the fact that they appear here, most of these names mean noth-ing at all to us. Clearly, we are tempted to say, such a pas-sage has no significance; it is simply an appendage—and an almost unintelligible one—to the body of Paul's letter.

But reflection suggests another verdict.

Here is proof positive that the "author of Christian theol-ogy" is deeply concerned with *persons*. Here is the most extensive and convincing piece of evidence in any of his letters, witnessing to the fact that he sees himself as a bridge over which specific individuals (and not a vague "humanity in general") can walk in order to find trans-forming encounter with the Saviour who is in the process of making Paul a "saint."

This evangelist is daily—hourly—concerned with the im-mortal souls of Junias and Ampliatus, with all their faults and failings! His one life-dominating concern is to persuade them to enter new life, through the divine-human Saviour. All his theological arguments, fine-spun as they sometimes are, have emerged as by-products of his passionate desire that folk like Aristobulus' family and Paul's relative Herodion should so surrender to God, through Christ, that the Creator will enable them to trample Satan under their feet!

Individual men and women, made in the likeness of God and having potential for godliness as a fruit of divine rescue, have evoked The Letter to the Romans. It is for precisely such persons that God sent the supreme messenger to whom Paul points. This is the reason the Old Testament and the New Testament exist: in order that ordinary mortals— namely, you and I—may be impelled to enter that state of faith through which God can provide rescue of such order that we may become blameless in his sight.

From I and II Corinthians through Philemon

Paul's Letters to the Church at Corinth

Julius Caesar himself founded the modern city of Corinth in 46 B.C., and made it the capital of the province of Achaia. Located at the end of a narrow isthmus that linked Europe with the Peloponnesus, it was a major trading and manufacturing center even under the Phoenicians. As a Roman center, it played a role roughly comparable to that of modern Singapore.

Paul made his first visit to the city about the year A.D. 50, and remained for eighteen months. He returned at least once, five or six years later, and wrote at least four letters to the congregation he had founded there.

Partly because they are highly personal, the little "books" of I and II Corinthians are as vivid as they are direct. Paul makes no effort to organize a systematic treatise, such as that which makes up his Letter to the Romans. Instead, he deals with whatever practical issues happen to occupy him at the moment.

Filled with everyday advice about personal Christian service and the organized life of the Church, these short documents dispel the myth that all early Christians were saints! These Corinthians were folk like us. Had it not been for their arguments and dissensions, theological errors, and abuses in public worship, Paul would have had no occasion to rebuke, correct, and encourage them in the documents that also speak directly to us in our present-day attempts to follow Christ individually and as members of congregations.

First Day   **Read I Corinthians 1-2**

Individually, those whom Paul addresses here are persons consciously engaged in pilgrimage toward the City of God. Collectively, they form a church that is an outpost of the Kingdom. In spite of their high calling, these men and women are weak—prone to fail and fall. That is, they are exactly like the persons who make up congregations today!

Divisions among the Christians grow out of the fact that many of them have elevated human leaders to first place in their thought, thereby reducing the fervor of their devotion to Jesus Christ. They have tried to master the secrets of the faith—reduce the sublime promises of the Good News to human dimensions. In doing so, they have turned their backs upon the goal to which the Christian pilgrimage leads and have actually walked away from the Cross, which is *never* comprehensible.

There are two realms of knowing, Paul reminds his readers. In doing so, he simply repeats in fresh language an emphasis that runs through the Bible from beginning to end. Worldly wisdom is distinct from spiritual sensitivity. Consequently, the meaning and value that a person discovers in any situation will depend upon the mood and goals with which he assesses it. Spiritual truths constitute "a secret and hidden wisdom of God" (2:7), which can never be reduced to the level of ordinary flesh-oriented knowledge without major distortion. That is why paradox is the language of faith.

The problem is somewhat like that of making maps. In order to project a round globe upon a flat piece of paper, an orderly method of distortion is necessary. When the geography involved is that of the solar system or the universe, the problem is even more complex. There simply is no way to devise a "map of the solar system" that is accurate for more than a few selected factors. Just so, it is impossible to put the glorious truths of the Gospel into logical and prosaic language; in order to "know" the good gifts of God through Christ, one must turn his back upon human wisdom and rely upon seeing spiritual things with the eye of the spirit.

Second Day   **Read I Corinthians 3-4**

To call one's self a disciple of Paul (or any other man) is to insist upon remaining in the childhood of faith. All missionaries and evangelists and pastors are merely agents—spokesmen proclaiming a message not their own. Ideally, the witness so empties himself that he functions as a channel for the flow of continuing self-revelation by God. Practically, so exalted a state is rare and brief, for the witness himself is caught up in the stream of humanity. That is precisely why Christians need to avoid forming parties and putting their trust in mere men (or their doctrinal systems or religious organizations or patterns of religious experience) instead of the Saviour to whom their leaders only point.

A leader—even a St. Paul—is to be regarded simply as a steward who, for a little while, has been entrusted with a few of the mysteries offered to men by God. He is *not* a master of knowledge. On the contrary, in order to function at his highest, he must himself be captive of his message—directed by it, rather than controlling it.

To discover this fundamental aspect of human knowledge and leadership and live in the light of that discovery is to conquer pride and the flesh and "live according to scripture" (4:6).

Third Day　　　　　　　　**Read I Corinthians 5-7**

Paradoxically, these chapters are at the same time chastening and encouraging. They warn us that human nature is the same in every epoch. Just think! Men and women whose ears throbbed with burning words from the lips of Paul himself descended from their mountain peaks of religious experience to engage in lawsuits and immorality!

At the same time, these chapters offer hope. For it was from such weak vessels as those who are chided here that God forged the mighty apostolic Church!

Clearly, the Church partakes of the double nature of humans who form it. It is of God and dedicated to God; yet men and women are the only raw material from which God can form saints, through the Church. So it is at one and the same time the most sublime and exalted of all institutions, and a context in which humans can offer proof positive that sin is indeed universal.

That is, the Church echoes the impossible demands of the Saviour whose message she seeks to transmit and to whom she points. The Church calls men to live in a fashion impossible to flesh-bound creatures. It is for this reason that such matters as sex and marriage are basic. To stress Christian doctrine in the abstract, and neglect to emphasize practical purity and control, is to pervert the Good News. For it is precisely the high demands of the Church which serve to convict us of our sins and failures and call us, once more, to seek divine grace in order to be lifted into that state of "perfection" we can never enter by dint of our own efforts. Always, the Church *must* require of its own more than they can possibly expect to achieve.

Fourth Day　　　　　　　　**Read I Corinthians 8-9**

Knowledge, in the sense of consciousness of being an expert, is exceedingly dangerous! Possession of it is likely to persuade one into a state of pride, in which he trusts himself instead of divine grace. If the "wise" man does not fall into that error, he may commit the sin of ignoring his influence upon other persons.

Perhaps the closest modern parallel to the first-century issue is the use of tobacco, by persons who consider themselves good followers of Christ. Can you succeed in following the Pauline reasoning, as it applies to the present-day controversy? In the light of Paul's analysis, regardless of whether or not you accept the Apostle's conclusions, do you think a minister (of any faith) blameless in using tobacco? What about a church officer? an "ordinary" church member, holding no office but under a vow of fidelity to Christ?

No matter what your conclusions may be, you will probably find a personal challenge in Paul's personal confession. As a witness who speaks under divine compulsion, he never achieves a state of complacency, or even ease. His Christian life is a constant struggle. He never finds it possible to rest on his laurels. He is continually revising his judgments and re-examining his personal conduct.

Anyone who adopts the Apostle's attitude in this respect will be perpetually bombarded with questions and problems. When the tobacco issue is settled to his satisfaction, an equally vexatious one of different sort will take its place!

Fifth Day   **Read I Corinthians 10-11**

It is almost absurdly simple to see the fallacies involved in idolatry—as practiced by someone else. But it is fearfully hard to escape paying homage to less than God—and, regardless of its form, such prostration before any finite goal or set of values constitutes idolatry.

All men of every epoch are tempted and tested. It is a temptation to look back to some period which seems to constitute "the good old days," and to conclude that it was comparatively easy to seize the prize of life in such a simple, pious period. Actually this is nonsense. Christians of first-century Corinth faced problems just like ours today! Specific ways of falling away from God differ from one epoch to another, but the ultimate choice between serving God and serving other-than-God is the same in every generation.

As with individual seekers, so with the Church. Every age has its own pressing issues. In a day when the question of headgear for women seems trivial and academic, the matter of interracial worship is not. Whether in the first century or the twentieth, the highest and holiest heritage of the Church (no less than the Supper of the Lord) invites abuse as well as use.

Once more, we are reminded that even in the house of the Lord—perhaps especially there—we retain our human limitations. We are creatures upon whom the divine image has been stamped. We have feet of clay, but our hearts yearn for the heavens. Perpetually dissatisfied with ourselves, we are prone to try to win victory by dint of striving, instead of as a result of accepting divine rescue. To see ourselves as poor, blind, and naked, even in the band of pilgrims that forms the Church, is to recognize anew that something must be done *for* us as well as *by* us. Though the term does not occur in these chapters, here is a vivid example of the necessity for "justification by faith"!

Sixth Day   **Read I Corinthians 12**

Because we take our humanity with us into the worship and work of the Church, we are prone to engage in idolatry before the very altar of the Lord. That is, we find it difficult or impossible to avoid putting God in second place, by virtue of concentrating our interest and attention upon such matters as forms of worship and varieties of spiritual service.

One person likes formality and solemnity in his worship; because it seems to him to be the most effective path toward God, he is easily persuaded that he should insist upon use of this path by fellow pilgrims. If his insistence reaches the level at which he attaches more importance to ways of worship than to the God of whom worship witnesses, he has become an idolater. Worst of all, he may feel that any person who refuses his form of idolatry is a blind and stubborn sinner who will be condemned in the Judgment!

This monumental chapter is a prelude to the more familiar Chapter 13. Beautiful as the latter is, and comforting, in some respects it is less important for Christian thought than is Chapter 12. For many of the sad divisions of Christendom stem from the very errors that Paul underscores here. A limb or an organ of the body which makes up a congregation or a denomination becomes proud and self-centered. Soon there is a demand that the rest of the body pay homage and come into conformity. Fresh division is the inevitable result.

Tolerance is here demanded, of course. But it is not tolerance for the sake of tolerance. Rather, it is tolerance that grows out of unswerving concern for continuing divine rescue. That person or group who is consciously under the Judgment is not likely to sit in judgment upon others. He who knows himself to be perpetually failing and falling recognizes that he is no better than those who have stumbled over other obstacles and fallen in different ways.

Provided that we unite in our zeal to serve God through Christ, our individual differences becomes unimportant. This applies not only to "spiritual gifts," but also to racial, educational, and economic factors. When we become truly united in our surrender to God through Christ, all of our differences will dwindle into insignificance, and we will cease our squabbling.

Seventh Day   **Read I Corinthians 13-14**

I Corinthians 13 is among the chapters most favored for memorization. Like the greatest of the Psalms, it is powerful in its own right. But like every other passage of Scripture, it is most meaningful when read in context.

Early Christians who broke away from the restraints of tradition and religious law were impelled to give great weight to religious experience. Personality make-up is so varied that men and women of equal piety gave quite different expression to their surrender. Those who succeeded in reaching such a state of ecstasy that their speech became incoherent began to boast of their superior devotion. It was this practical problem—namely, the merits gained by "speaking in tongues"—that stirred Paul to write about the superiority of love over any and all other spiritual goals.

Here is a focus of an inescapable dilemma. Institutions cannot function without structure. Men who throw off the rule of religious law (ancient or modern, Jewish or Christian) find themselves under the necessity of establishing a new system of authority. Enthusiastic over some potent gift of the spirit, such as "speaking in tongues," devotees confuse cause with effects and begin to seek spiritual ecstasy for its own sake, rather than as a by-product of encounter with the risen Christ. So the end result—still another variety of idolatry, centered in customs and practices of a given group of seekers—becomes pernicious. The last state of these folk is worse than the first.

Eighth Day   **Read I Corinthians 15-16**

Neither speaking in tongues nor any other gift of the spirit is of the least importance unless the seeking one continues in a state of surrender to Christ. It is what Christ has done for him, not what the disciple himself accomplishes, that is paramount. Having given himself into the power of death (paying to death the price demanded of every human) and having risen again from the dead, the divine Christ offers life to every human who will accept it *in him.*

No man can offer an acceptable intellectual exposition of this mystery. Paul himself is not for an instant under the delusion that he is here explaining immortality. Rather, he is using metaphors and figures that point toward aspects of life that, seized through faith, defy all man's attempts at full understanding and explanation. There is a mystery here—the mystery that gives mortal man potential for transcending all the limitations of mortality. Here is the grand prize of the Christian endeavor, the reward for entering into surrender that makes rescue actual instead of potential. It is for this that the whole of *salvation history* has been ordained.

But, glory over cosmic victories and ecstasy at the prospect of achieving enduringness and significance like that of the Creator do not relieve the creature of present responsibility. Instead of reducing the importance of "practical" good works in this life, the sure hope of heaven magnifies them. Nowhere in Scripture is there a more vivid example of the fact that man, the individual who stands alone before God, is also in organic relationship with his fellow men. Chapter 16 affirms that to be human means to have a set of bonds with other humans who form social systems, organize churches and other institutions, and depend absolutely upon one another as well as upon God. Man must enter the Kingdom in company with other men, or not at all.

Ninth Day Read II Corinthians 1-3

Humans, including those who band together in the Church, are at one and the same time totally individual and completely social. It is therefore not strange, but natural, that the society of the redeemed should reflect both the limitations and the glory of man.

For the Church to exist, there must be an evangelist and a group of converts; the relationship between pastor and people is analogous, but not identical. But, in the pastor-people as well as in the evangelist-converts relationship, mutual interdependence is the rule. Each depends heavily upon the other. Paul could never have become what he is in a spiritual vacuum. Lacking the influence of those to whom he witnesses in general, and of the Corinthians in particular, he would have developed along quite different lines.

As a witness, he never forgets the urgency of his divine commission (1:21-22; 2:17; 3:6). He is sent to persons who are so typical that they are prone to become involved in quarrels and divisions—but who also form a "divine letter," a sort of "living epistle" written by God to the world (3:1-3).

In practice, therefore, the Church is as paradoxical as the Gospel from which it springs. It is headed toward heaven, but walks with feet of clay!

Tenth Day   Read II Corinthians 4-6

Paul, the witness, sees himself as a channel through which divine messages may flow. He is utterly convinced that they actually do proceed through him, in the sense that his words are not fully his own. This is the source of his power —and perhaps a key to some clashes with converts and fellow workers.

Were absolute victory possible, he consoles himself, we should cease to depend upon God. So even our failures and afflictions can be turned to good ends! Through dedication to eternal spiritual goals, all temporal and finite issues— including health vs. sickness and affluence vs. poverty— become secondary.

Notice that closing lines of Chapter 6 again reveal a man shaped by life-long absorption with the Scriptures. He does not so much "quote" sentences and phrases as he spontaneously uses Biblical language to express ideas he wishes to convey! Few of us in the modern Church will ever achieve such unstudied skill, but every one of us can facilitate the life-giving work of the Book of Life.

Eleventh Day   **Read II Corinthians 7-9**

It is a source of considerable comfort to discover that Paul himself has to give considerable attention to a vexatious problem of Church administration—namely, special offerings! His letters, which soar so high into the heavens, are yet linked with earth. Instead of serving the risen Lord in an ideal situation where there are no mundane problems to vex him, he is working in a "normal" context. That is, the congregations are plagued with frictions, and the need for money is so great that the evangelist is forced to put on the pressure!

Viewed from this perspective, the life situation in which Paul works is seen as playing a vital part in his transmission of the Good News that has made a new man of him. Because the goals and values linked with that Good News are wholly spiritual, all material barriers are temporary hindrances only. That is the basis on which the much-troubled and always-beset evangelist can exult: "With all our affliction, I am overjoyed" (7:4).

Here the disciple of the risen Lord, who has demonstrated his victory over death and all evil, offers a convincing case history. That radiant faith which is reflected in many of the Psalms is actually an achievable way of life! In and through the search for holiness that is grounded in "the fear of God" (7:1), we puny mortals actually can achieve peace, victory, and joy here and now!

268

Twelfth Day   **Read II Corinthians 10-11**

Who is this impassioned witness whose words still ring after twenty centuries? Why did God choose to use this special channel through which to pour messages that form about one-third of the New Testament?

His name we know well enough: Saul, who became Paul. And fragments of his personal history are preserved here and elsewhere. But what of the man himself—the inner self?

Clearly, he does not think of himself as eloquent. He is "unskilled in speaking" (11:6), and stands a bit in awe of some noted colleague "who is famous among all the churches for his preaching of the gospel" (8:18). (Who that "famous one" might be, I confess that I have no idea!)

Measured according to any material scale of values, the messenger named Paul, who feels himself commissioned by God, has made a very poor showing. His famous and familiar summary (11:23-33) reads like an account of failure rather than of success.

Yet in the whole history of the Christian movement, Paul stands head and shoulders above every other witness. Why? Precisely because of the depth of his surrender, the unqualified passion of his ceaseless search. It is not so much what he *does* that counts, as what he *is*. Failing and falling, he yet remains eternally true to the one purpose of so serving God through Christ that he is an instrument of *salvation history*. He manages so to empty himself of self that he becomes a vessel in which the water of grace may be conveyed to men. He is a human agent in the divine-human process for which the world was created—namely, accomplishment of the marriage between God and man (11:2), by which the creature made in the divine image is lifted to the level of the Creator himself.

Thirteenth Day   **Read II Corinthians 12-13**

Paradox and contradiction is the mood of these closing pages. In the *salvation history* whose stream includes Paul of Tarsus, you, and me, there is always an "intermingling" —which sometimes baffles us. Power comes through weakness rather than strength (12:9, 13:4). Victory is won only when the smell of defeat is strong in the air (12:20-21). "A thorn in the flesh" may prove to be a potent instrument of grace (12:7).

Conscious dependence upon God is absolutely essential to spiritual growth. Israel's history provides abundant instances of conspicuous failure on the part of the Chosen People during times of peace and prosperity—and numerous cases of re-entrance into the Covenant in times of failure and defeat.

As with nations, so with men. That is why it is foolish and dangerous for any seeker to boast about his victories. Incredibly, weakness, which requires one to accept grace, is the only valid ground for spiritual pride! It is this grace that Paul invokes in his benediction, which is destined to mark "finis" to his correspondence with his so-human converts in Corinth.

St. Paul's Short Letters to Congregations

Like the longer letters of the missionary evangelist, Paul's short letters to the churches grow out of life situations. For the most part, they are evoked by problems. Had all gone smoothly with Paul, he would have had no reason to put into writing the arguments and exhortations and promises that make up the bulk of these documents.

The very fact that these brief letters reflect the kinds of crises and opportunities that still confront congregations and individual seekers for God through Christ is a source of great consolation. We are perpetually tempted to think that we have fallen upon evil times; that the clock of history is running backward; that men are day by day getting worse and worse. Such a pessimistic verdict concerning God, man, and the universe is thoroughly demolished by a sensitive reading of messages sent by Paul to the Ephesians, Philippians, Colossians, and others of their day. Even in the period when the glory of the resurrection was still bright in the eyes of men, those who heeded God's call and tried to obey it were still . . . men!

In this aspect of the first-century situation, we discover a fresh opportunity to dwell upon the central message of Paul. Without exception, all of us, in every epoch, need something done *for* us as well as *by* us. We must strive with all our might to live as God demands, but in the midst of our striving we must also be forever in the act of yielding. Not one of us—now or then—stands blameless in the sight of God. But each of us can accept from him, through Jesus Christ, the righteousness we can never earn. In the first century as in the twentieth, the unfolding of the Covenant requires belief-powered turning to God for mighty acts which transform and literally "make new" those mortals who succeed in accepting what the Father offers.

Galatians

Fourteenth Day   Read Galatians 1-3

Never fall into that erroneous point of view according to which the Gospel is altogether easy and entirely simple. For its ease and simplicity are matched and accompanied by its difficulty and profundity. Its truths are not so much to be learned, as accepted (1:12). Even a band of first-century zealots converted under the preaching of the Apostle Paul quickly begin to pervert the Gospel! (1:6-7; 3:1-5). Even Peter and Paul find it impossible to agree with one another on all major issues! (2:11-14).

Paul's own spiritual biography reveals the fact that God confers his best gifts only to those who are forever seeking and struggling, never complacent. Indeed, it is essential to

271

identify one's self with the Saviour, even to the point of participating with him in the fearful agony of Calvary (2:19-20).

In and through acceptance of divine grace offered by God's own Son, the ancient Covenant is fulfilled. It is not canceled, as logic seems to indicate. Rather, it gains new depth and invites participation by a new and larger "chosen people." Thus, the way faith supersedes law is the key not only to the work of Christ, but also to the centuries-long unfolding of *salvation history* in its entirety. It is for this that the events recorded in the Old Testament took place. It is for this that God created the world and put in it a creature shaped after his own image.

Fifteenth Day   **Read Galatians 4-6**

Saul, so long a zealous student of the religious law, has become Paul—convinced that nothing a man can do will cause him to earn or win the commendation of God. The Old Covenant of the law, symbolized by Hagar (4:24) was not so much "false" as incomplete or immature. It was a preparatory stage—and an essential one. Without it, men could never have been made ready to enter the New Covenant erected from constituents that included both the Old Covenant and Jesus' death upon the Cross.

Now that men are confronted with an invitation to enter the New Covenant relationship, the choice is not between law and freedom—but between the flesh and the spirit. To enter into a state of continuous striving for larger surrender to the spirit is to accept the invitation to Covenant. He who does that participates in the events of Calvary, so that he is in the process of "crucifying" flesh-born yearnings (5:24). To do this is to sow eternal life (6:8).

This is the victory. It is for this—and nothing less—that you and I were born. Here is our reason for being.

Ephesians

Sixteenth Day   **Read Ephesians 1-3**

God's choice is the central fact of the universe. That choice was made "in the beginning," but it includes human freedom. Therefore the primeval choice of God becomes actual, rather than potential, only through purposeful responses of individual men and women.

Exercise of the option to "choose God" involves acceptance of unearned grace. In and through the act of acceptance, the mystery we call *salvation* occurs (2:4-10). This salvation is offered to all men who will accept it, and not simply to the physical descendants of Abraham. Therefore, practically speaking, since Calvary "the chosen people" consists of all human beings. Without exception, God yearns to confer grace.

It is to proclaim the incredibly radical message here outlined that Saul of Tarsus was seized in the hand of God and "made a minister" (3:7). Through lips that no longer belong to him but are "captive to God," he pours out a message not his own. That is how the letters of a missionary-evangelist to his converts and colleagues rank as Holy Scripture. They are shaped by God himself for the purpose of imparting divine things to mere men who, responding and accepting, form a society of the redeemed that we call the Church.

Seventeenth Day   **Read Ephesians 4-6**

Continuous radical change is the hallmark of surrender. We must perpetually be in the process of discarding our "old nature" (4:22) in favor of a radically different "new nature" that is more a gift than an achievement (4:24).

There are vast and radical implications for everyday life as well as the goal of life. Some practical issues for the

273

first-century Christians are discussed in the vivid section (4:25-6:9). Because Paul's exhortations rest on a foundation of application to specific persons in a definite cultural context, "the letter of the law" does not always apply in other situations. It is the spirit that matters. If you and I can succeed in achieving the state of continuously transforming surrender/rescue of which Paul witnesses, we will make our own practical applications.

Let us not be under the delusion that such surrender/rescue is easy or once-for-all. Rather, it involves a ceaseless fight against both visible and invisible forces of evil (6:12). Victory does not mean overthrow of Satan in such fashion that he never again threatens. Rather, it means continuous faithful resistance with every defensive and offensive weapon available!

In this sense, personal salvation simply echoes *salvation history*. Struggle, by both God and man, is the essence of it. Continuous divine-human interaction, of such nature that the work of creation unfolds thereby, is the context in which salvation becomes tangible and mortals put on immortality.

Philippians

Eighteenth Day   Read Philippians 1-2

God's continuing act of rescue, oriented toward individual human souls, takes place "within history." Grace can be, and is, conferred within time and space. Yet there is also a sense in which the work of salvation—which alone gives meaning to human existence—centers beyond history. To surrender to Jesus Christ is to seek to be blameless both today and in the "day of the Lord."

Never fall into that pernicious and perennial error—if not, indeed, actual heresy—according to which "salvation is easy and cheap." To be in the process of attempting to live a life "worthy of the gospel" (1:27) is to be forever striving, failing, and yearning for a fresh act of divine rescue. It is almost laughably easy to mouth pious words about "having in ourselves the mind of Christ Jesus"; it is fearfully hard to apply those words to actual decisions we face in our daily life and to actual relationships in family, community, and congregation.

Nineteenth Day   Read Philippians 3-4

Here, and in the two preceding chapters, we catch an illuminating glimpse of the relationship between Paul and those who felt indebted to him for their knowledge of Jesus Christ. Both Paul and members of his congregations were very, very human! Clearly, individuals and groups sometimes brought great sorrow to the evangelist. Just as clearly, he sometimes spoke and acted a bit hastily if not actually angrily.

Paul's ceaseless stress upon personal surrender to Jesus Christ and continuous spiritual growth are essential to the creative relationship that exists between the evangelist and his converts. Though he prods and challenges and scolds them, he never does so in pride or self-righteousness. Always, he goads himself more zealously even than he urges those to whom he witnesses. Whatever else he may be, Paul is a man with a burning consciousness of commission who never flags in his zeal better to serve his Saviour. He stands as an all-time challenge to preachers, teachers, witnesses, parents, church officials, and all others who seek to influence their fellows for good.

Colossians

Twentieth Day   Read Colossians 1-2

Paul here presents a poetic and impassioned plea that also forms one of his most vivid theological tracts. To a degree

275

seldom approached in other letters, he deals with many facets of the universe and life within a short space. While the treatment is not orderly and systematic, it approaches a "complete bundle of truth," instead of offering only fragments.

This world, he insists, is pervaded by the principle of dualism. While it has unity, it also has diversity. God is perpetually opposed by forces of darkness and evil. It is in this context of "cosmic conflict" that man lives as a free agent whose choices and acts of surrender will affect not only himself, but also the fate of the whole world.

All the creative work of God, not simply "in the beginning" but also in the living present, centers in the God-man whom we revere as Jesus Christ. Nothing that has ever existed did so apart from Christ. (In this principle, we find a new door into the Old Testament. He who, trembling, enters that door, can never again read the Old Testament as merely a "pre-Christian document." Jesus Christ permeates it as truly as he does the New Testament, though in quite different fashion.)

Christ the Creator, who makes and sustains all that is, has a special role—no less than that of effecting the transfer of human souls from the kingdom of darkness to the Kingdom of light. Through two-way "identification," or mutual yielding and surrendering, Christ and his follower "become one." In and through this grace-powered act of salvation, the rescued one makes the latent divine image real, AND THE PURPOSE FOR WHICH THE WORLD WAS CREATED IS REALIZED!

Twenty-first Day   **Read Colossians 3-4**

There are earthly, flesh-linked consequences of spiritual victory through Jesus Christ. He who has "been raised with Christ" (3:1) out of death into life must act accordingly. He must live as a citizen of the Kingdom of light, no longer being enslaved by darkness.

This radical transition as a consequence of rescue affects the whole person and every compartment of life—hopes, goals, conversation, family relations, daily work, prayer life, and all other activities and relationships.

Though he does not specify such a conclusion, the evangelist everywhere implies that "the social gospel" is a by-product—but an essential one—of individual surrender to God. Those persons or congregations or societies claiming to be Christian must show it in every aspect of daily life. One cannot—simply cannot—have his eyes "on things that are above" (3:2) and not be noticeably, tangibly different from a neighbor still captive to Satan. Of course, to concentrate upon social reforms and a high moral-ethical code, without having entered into the surrender which alone gives life a new goal, is futility compounded.

Thessalonians

Twenty-second Day   **Read I Thessalonians 1-3**

Some emphases and ideas that occur everywhere in Paul's letters are here especially prominent and vivid. Perhaps partly because of its brevity and intimacy, this letter reveals the organic bond between the evangelist and his converts. Without them, he could not be what he is. Two-way intercessory prayer—Paul's praying for his converts, and their praying for him—is high on the list of potent factors affecting all who are in this relationship.

These chapters also echo with a note of radiant joy (1:2; 2:13; 3:9) so clearly linked with struggle that one wonders whether it could be evoked by a calm and placid life. Paul is never at ease. He faces abuse (2:2), disappointment (2:17), and affliction (3:4, 7). Not so much "in spite of" these factors, perhaps, as *because* God's continuous deliverance is made vivid only in a context of struggle, the Apostle's joy frequently rises to the level of ecstasy.

Twenty-third Day   **Read I Thessalonians 4-5**

Paul's own life vividly illustrates one of his chief emphases. Having had some intimation of what one should do in response to God's call, it becomes the believer's life-long task to "do so more and more" (4:1, 10), ceaselessly keep awake (5:6), and "hold fast" (5:21). That is, ceaseless growth is a condition of the Christian pilgrimage.

Once more, we glimpse a capsule delineation of *salvation history* in its entirety. Abraham, chosen by God for special instruction and a unique Covenant relationship, does not reach a terminus. Instead, he launches a movement destined to become wider and deeper, not for a generation or so, but throughout history.

There will be a climax, or consummation, to the entire process. Just as thought requires a beginning, a primeval "day of creation," so we instinctively demand that there also be an end—a Day of Judgment. Because God has ordained it, that day will be entirely good. It will see all wrongs made right and every inequity wiped away. In that prospect, the Christian can rejoice. But time and thought and energy needed for today's pilgrimage should not be wasted upon idle speculation about the day and the hour or the specific details of the day of the Lord. Our task today is to believe, accept God's mercies, and move forward. This *is* salvation!

Twenty-fourth Day   **Read II Thessalonians**

In the first century as in the twentieth, one of the sugar-coated temptations of Satan is the offer of secret knowledge. Oh, how it appeals to our pride to be able to say with assurance that we know hidden things of God which have not been given to other men! Especially in the dark realm of mystery which we see only dimly at a distance, namely, "the coming of our Lord Jesus Christ" (2:1), there are riddles and obscurities enough to baffle the wisest.

Therefore, urges Paul, take care. Avoid the temptation to loaf upon the excuse that the coming Day makes all human effort meaningless (3:6-13). Guard with your life the tendency to question God's goodness in sending present suffering (1:5-8). Never forget that more-than-human forces of evil are at work; namely, the minions of Satan himself. They must and will be overthrown by God.

In this assurance, the believer can face whatever comes and triumph. This task demands much of one's energies—indeed, *all* his time, thought, and effort—and leaves no place for idle speculation about the day and hour, or empty boasting of secret knowledge. God is faithful, and his living word is potent; to know that, and live accordingly, is to pursue the path that leads toward the Kingdom.

Personal Correspondence of Saint Paul

Four of Paul's letters to his individual colleagues have been preserved. Like the letters to his congregations, they are intensely practical, and yet they are "soaked with theology." Paul can hardly fashion a phrase dealing with a problem confronted in daily life without also offering profound theological ideas.

He is a living example of the effects of his message. He is so dominated by a single set of goals and loyalties that he cannot open his mouth or take up his pen without instantly betraying where his heart lies. He is a man under orders, and though he several times acknowledges consciousness of this role, his indirect witness is actually more convincing and contagious than the direct. Of those whom he instructs, the missionary-evangelist demands no less than the devotion he exhibits: so absorbing an orientation toward God through Jesus Christ that every act and each word serves as a witness.

279

Twenty-fifth Day   **Read I Timothy 1-3**

However glorious it may sound in theory, the practical organization and functioning of a church always involve problems—human problems! For a group of men and women to band themselves together as pilgrims toward the King-dom, some kind of structure is essential. Structure means a division into various levels of leadership, along with ordered categories of followers. When the raw material for leaders and followers is mortal, there is no escape from the tendency to quarrel at public prayer and the temptation to make a man a bishop or a deacon from less than the noblest mo-tives.

Is this a cause for despair—on the part of Timothy, of you or me? By no means! Once more we are confronted with the challenge/promise of "justification by faith." In the Church as in the world, men cannot save themselves. It is my task and yours to recognize ourselves as "foremost of sinners" (1:15) in order that, confronted and convicted, we may join Paul and Timothy in continuously accepting divine mercy, while we do our poor best to serve as church-men!

Twenty-sixth Day   **Read I Timothy 4-6**

For the witness of whatever type and epoch, it is imperative that there be use of the head as well as the heart in the service of Christ. Every age has its own set of "godless and silly myths" (4:7); to distinguish and repudiate them is no easy task.

Neither is the work of church administration to be taken casually. Any person in a place of responsibility—as an evangelist, preacher, teacher, or congregational leader—must be firm and gentle, ardent and patient in his dealing with people. In every congregation there are widows . . .

and widows! All groups include individuals who have a fondness for "disputes about words" (6:4; *see also* 6:20-21) and controversy of every shade and hue.

Therefore, the person who thinks of himself as God's man, not his own, must aim impossibly high and strive with more than mortal strength! This is the call to discipleship! Each runner in the race for life must snatch the baton from the hand of some elder brother in the Lord and dash forward to seize defeat in order that victory may be conferred upon him.

Twenty-seventh Day   Read II Timothy 1-2

As a prisoner for faith's sake, Paul is helpless to do anything but watch from a distance. One by one, the structures he has erected begin to topple, until it seems that "all who are in Asia" have turned away (1:15).

Is this defeat a cause for despair, for ceasing to strive?

By no means! On the contrary, this situation evokes the metaphors by which the disciple of Christ is compared with a soldier, athlete, and farmer (2:3-6). Struggle is the context in which discipleship must mature!

If that struggle is to be within endurable limits, so that the disciple is continually growing stronger but is never overwhelmed, he must have help. He has precisely that in his certainty that he is indeed "one with Christ," sharing with him in his triumphs and glory.

Twenty-eighth Day   Read II Timothy 3-4

So personal are the miscellaneous exhortations here, that they can be read as applying directly to every one of us today.

If Paul's analysis is taken literally, we can always regard

281

our own epoch as "the last days," for the conditions he describes in 3:1-7 are universal! So are human tendencies to exalt false teachers whose doctrines are more pleasing than convicting (4:3-4).

It is under precisely such circumstances as these that the Church unfolds and displays her glory. For in a context of misunderstanding and difficulty, God provides that aging Paul should find some young Timothy to carry on when he is gone.

You know, of course, the oft-quoted question and answer:

> Q.—But if the next generation of the Church should fail, what other plans does God have for the salvation of the world?
>
> A.—God has no other plans.

Twenty-ninth Day   Read Titus

In these brief lines, there are enough challenges and suggestions to keep any Christian worker busy for the rest of his or her life! For in the first century as in the twentieth, persons are the only raw material with which God has to work in building the Kingdom. Always, he sends his messengers and envoys into impossible situations. Without exception, he commissions his representatives and then requires them to live as angels—all wise, ever faithful, ceaselessly true.

Obviously, no man can do that. Neither Titus (nor Paul) nor you nor I can go through even one week as leader of a congregation and not fall short of "the perfect man" here demanded. What, then, shall we do? Shall we lower our standards for ourselves and for others—compromise, and accept some level of accomplishment that is possible rather than impossible?

God forbid! The fate of *salvation history* is at stake here. Whether within the framework of the Jewish legal system or the Christian code of morals and ethics, the seeker who adjusts the demands of God to his own capacity is doomed. Here (and everywhere) the answer is to recognize defeat, admit failure, and enter the state of rescue which God wove into the structure of the universe, but which men (especially those with a reputation for wisdom or piety) are perpetually reluctant to accept.

Thirtieth Day   Read Philemon

There is no situation or condition from which Christ is absent. Regardless of the human dilemma, faith will find a firm answer.

Here is part of the glory of discipleship! He who is surrendered in any state approaching the surrender of Paul is no longer his own master. He belongs to Christ, and looks to him for solutions and answers. Out of his surrender he gains power. From his abasing of himself he receives a dynamic sense of authority. Therefore, he can speak boldly and unequivocally upon any issue whatever. It is not his own wisdom that he offers to a slaveowner with a valid claim for redress—but a solution "given" to him by his Master.

Precisely here, in the briefest of Paul's letters, we find the source of his dynamic authority. He is never baffled, never at a loss. He is always confident, perpetually sure. He always has a message—but it is never his own!

Hebrews, Brief Letters, The Revelation

The Letter to the Hebrews

Except for a few favorite passages that are often memorized, this brief book is much neglected in the modern Church. Actually, it is among the most important and illuminating guides provided us in the entire Bible.

The very title is symbolic and suggestive.

Here is a work addressed to "Hebrews." It is all but meaningless to those who have not soaked themselves in the fruits of *salvation history* in such fashion that they are at home with the vocabulary and metaphors of the law and the prophets. (Precisely so, the modern Christian must saturate himself with the whole Bible in order that each section and portion may "come to life" and convey rich meanings that no single book of it can afford.)

But the "Hebrews" who are here addressed are not only the recipients of a centuries-long stream of revelation; they are also the human agents upon whom God is depending to receive, interpret, and transmit the final and definitive message he has given through his Son. Therefore, the "Hebrew," whether a first-century inheritor of Jewish things or a twentieth-century inheritor of Christian ones, stands in a special position. He is "in" the doorway that is Christ. He has one foot in the past and one in the future. He must balance his weight upon both feet in order to maintain his equilibrium in the living, creative present.

Though the figure of speech is artificially simple, it is this "creative equilibrium" that the Letter to the Hebrews seeks to establish, in order that men may find in Jesus of Nazareth the long-awaited Christ of God.

First Day   **Read Hebrews 1**

In order to gain the full sweep of this chapter's glory, you must read it not once, but many times. Turn to Gen. 1 and John 1 in order that those passages may help you enter the secret door so artfully fashioned by today's reading.

Jesus of Nazareth, the Son of God, is in a sense that brings both awe and joy "the last word of God." He is ultimate, absolute, and final. God has no more to say to man than he is in the process of saying through the Son. For him and through him, the Covenant came into being. In him, it finds its meaning.

Jesus Christ is totally communicative. Not simply his words, but also every act and deed, constitute revelation at its highest. Anything divine that man in general or men in particular are unable to receive through Jesus Christ is forever hidden. He offers God in his totality, and each seeker and believer receives fragments and portions according to his ability.

Jesus Christ is the essential central Person in the total divine-human relationship for whose unfolding God called the world into being. Everything "before" him (humanly speaking) flows into him and through him. Everything "after" him has proceeded from him. Human history, of which salvation is only a portion but the portion that gives it meaning, is like a beam of light. Focused in such fashion that it falls upon a lens (Jesus Christ), it is totally transformed thereby. All that was, is, and will be, gains its meaning—indeed, its very existence—from this relationship.

All the angels of heaven and the kings of earth are as nothing before Jesus Christ, altogether human and entirely divine, embodying absolutely in himself that creativity which transforms every man who remains in the act of surrendering in order to be rescued.

Second Day   **Read Hebrews 2-3**

Whoever first suggested that the Gospel is absolutely simple did mankind a great disservice. It is simple, but at the same time it is profound. The Gospel partakes of the paradoxical nature of Jesus Christ, from whom it flows. Even those high-level moments of inspiration and revelation which convince us we have been visited by angels are not to be taken as definitive. Jesus Christ alone is definitive. And though he is "simple" on his human side, he is unutterably far away and mysterious on his divine side. Therefore, even when they are offered to men through the lens of the divine-human Saviour, the things of God must forever remain obscure and baffling, while at the same time clear and understandable.

Having entered into suffering and death, Jesus Christ, who forever creates and conquers, serves as a human-divine doorway through which mere men may penetrate a little way into divinity. It was for the coming of Jesus Christ that God entered into Covenant with his faithful servant, Moses. Only a prepared people, self-conscious in their special relationship with God, though blindly unaware of the final consequences of their contribution to *salvation history,* could provide a social womb to nurture and yield a Babe at once man and God. Moses and the law were essential forerunners of Jesus Christ and the Gospel.

Belief is the key that unlocks the door. It, too, is paradoxical, for at one and the same time it is easy and hard. Only vital belief, pulsating through the soul in the living present, enables man to appropriate the gifts offered through Jesus Christ. Regardless of what ecstatic victories lie in the realm of the past, the pilgrim who expects to reach his destination must be perpetually in the process of believing more deeply. It is therefore the chief work of the Church to provide a context in which those whose appetites are whetted by feeding may "exhort one another every day, as long as it is called 'today'" (3:13).

Third Day   **Read Hebrews 4-5**

Make no mistake. The going is hard here, intellectually. Fibers of thought and of faith are interwoven in complex patterns. None stands alone. Each requires all the others to form the fabric which offers a capsule interpretation of the Good News that is the motif of Scripture in its entirety.

"Difficulty" of the Letter to the Hebrews is vividly apparent in terms of its high-level theological exposition. At the same time, a single simple word also points to the way in which Hebrews challenges the idea that one can be a good follower of Jesus Christ by surrendering his heart, while making no dedication of his head. Strangely, this all-important word keeps its head bowed in humility, with the result that a casual reading may not even reveal its presence—to say nothing of its role.

Notice that in the Revised Standard Version, today's reading begins: "Therefore . . ." Skim hastily through Chapters 4-5 and observe the vital role of this word in their unfolding. Now turn back to Chapters 1-3 and focus your attention upon this key word until it "jumps out at you" from one hiding place after another.

Almost, the word *therefore* in the Letter to the Hebrews serves singlehanded to overthrow widely-held notions that one can "know the Bible and the Gospel" by centering upon scattered verses and phrases. No mere accumulation of disconnected fragments, the Bible (and the Gospel it pours out) is an organic whole. Each grand theme and every exalted concept is essential to all others. Because God has performed mighty acts through the Hebrews, *therefore* the whole world is the beneficiary!

Precisely here, near the end of our year-long journey through the pages of Holy Writ, we begin to gain new understanding of the fact that the New Testament yields its richest treasures only to those who have digged faithfully in the Old Testament. When we catch a glimpse of the way in which David contributed to God's unfolding purpose, we see the Son of David in an entirely new light. Given some faint understanding of the way Aaron and the Jewish priesthood helped to level mountains and fill valleys in the human mind and heart, we achieve a new dimension in our personal encounter with our "great high priest who has passed through the heavens, Jesus, the Son of God" (4:14).

Fourth Day   **Read Hebrews 6-7**

God's oath confirming his promise to Abraham constitutes the nucleus about which the history of the Hebrew people clusters. It is impossible even dimly to glimpse the idea of *salvation history,* to say nothing of beginning to "understand" it, without having been personally captured by the grandeur of this initial act. Through Jesus Christ, God entered history—absolutely, without qualification or reserve. But this definitive "pouring of divinity into humanity" was no isolated act. Rather, it actually had its organic beginning in God's promise to a patriarch. Calvary was foreshadowed—though dimly—at Mt. Moriah.

For twentieth-century Christians not "soaked in the Scriptures," the role of Melchizedek and the Jewish priesthood is not so vivid and compelling as that of Abraham, Moses, and the law. Many contemporary worshipers have little or no firsthand experience with holy mysteries solemnly guarded and transmitted by men whose chief work is to offer God to man by way of sacraments, rites, and ceremonies. Therefore, we find it difficult or barren to magnify Jesus Christ as one "in the likeness of Melchizedek" (7:15).

First-century seekers, steeped in the customs and traditions of Israel, never could have accepted the idea of a Saviour who did not have as one of his chief functions the work of an ideal "high priest." Reflection suggests that many of today's disciples may be much the poorer for their lack of handles with which to grasp this idea. Life-long habits of Bible reading will do much to raise one's level of receptivity at this point. Here we glimpse, though "through a glass darkly," some fruits from our having gained a surface acquaintance with the Book of Leviticus.

Fifth Day   Read Hebrews 8-9

In his role as great high priest, Jesus Christ functions somewhat like earth-bound priests who serve as intermediaries between God and man. That is, he offers sacrifices to God in order to atone for the sins of men. By giving *himself* he became an eternal sacrifice, establishing a means by which every man may escape the death penalty that he invokes upon himself by virtue of being born a man.

So viewed, Jesus Christ is "the mediator"; he himself serves as the sacrifice (offered upon Calvary) which he presents before God in order to make up the deficit in man's final rendering of accounts. So important is this work that Jesus Christ's performance of it marks a radical new point in *salvation history*—no less a peak than that which reveals the ratification of a Second Covenant between God and man.

Now, the very idea of a covenant—or solemn agreement—suggests the necessity of orderly procedures. There are certain things required of the contractual parties, and these must be clearly understood on both sides. Among the chief stipulations of the Covenant with Abraham was the provision that God would permit his people to make sacrifices to him in order to make up for their failures and fallings. Interpreted and re-interpreted by generations of the faithful, growing in complexity and obscurity, ceremonial rites and laws concerning them came to dominate the life of Israel. Always, the concept of blood sacrifice remained central. Once a year the high priest went into the "most holy place" and poured blood upon the altar in order that his people might be washed from their sins.

Jesus Christ, the great high priest who presided over the most solemn sacrifice the world is capable of containing, poured out his own blood upon Calvary. It is this continuing act of sacrifice that enables a follower to rejoice that he is "washed in the blood of the Lamb." This self-giving of the divine-human Saviour is the watershed of both *salvation history* and of the whole unfolding universe. Participating as humans in the sacrifice of the Man on the Cross, mere creatures enter into the victory of the Son of God and thereby find meaning for themselves and this world.

Sixth Day   **Read Hebrews 10**

Noble as it was, and essential as it was to the developing of God's purposes nurtured within the Covenant, the law of Moses was not the final word of God. Instead, it was the essential base from which that word might spring, the foundation upon which God's finished structure might rest.

Men had to slay bulls and goats for centuries before they could be made ready to conceive of God's blood being poured out upon Calvary in a once-for-all sacrifice.

We must not be too impatient with ourselves if we do not gain from such a line of thought the heady inspiration that comes from following, say, St. John's interpretation of the life and message of his Master. At the same time, we must not be too quick to turn aside from such passages as this, rejecting them as barren for present-day Christian life and thought. Re-read after having struggled through the Letter to the Hebrews, Paul's Letter to the Romans echoes and re-echoes with new overtones that combine to form subtle harmonies you may have failed to hear when you listened there a few weeks ago.

As one who would quench his thirst from the living water of Scripture, "you have need of endurance" (10:36) here, as well as in holding fast to your confidence in God's great rewards. Discipline—archaic practice though it seems to many a modern churchman—is essential. Simply to stay with your purpose, not simply of reading the entire Bible this year, but of rooting your life in it, is in some degree to achieve your ultimate goal.

We cannot—we simply cannot—begin to cultivate an appetite for God's most tasty gifts until we have read, pondered, re-read, and assimilated the whole Bible in such fashion that we can, in faith and trembling, step forward, asking in no glib use of easy lingo that the shed blood of Jesus Christ be accepted by God in lieu of the Godlike lives he demands of his children.

Seventh Day   **Read Hebrews 11**

Endurance in faith is essential to any grand enterprise— whether that of journeying through the Bible in order to be in the act of meeting God, or of desperately hanging on and waiting for God to bestow power and victory in a context of defeat and despair.

Faith, moreover, is an essential ingredient in that sublime salvation. It serves as the magnetic field which pulls together the human pole and the divine pole. Nothing can substitute for it here. No other glue will hold the components together.

All the grand achievements and noble exploits of the past are monuments to faith. Name the heroes over, one by one, and each is seen to have reached his niche because he believed in ideals and values he could not see with his eyes. Yet all the most radiant hours of the past were but preliminary. Each is a lighted highway sign that pointed forward. Through the whole torturously sublime struggle that constituted the period of the First Covenant, and indeed before he brought into existence a world that could nurture a People of the Covenant, God had something better in mind: the sending of his Son.

Eighth Day   **Read Hebrews 12-13**

You are surrounded by heralds who shout to you of God's ceaseless creative striving on your behalf. That being the case, it is time to stop attending to distractions and hesitating over difficulties. Having been assured the victory through our divine champion, Jesus Christ, "let us run with perseverance the race that is set before us" (12:1).

The race will never be easy. Thank God that this is so! It is through the faithful, if sometimes painful, work of discipline that flabby muscles become hard!

However long and rough the road ahead, you must not shake your head and ask to be excused from running this race. You are under a divine imperative. God, whose voice shakes the earth itself, has called you. It is for this that you were born. It is for this that all previous history, pouring

into you as though through a funnel, has run its course. It
is for this that the world was created!

Yet the vision of eternal and invisible rewards laid up
for you at the end of the race must not serve to make you
contemptuous of this present life and other men. Acts of
love are not to be scorned, for there is no way to reach the
world to come except by passing through this world. Be
obedient to God, therefore, in your daily life. Put faith to
work here and now!

Miscellaneous Brief Letters

Some of Paul's short letters are more important because of
having come from the Apostle than for their contents.
Judged by the standard of sheer capacity to evoke dedication to Jesus Christ and aid the seeking pilgrim, II Thessalonians, for example, falls far short of the peaks attained
in *The Imitation of Christ* and other classics that do not
have the authority of Scripture.

Much the same thing can be said of the miscellaneous
brief letters that are grouped after The Letter to the Hebrews and before The Revelation of St. John. They are
priceless treasures from the experience of men who either
walked about Palestine with Our Lord or absorbed inspiration from his life and teachings at second or third hand. Yet
even the most ardent advocate of Biblical literalism will not
go so far as to suggest that the Third Letter of John is on a
par with the Psalms or St. Luke's Gospel.

In a sense, therefore, the very structure of the Bible itself
serves here to remind us that we are (necessarily) dealing
in history with a Gospel that transcends history. Because the
Word was made *flesh,* the drama of salvation was enacted
in a particular place at a specific period. It was not some
vague "mankind in general," but particular men who were
(in the flesh) permitted direct encounter with Jesus of
Nazareth. God used these men, and those whom they in-

fected with the contagion of their own discipleship, as agents through whom to offer the New Testament to the world. Thus, in a sense, the Book that is the vehicle for transmitting the power of the New Covenant is also limited by the humanity of the contracting parties.

If, therefore, The Letter to Jude yields less direct "inspiration" than any chapter of The Gospel of St. John, with its cluster of companions it yet serves vividly to persuade us that in Jesus of Nazareth, God entered humanity and history.

Ninth Day   **Read James 1-2**

"Testing" is the fire which serves to harden the metal of faith, producing an alloy that cannot exist without having been heated! This is the divine alchemy through which trials are transmuted into joys!

This, indeed, *is* the victory—no less than that of standing with bowed head to receive from God "the crown of life" (1:12).

On the foundation of so victorious a statement of faith, James erects a set of guides for practical conduct. It is not easy to decide precisely which of his rules apply in a given situation, and which should be modified. That is perhaps one of the reasons that so God-intoxicated a seeker as Martin Luther should have considered this epistle as having little value.

Ponder the challenges of James with a receptive heart, however, and you are likely to agree with me that he quickly brings you under conviction. Practical-minded as he is, the Apostle makes demands that require every hearer to confess himself impotent to "keep the law" and therefore in need of grace. Compared, say, with The Letter to the Romans, this tract certainly is thin in its theological content. But the same man who (many of us would say, properly) insists that "faith apart from works is barren" (2:20) has already trumpeted the warning that failure at any point brings guilt everywhere (2:10).

Perhaps, therefore, the Church of the first century and of the twentieth needs the corrective emphasis of James as desperately as the clarion call of Paul. We are indeed made just only by faith—but "faith apart from works is dead" (2:26).

Tenth Day   **Read James 3-5**

Every aspect of life and conduct involves challenge and struggle. The tongue, for example, is one of God's richest gifts to man. Yet it throws man into an arena in which there is no peace or quarter. Because the tongue illustrates the way we can use our gifts for good or for evil (3:9-10), it furnishes God with an opportunity to test us in order that, through fortitude under stress, we may grow more like him (1:2-3, 12-15).

As with the tongue, so with every hope and wish. Ambition, without which man will do nothing, can easily defeat him.

Our total inability to master ourselves should serve to make us vividly aware of our limitations, and hence cause us to depend only upon God. Such a mood is hard to enter, and even harder to maintain. By concentrating our attention upon the coming day of the Lord, we will gain power to be steadfast in the struggle now.

Another powerful source of help is the fellowship of other pilgrims. Though each of us is frail, he who could never stand alone may succeed in remaining vertical when he helps hold up his comrades and in turn is bolstered by them.

Eleventh Day Read I Peter 1-2

We modern readers tend to think of ourselves as the best—
or at least the normal—people of a society which itself has
accepted Christianity as its guiding principle. Except in
special instances, it is hard even to imagine ourselves in the
role of "exiles of the dispersion" in remote outposts of a
pagan culture (1:1). Nor is it any longer typical for the
churchman to have his daily life dominated by his consciousness of being "chosen," "destined," and "sanctified"
(1:2).

Really to seize Peter's meanings here, we must try to
be the kind of readers he addresses! We must be vividly
aware of the gulf between the Church and the world, conscious of our own alienation from the culture that includes
us. Only to the degree that you succeed in becoming, as it
were, a little island whose shores are perpetually assaulted
by tides that threaten your existence, will you achieve transforming encounter with Peter's Lord through his brief letter.

Fearful though it is, the Apostle asserts, this time of exile
(in the flesh, separated from purely spiritual encounter with
the Father) is not to be taken seriously. It is transient and
passing. It will be swallowed up in the new creation whose
existence is guaranteed and revealed by the resurrection of
Jesus Christ. In the light of so great a victory—not limited
to the future, but being bestowed in the present—a sober
but joyous life of endurance in hope can overcome all adversaries. Not simply those foes on the outside, but also—
and especially—those on the inside—everything included under "the passions of the flesh" (2:11)—may and must be
overcome!

Twelfth Day Read I Peter 3-5

How clearly these chapters reflect the paradoxical nature of
the Gospel from which they spring!

For Peter's words are maps indicating highways that lead in opposite directions simultaneously. Here are sources of comfort and solace—that also serve to prick and goad. Singing sentences that offer power are also sources of condemnation. For it is only in glimpsing the glories of spiritual mountain peaks which we know we can climb with God's help, that we are impelled to look at the ground under our feet and discover how short a distance we have yet come.

Brief as this letter is, it exemplifies the fact that *salvation history* unfolds to engulf you and me in a creative field of tension, where one must perpetually be in the act of choosing between spirit and flesh, where failure runs like a red thread through the whole mortal coil, and where response to God's ceaseless overture brings victory in past, present, and future tenses simultaneously.

Thirteenth Day   Read II Peter 1-3

Those who take fragments of the message conveyed by God through Christ and elevate those bits of it into a "gospel of their own making" are living with futility compounded. But such persons often attract weak and silly followers in substantial numbers (2:17-22).

Instead of chasing after myths and emphasizing some one phase of the Gospel to the exclusion of all others, it is imperative that we wait as well as act. Not everything depends upon you or me. God will usher in "new heavens and a new earth in which righteousness dwells" (3:13) regardless of how much or how little we do. There is a sense in which he demands passive submission as fully as active striving.

Once more, we are confronted by a demand for a coherent and systematic pattern of belief, thought, and action. Fortunately for us, the very inter-connectedness of salvation's aspects presents us with an advantage as well as challenging us with its immensity. Provided we will be in a state

297

of mingled striving and surrendering, God will set chain reactions in process. Faith will co-mingle with virtue, and virtue in turn will produce side effects upon knowledge. Increase in knowledge, whether oriented toward self-control or not, will affect the pilgrim's balance and steadfastness— and so on (1:5-6). All of God's stupendous promises, therefore, have capacity to transform not simply one aspect of belief and conduct, but the entire self. This mysterious work of Providence, meditated by Jesus Christ and so magnified in him that we can see it even with our bleary eyes, operates to offer salvation to all who will continue in the process of dedicating mind, heart, and soul. It is the whole man, and no mere portion, that God offers to redeem!

Fourteenth Day   Read I John 1-3

Gloriously and incredibly, mere man really can come into meaningful encounter with God! That is the message of the entire Bible. If everything else had to be omitted, the reader saying just one thing as a result of being made captive by the total verbal record of unfolding *salvation history,* this central proclamation would have to stand. Earth-bound creatures really can hear the Creator's voice with their ears, and with their hands can touch the evidences of his presence (1:1-2).

Second only to this great central affirmation is the assurance that man's coming into transforming encounter with God is best effected through the God-man, Jesus Christ.

All else is subsidiary and derived. Here is the core of the Gospel.

Really to come into meeting with it as an item of personal experience, rather than secondhand evidence gathered at a distance, one must have thought and hoped, struggled and dreamed with stalwarts of the mind and spirit. Then, and only then, the seeker gains capacity to see—really—the light in which he has been bathed all the while. In the glory of his vision, he must strive harder than ever to see more light —to "abide in him" (3:24).

It is for this state of victory under tension, as a result of being in the process of accepting rescue through striving, that we have read the entire Bible. Precisely here, in John's so-brief epistle, we see clearly that in nearing the end of our course, we have just begun. Instead of ceasing to run, we must pump harder than ever with muscles made firmer by our striving!

Fifteenth Day   **Read I John 4-5**

Divine love is beyond our experiencing or describing in its entirety. Yet, paradoxically, it is ours for the acceptance. God's ceaseless outpouring for us and to us partakes of the both/and nature of his supreme self-disclosure in Jesus the Christ.

This love may be claimed here and now, but it does not reach its absolute in this life. Nevertheless, it is tasting of it now that enables mortals to lay hold of eternal life then!

Any attempt at systematic explanation of so exalted a set of ideas as those that cluster about the experiencing of divine love, is necessarily inadequate. To talk of God's love is, inescapably, to overlook some aspects of it and to distort others.

God, therefore, sent his Son to exhibit that love which defies description. By laying hold of love through faith in Jesus Christ, the surrendered and rescued believer experiences love in a fashion so sublime that he transcends the limitations of thought and language. Such entering into the revelation of personal religious experience is the highest state mere man can attain. In the process of making such encounter with God his aim, he overthrows the evil one and enters into eternal life—here and now!

299

Sixteenth Day   **Read II John, III John, Jude**

Clearly, these documents are but snippets and fragments. They point to a way of salvation. Uniquely, though momentarily, they serve as heralds for the church. Notice, for example, that one of the most powerful of all benedictions appears in the final verses of Jude's little-read letter.

Alone, no letter in this trio offers the whole Gospel.

Still these little "books" are Scripture! We are here dealing with the inspired word of God. We are not permitted to judge it, for it sits in judgment upon us!

In the dilemma we here encounter—one which we cannot in honesty side-step—the Bible itself offers a potent illustration of a perennial danger. We are men, caught up in our mortality. Hence we can distort and pervert and twist even Scripture! Just three days ago, we were startled by the vehemence with which Peter makes this very assertion.

Because we are frail and human, even the most devout reader of the Bible may mangle its message. He who selects a few fragments (perhaps not so long as The Letter of Jude), and proceeds to make them the measure of the measureless Gospel, has consciously or unconsciously "edited" the Bible. Through such a process, one can "prove" almost any doctrinal position whatever, and find support for almost any rite or practice.

Once more we are persuaded that for balance and perspective, we need the panoramic view that comes from surveying, over and over, the whole Bible as well as all of its parts.

The Revelation to John

It would be possible, I think, to make some changes in the sequence of its individual books without substantially altering the nature of the Bible. For example, Paul's letters are arranged in the approximate order of their length. If they were grouped according to time of writing, sequence would be quite different, but their total impact might not be greatly altered.

That is clearly not the case with the first and the last books of the Bible. The Revelation is just as essential to the closing pages as is Genesis to the opening lines of those crucial centuries that comprise the kernel, or nucleus, of *salvation history*. Like Genesis, the Revelation points both backward and forward simultaneously. And like the matchless account of the beginning of things, this scintillating summary of meanings that converge in the end of things is great literature as well as an eloquent witness of things divine.

No book of the Bible has been more greatly abused than this one. Because of its difficulty and obscurity, many readers have opened its pages only long enough to whiff the aroma of sanctity that lingers here, in somewhat the same fashion that ozone remains after lightning has struck. At the other edge of the spectrum, seekers for light have been dazzled by gazing into the pure red of John's masterpiece painted in blood and fire. As a result, many have become so enamored of The Revelation that they have, in effect, elevated it to the place of "a Bible within the Bible." Insisting upon using it as the one key with which to unlock all doors leading into places of holy mystery, such readers have wantonly and violently committed the precise errors condemned in the brief letters that form stepping stones leading to The Revelation!

Strangely and significantly, the very title serves as an index to the promise/warning that must here be heeded.

For in the Revised Standard Version we are invited to immerse ourselves in The Revelation *to* John, and, in the King James Version, we are asked to view ourselves and the world through the lens formed by The Revelation *of* St. John. Which preposition is "right"?

Both—and neither!

301

Indisputably, it is God's self-revelation *to* John with which we are dealing here. But it is equally certain, and equally essential, that we recognize how the unique vessel, John, received and held the divine outpouring in order to offer it to the world in a form possible only to this one listener/speaker. In this sense, the verbal witness that comes to you and me is surely The Revelation *of* John.

Even the gross distortion of title by which many a pious pilgrim has spoken of this book as "Revelations" is not to be dismissed lightly. For John's body of witness is as clearly plural as it is singular. It really does deal with hidden things as well as with that one sublime secret in which the meaning and fate of the world are engulfed.

Not simply in this book, therefore, but in its very title, we are again confronted by the paradox of the one and the many. Here is the both/and factor that has emerged so many times in our striving to burst the outer kernel of confining words and enter into the heart of the Good News that deals with Jesus Christ: altogether divine and utterly human.

Again, both the opportunities and difficulties that cluster about the title serve as highway signs into the book we are about to enter. Guard with your life against too great an absorption with one word, or a few phrases, or some potent visual image, or a mind-dominating number such as 666 or 144,000. Like the little prepositions "of" and "to," these symbols are fluid rather than static. They issue great invitations and pose grave threats; a reader can become so fascinated with the antics of a squirrel on the limb of an oak that he no longer sees the tree—to say nothing of the enveloping forest.

We would be far the poorer not to make our way through the turbulent waters of The Revelation, but we must not spend our lives here. Once more, we need the balance and corrective that comes from living with the whole Bible—but when we next approach the Psalms or Romans, our eyes will be sharper for having peered at the heavens through the unduplicated telescope fashioned by St. John in response to God's urging and prodding of the Apostle's soul, heart, and mind.

Seventeenth Day	Read Revelation 1

Belief in meaningful encounter between God and man is basic to the Jewish-Christian point of view. Without such belief, there could be no Covenant and no unfolding of *salvation history*. Revelation, or the self-disclosure of the Creator to the creature made in the divine image, is the door (and the only one) through which man can walk into an atmosphere in which he and the universe have more than finite meaning.

Revelation is the basic work of all Scripture; again it is the central role of Jesus Christ in whom "the Word was made flesh" in order that flesh-bound men might hear the things of God. Revelation can and does proceed through every work of the Creator; the world of nature sings the praises of our Maker (Ps. 19). And Revelation flows through God-centered men who serve as megaphones through whom our Creator shouts, in order to be heard and understood by men too dull to catch the voice of their Lord except when mediated through personality.

Because John of Patmos stands at the very peak of disciplined listeners, his proximity to God makes it difficult for us ordinary mortals to grasp the full import of the secrets and warnings and promises he would transmit from heaven to earth. It is dreadfully easy to become so absorbed with, or puzzled by, the figures and symbols of this witness that his God-given message is obscured instead of clarified.

In this opening chapter, we are likely to be repelled by shadowy metaphors, if we are not wooed into that fierce spiritual pride which centers in claiming mastery over the occult and hidden.

Speaking for God and not for himself, John clearly has a message for those who seek to apply Calvary's poultices to wounds of their souls. Precisely which historical churches he addresses is a matter of no consequence whatever. His audience here is the human heart: everywhere, in all epochs. John has a message so potent that he can hardly make it articulate. He has seen a vision so stunning that he was thrown into a trance. He would speak to the sons of men about the things of God, and, in order to do so, he will perforce use images and symbols, metaphors and double meanings. He is trying to utter unspeakable things; that is why, even in this comparatively sedate first chapter, we recognize ourselves to be in a strange and almost alien atmosphere.

Eighteenth Day   **Read Revelation 2-3**

John's brief letters, or proclamations, address not simply a group of seven first-century churches but all Christian congregations everywhere. Since the imagery of these two chapters is less obscure than some later ones, the going is comparatively easy here. We do not have great difficulty in seizing upon shining clusters of promises and grim bundles of warnings that seem directed especially and particularly to us who read.

Notice that using seven, "the perfect number," John has shaped a seven-sided delineation of qualities which cluster about Jesus Christ. For a breathtaking glimpse of the Apostle's intoxicating view of his Saviour, meditate upon descriptions included in: 2:1; 2:8; 2:12; 2:18; 3:1; 3:7; and 3:14. Jesus Christ, whose fullness is so far beyond us that we can only absorb snatches of it, as it were, is all that John says— and infinitely more. To take these "descriptions" in literal sense and try to define the physical or spiritual nature of the Saviour by combining them is worse than useless; it is heresy. For each individual set of clusters, and all of them together, will "illuminate the mind and spirit" only if treated as a *pointer to divinity*, rather than a vessel holding a frozen portion of it.

How superbly John the listener becomes John the speaker! With unmatched grandeur these seven little "letters" exhibit the both/and character of the Gospel in their organic combination of warnings with promises, condemnations with commendations!

Nineteenth Day   **Read Revelation 4-5**

Every attempt to know God, and to communicate what is known, requires the seeking one to recognize two sets of limitations. On the one hand, human thought is not big enough to explore divinity; likewise, human language is so geared to the realm of created things that it cannot speak of the Creator without distortion. That is why worship at its highest has always leaned heavily upon symbols, figures of speech, ritual, music, and other media that (to a degree) liberate us from the tyranny of words. But the more exalted a particular piece of material is, the harder it is for "ordinary folk" to use it without gross twisting and bending of its sublime meanings.

Because John was granted a vision so exalted that he pressed far up the Mt. Everest of religious experience, his report of that vision sounds almost incoherent to persons who have glimpsed the mountain only from a distance. Even those who have climbed its lower slopes are likely to be dazed and bewildered.

Here we must not—we simply dare not—let ourselves be blinded by sunlight reflected from snow fields at the crest

305

of the mountain. We must put on our dark glasses and admit only enough light to make out some prominent landmarks.

So viewed, in these chapters we find: (1) that mere men (John, for example) actually can press through the door into God's realm of glory; (2) confronted by God, the presence of his grandeur is so overwhelming that it can be hinted only by means of mystical symbols and figures of speech; (3) the supreme work of the God-man, Jesus Christ (Lion of the tribe of Judah, Lamb of God slain from the beginning of the world), is to transmit the things of God to the sons of men. The Incarnation is indeed the axis of existence—the central point of the whole unfolding creation in general and of *salvation history* in particular. Incredibly, illogically, unbelievably, in and through the God who was man, all men may know God. This is the Gospel. This is salvation. This (and this alone) gives meaning to a creature made in the image of God and placed within a context of time and space—bound to the earth by his body, and potentially one with God through his soul.

Twentieth Day   **Read Revelation 6-7**

Jesus Christ, who reveals the things of God to the sons of men, pours out a message that is "both one and many." He opens many seals, disclosing a multitude of truths—all of which come from God and point to God. Like the Creator of whom they witness, these messages "give light darkly." They reveal—but not to the naked eye of the first-time viewer.

God is majesty, power, justice, death, and life. His outpouring of himself is not "all sunshine and joy"; in his self-revealing there are elements that strike dread into the hearts of all who behold.

In the midst of the "falling of the mountains" which occurs over and over to civilizations as well as to every individual, there is stability. Face to face with death, a great multitude will enter life. (The number 144,000 is figurative and symbolic, not literal.) Many who are rescued by God will come from the Chosen People of the Old Covenant, but hosts of others from "all tribes and peoples and tongues" (7:9) will join them. Salvation, though mediated through Israel, is universal. All who believe in Jesus Christ thereby enter through him into the company of God to know their Creator in a state of surrender that includes unspeakable joy.

Twenty-first Day   **Read Revelation 8-9**

Revelation proceeds from God to man; communication proceeds from man to man. In his capacity to receive divine things through revelation, and his God-given power to transmit intangible ideas to his fellow, man is unique among creatures. But because communication as well as revelation is so sublime a process that it "smells of divinity," there are a hundred ways for every message to run aground. In these chapters (and perhaps the bulk of this book), John offers such scintillating metaphors and such brilliant flashes of thought that for most of us he dazzles rather than illuminates.

Clearly, these chapters "say" that terrible woes will come to mankind in the day of the Lord. Even more clearly, they underscore the conviction that though men know Judgment is inescapable, only a minority will ever order their lives in keeping with that certainty (9:20-21). These two fundamental proclamations are at the heart of today's reading. If we try to decipher details, I fear that we will be in danger of losing our way in the subtleties of John's thought and the exuberance of his imagery. We must not, we dare not, become absorbed with tracing brush strokes of this

307

master painter and thereby take our eyes off his masterpiece as a unified whole.

Twenty-second Day	Read Revelation 10-11

Clouds of glory, like vapor above the surface of a mountain lake, hover here and make vision difficult. Yet, if these chapters, and their companions, had to be summarized in one exclamation, I think you and I would agree on the message if not the language: "How great is our God!"

Allegorical allusions (clearly stipulated by John in 11:8) which must have had obvious meaning to first-century readers puzzle us, when we do not overlook them altogether. We cannot, by any amount of striving, read these pages through eyes of early Christians expecting martyrdom at the hand of Caesar. But if we have lost something, we have gained much.

Precisely because The Revelation does not have for us the immediacy it surely possessed for those who first read it, we are the better equipped to penetrate beneath the surface of this book and find its rich veins of ore. Because we do not vibrate to the tread of Roman legions, we can center our attention on every clue that will help us reach that pinnacle on which, with our own ears, we can hear the seventh angel blow his trumpet as a prelude to joining our voices to the heavenly chorus that proclaims:

"The kingdom of the world has become the kingdom of our Lord and of his Christ, and he shall reign for ever and ever" (11:15).

Twenty-third Day	Read Revelation 12-13

It is futility compounded to attempt to discover precisely what details may be signified by each of the ten horns and the seven heads of the beast that rose from the sea (13:1). Such allusions give power and grandeur to the imagery of this mind-absorbing vision, but they are not to be regarded as doorways into secret realms.

Whatever else he may be telling us here, John is using every resource of the poet-prophet to warn us that we cannot extricate ourselves from involvement in cosmic forces. There is a more-than-human struggle between the powers of good and evil, between the ongoing work of creation and the forces of degeneration.

You and I are caught up in combat that, for us, is mortal. We are tested and assaulted by one "beast" after another. There is no peace in this life. Yet, paradoxically, we can have absolute peace through participation in the conquest effected by "the blood of the Lamb" (12:11). Thus the battle is won before it begins; absolute victory by God and good is assured, in spite of the fact that, for you and me, the struggle for life is personal, ceaseless, and to the death!

Twenty-fourth Day   Read Revelation 14

As with poetic metaphors, so with symbolic numbers. To treat figurative language literally is to drive out the spirit and leave an empty shell. Far more than 144,000 readers of John's book have wandered off the path to life by trying to determine precisely what twelve groups of twelve thousand persons have God's signature upon their foreheads!

Men, John is saying, are divided into two categories. Some tune their ears to God's melody ("the music of the spheres" as well as formal systems of verbal witness, such as the Bible). Others prostrate themselves before created things and thereby witness their unwillingness to attempt to hear the divine harmony.

Members of both groups are marked by their goals. Some

men bear the mark of God, while others exhibit the mark of the beast. This inevitable and perennial dichotomy, or state of division, is itself cause enough for ceaseless strife and woe. Even if there were no divine agents of judgment, wielding their sickles in the harvest day of the Lord, men would be perpetually in turmoil and strife because the seeker after God *cannot* be at peace with adherents of the beast.

Here the whole problem of evil and the doctrine of Providence are brought to focus. God is wholly and altogether good, and he has nothing except bounty for the creature made in his image. Yet it may be that God could not give his richest gifts to man without placing him in a growth-inducing context of struggle. So viewed, evil becomes a tool of Providence, an instrument of a larger good in which it is included. God's work of creation continues in and through man, spurred to creative striving by being forced to work out his destiny in an environment in which there is no peace except through ceaseless struggle.

Twenty-fifth Day   **Read Revelation 15-16**

In the chorus that constitutes the Good News, the songs of Moses and of the Lamb become one. Separately and together, they help man heighten his capacity to listen; and, listening, to understand hidden things.

One of the heavenly mysteries, revealed since the beginning of divine-human dialogue but perpetually requiring individual and cultural rediscovery, centers in "the wrath of God." Altogether good and so prone to forgiveness that he sent his own Son to pour out his life for your sake and mine, God is yet a God of justice. His tenderness is that of a mother who in agony must punish her child in order to implement the flow of her love for him whom she bore.

Always, it is easy for us to stand and cheer as God takes the offensive against beasts, dragons, and foul spirits. Always, it is *infernally* hard for me to see myself as a patriotic citizen of Babylon, my allegiance to that great city making me—even me—a rebel against God. Part of the work of John in his gloriously obscure and radiantly dark book is to give me new perspectives whereby I will be enabled to see that the warning/promise of the Gospel is written especially and particularly . . . for me.

Twenty-sixth Day · Read Revelation 17

Who is this so great harlot who lures men away from God?

Ah! John is too sensitive a listener to God, and too skilled a singer to men, to be trapped by the specific, the concrete, the created. Deliberately he has framed harmonies that lend themselves to a great variety of stanzas. Instead of being merely a specific time- and space-linked power of evil, the harlot *is* (not simply "stands for") evil itself.

She is Rome, sprawled over her seven hills, of course. She is also Caesar lying awake at night to map new conquests by his legions. She is imperial tyranny and official corruption in the first century. She is idolatry flourishing in temples scattered about the shores of the Mediterranean. But the harlot and the beast are also evil in high places within twentieth-century democracies. This professionally-soiled woman is official corruption within Christian institutions. She is lust for power and for sensual experience, bidding for the allegiance of all men everywhere. Most fearfully of all, she is the jeweled one who will occupy the throne of my own heart if I do not remain in the act of surrender to Jesus Christ in order that he may unseat her and rule in her place.

311

Twenty-seventh Day   **Read Revelation 18**

God's call to "come out" is both specific and general.
Through John of Patmos, he does indeed challenge his own
to separate themselves from the Babylon of empire that
surrounds and includes them. But the imperative is not
limited to a demand that Christ's own refuse to sell themselves to the Roman Empire in return for her favors.

God's very act of entering into Covenant with a *Chosen*
People implied and involved their separation from other peoples. God called on Abraham's descendants to separate
themselves from the death-conferring security of Egyptian
slavery. Perpetually and perennially he calls to the Church,
bride of Christ, to separate herself from all her lovers. With
a yearning that never takes "no" as final, he calls upon you
and me to go apart—deliberately to renounce "the world,
the flesh and the devil" in order more perfectly to love and
serve our God.

Perpetually and perennially, men—all men—enter into
commerce with Babylon. "The great city," wherever it may
be and whatever forms of power are concentrated there,
must and will fall. But we find it woefully hard to order
our lives in the light of this certainty. It is to fortify us, convict us, and encourage us in fear and trembling to be continually in the act of separating ourselves from her—now—
that John pens these lines.

Twenty-eighth Day   **Read Revelation 19**

Throughout this book, visions take place in sequence. Every
time we think we have reached the final pinnacle, another
and higher peak looms in the distance. When it seems that,
with John, we have been wrung dry, spiritually and emotionally, we are urged to lift our eyes and glimpse new
cataclysms and fresh glories.

312

That the time sequence of The Revelation is not to be taken too literally is indicated by the fact that 19:11-21 echoes the earlier report of Chapter 18. Still, there is a special quality in the ringing "After this . . ." with which the present chapter begins. Babylon is fallen. Evil has been unhorsed. Almost, it would seem, the logical next step would be to write "The End."

Though the end is in sight (though as through a glass darkly), we are not yet upon it. There is more. Heaven and earth must join in a glad chorus of praise to God, who in his triumph over evil has won the cosmic battle—not simply for himself, but also for John and his intimates, for you, me, and Everyman. Now the marriage feast may be held. Now the true union of heaven and earth, divinity and humanity, God and me, may take place!

Twenty-ninth Day   **Read Revelation 20**

Yesterday we noticed the (admittedly) vexatious problem of sequence in John's account. From one perspective, it almost seems that events of the day of the Lord are hopelessly scrambled.

Part of the dilemma is due to the nature of verbal communication. John cannot put everything before us at once, in the fashion that Rafael, at one fell swoop, confronts the viewer with each and every detail of his painting depicting "St. George Slaying the Dragon." In order to write at all, John must describe first one detail and then another. This factor becomes confusing if we permit human limitations of the Apostle to persuade us that the sequence of his visions declares God to be incapable of doing *simultaneously* all of the things described in the entire Revelation.

Again, time does not limit or confine God. It is a necessary structure for ordered human life—at once conferring

313

great power and binding us in chains partly of our own forging. God is above and beyond time. With him, a thousand years are as a day—and a day as a thousand years.

With the troublesome time-factor transcended, these chapters (once more) echo with shouts of praise and victory. God has conquered, and in his victory men who believe in him through the Lamb find not simply rewards—but meaning for life. Here (and only here) is the way to personal significance not grounded upon transient created things, but rooted in the eternity and omnipotence which are the stuff which go into the compounding of deity itself.

Thirtieth Day   **Read Revelation 21-22**

It is the nature of the Creator perpetually to be creating—making "all things new" (21:5). That is why every human attempt to know God absolutely is futile, if not actually heretical. Such efforts assume a static universe, so small that the whole of it can fit within the human skull.

God is all in all; we are creatures—limited, cribbed about, confined within our humanity. But this humanity is only a husk that surrounds and for a little while nurtures the inner self that is made in the divine image. This second and higher man—the soul, if you please—has capacity to shake off all the limitations of the flesh.

In order to do so, and thereby achieve the end for which God created the world and me, I must seize hold of—appropriate—divine gifts that I cannot win or earn. Jesus Christ, Son of God and son of man, will enable me—if I will enter creatively into his whole cycle of striving, surrendering, suffering, and dying—to be in the process of becoming God's own. Fully revealed through words and deeds of the Word made flesh, the Good News of personal rescue that offers more-than-finite meaning to me is the secret shouted in every page of John's Revelation. Nowhere is it put more succinctly and more compellingly than in the final invitation of 22:17:

The Spirit and the Bride say, "Come."
And let him who hears say, "Come."
And let him who is thirsty come,
let him who desires take the water of life without price.

Conclusion

We have reached the end of our odyssey. Starting with a primeval act of creation that produced a world not yet fully formed, we are now in sight of the New Jerusalem. Its spires and turrets are too distant to be viewed in detail, it is true. Nevertheless, we cannot escape recognition that it is out yonder, a present reality rather than a not-yet-born dream.

But in coming to the end of the course, I think we have already realized that we are just beginning! Instead of being surfeited, our appetites are whetted. We are more eager, more curious, more zealous to know the Bible (and through it, God the Father, God the Son, and God the Holy Spirit) than when we started our course of reading.

One of the major television networks produced, a while back, an hour-long documentary on the Nile River. Starting at remote sources deep in the heart of Africa, a skilled commentator took his guests with him along the 4,000-mile waterway that has influenced civilization more than any other. He showed tumultuous waterfalls, enormous regions of near-stagnant lakes, and ancient Egyptian monuments scheduled to be flooded by backwaters of a dam soon to be built.

Finally and triumphantly, after an hour of suspense, each person who had "traveled the length of the Nile" emerged, with the river, on the Mediterranean coast. But the exuberance of having traced the course to its end faded into fresh wonder as the camera threw on the screen a vivid shot portraying the setting sun drawing water from the sea and sending it back to some new watershed, there to begin another journey in whose course it will move turbines to produce power, will support the vessels of voyagers, will slack

316

the thirst of parched farm lands, and once more will move out to sea.

As with the flow of water down the channels of the Nile, so with the pilgrim's progress through the Old Testament and the New. Having reached the end, it is time to make a fresh start.

There are many ways to read the entire Bible. If this has been your first complete journey "from cover to cover," you may decide to retrace your footsteps during another year. Should that be your decision, I hereby solemnly promise that your second journey will be far more exciting than the first.

If, on the other hand, you prefer to vary your quest by adopting a different pattern of reading, there are a number of tested plans available. Some of the best ones are offered by The American Bible Society. Address inquiries to Dr. Carl W. Larson, Study Secretary, 47 South 9th Street, Minneapolis 2, Minnesota.

Consult denominational headquarters for guides and reading programs endorsed by leaders in your own church. Or investigate some of the many plans available from private groups such as The Bible Study Hour, Box 2000, Philadelphia 3, Pennsylvania, and Scripture Union, 2136 Darby Road, Havertown, Pennsylvania.

This book came out of one congregation's quest. Strangely, it was first given national impetus along with two other study programs which also developed in downtown congregations of big cities. Quite different approaches have been made by these other explorers, both of whom offer study helps: Dr. Carl W. Berner, Faith Evangelical Lutheran Church, South Broadway and 95th St., Los Angeles 3, California; and The Rev. John D. Banks, Bethany Congregational Church, Coddington and Spear Streets, Quincy 69, Massachusetts.

Whatever you do—do something!

Should you decide against a return visit in company with *A Guide to Reading the Entire Bible in One Year,* and find

317

yourself not fully satisfied with any available published program—then develop your own! You might, for example, spend a month or two searching out and meditating upon the prayers of the Bible. Especially in the modern translations, poetic sections stand out so vividly that they may be read in one grand sweep that includes the Psalms along with many other noble verses not printed as poetry in the King James Version.

Personally, I find the "chain reference" approach less than satisfying. Most or all of these systems tend to concentrate upon isolated verses, phrases, or even single words. To use such an approach consistently over a period of years is, I think, to slip gradually into concentrating upon only a tiny portion of Scripture and consequently, in effect, to "edit" the Bible by neglecting whole regions of it.

Provided that the chain reference type of reading appeals to you, I doubt if it will do you any harm to follow it part of the time—say, one year's reading in every five or ten.

Biography is still another doorway; you might set out to re-read all the passages that deal with persons, as opposed to abstract ideas that predominate in the letters of Paul, for example. But after a season of tracing the footsteps of Moses and David, Simon Peter and Jesus Christ, you might—for balance—concentrate upon the great Biblical themes: sin, salvation, judgment, grace, fear, joy, and the like, tracing the development of each through the Old Testament as well as the New.

There are, in short, as many ways to read the Bible as there are personal interests. Whatever you do, regardless of programs that meet your needs and reading guides that leave you indifferent, I beseech you to continue the now-fixed habit of daily exposing yourself to Scripture as the word of God, thereby bridging the gap between creature and Creator in such fashion that you are bound to receive news bulletins from God almost every hour.

318

INDEX

319